STAKEKNIFE'S
DIRTY WAR

RICHARD O'RAWE grew up in the Lower Falls area of Belfast. He experienced the full force of the civil unrest that enveloped Ireland, spending eight years in British prisons for IRA activities from 1972 to 1983. In 2005, he wrote his first book, *Blanketmen*, about his experiences in prison, which became an Irish bestseller. His second book, *Afterlives*, was published in 2010, and in 2017 he wrote *In the Name of the Son*, a biography of his lifelong friend Gerry Conlon of the Guildford Four. His first novel, *Northern Heist*, was published in 2018, and his second, *Goering's Gold*, was released in 2022. Also in 2022, he co-wrote the stage play *In the Name of the Son*, which won the prestigious Aisling Award for literature.

STAKEKNIFE'S DIRTY WAR

THE INSIDE STORY OF SCAPPATICCI, THE IRA'S NUTTING SQUAD AND THE BRITISH SPOOKS WHO RAN THE WAR

RICHARD O'RAWE

MERRION
PRESS

First published in 2023 by
Merrion Press
10 George's Street
Newbridge
Co. Kildare
Ireland
www.merrionpress.ie

978 1 78537 447 0 (Paper)
978 1 78537 448 7 (Ebook)

A CIP catalogue record for this book is
available from the British Library.

Typeset in Minion Pro 11.5/18 pt

Cover design by riverdesignbooks.com

Front cover: © images4media

Merrion Press is a member of Publishing Ireland.

'A nation can survive fools, and even the ambitious. But it cannot survive treason from within. An enemy at the gates is less formidable, for he is known and carries his banner openly. But the traitor moves amongst those within the gates freely, his sly whispers rustling through all the alleys, heard in the very halls of government itself. For the traitor appears not a traitor; he speaks in accents familiar to his victims, and he wears their face and their arguments, he appeals to the baseness that lies deep in the hearts of all men. He rots the soul of a nation, he works secretly and unknown in the night to undermine the pillars of the city, he infects the body politic so that it can no longer resist. A murderer is less to fear. The traitor is the plague.'

Marcus Tullius Cicero
Roman statesman, lawyer, scholar and republican

'Culling agents was, of course, one of the [nutting] squad's key tasks, so Scappaticci's British Army handlers could have been in absolutely no doubt that he was involved in the murder of his fellow agents, time and time again.'

John Ware, 'The Spy in the IRA', BBC, 2017

CONTENTS

PROLOGUE

JULY 2021, COUNTY DERRY[1]

R O'R: Can you tell me about your history in the IRA?

IRA vol: I was fighting the Brits in south Derry and north Antrim with
Frank Hughes, Dominic McGlinchey and the south Derry boys.
We were more like a flying column than an ASU [Active Service
Unit] because we were constantly on the run, hitting and running,
hitting and running, never staying in the same place two nights in
a row. We very rarely travelled in cars; cars were too static. If you
ran into the Brits at a roadblock, they'd cut you to ribbons. So we
hoofed it, walked everywhere. Never on the roads, always around
the edges of the fields. And they were our fields. We knew every
ditch, every stream, every farmhouse. We were armed all the time
… rifles, usually. And we knew when Rebel the Dog would bark,
and if he didn't bark we knew something was wrong. The Brits
used to kill the dogs, y'see. Look: we knew who was friendly to us
and who was hostile. We usually moved at night and lay in ditches
during the day. Sometimes, at the end of the night, we'd go into a
barn and put our heads down on bales of hay.

R O'R: What did you eat?

IRA vol: Whatever there was. Tins of sardines, maybe a sandwich, or crisps, a coke to wash it down: small stuff you could carry in a rucksack.

R O'R: Did you ever get a hot meal?

IRA vol: Oh, yeah, sure. Sometimes, if we were staying with supporters, we'd be fed like lords. But that wasn't often 'cause the Brits knew who our supporters were, and you'd have been eating a meal with one eye looking out the window.

R O'R: You told me about a particular operation in the mid-eighties?

IRA vol: Intelligence reached me that a UDR [Ulster Defence Regiment, a local British Army militia] patrol walked the same stretch of road at the same time every Thursday night. It was a remote area, gorse everywhere, plenty of cover. I'd sussed it out for about two weeks … I looked at the terrain and worked out where to put my team to wipe out this patrol.

R O'R: Wipe out?

IRA vol: Well, we weren't sending them red roses, that's for sure. We were in the business of killing the enemy. So was the SAS [the British Army's Special Air Services regiment]. If they got us, we expected to be wiped out.

R O'R: That sounds as if you have some respect for the SAS.

IRA vol: Respect! They're a bunch of whores! They always had over-whelming numbers and firepower and they liked killing IRA vol-unteers, whether armed or unarmed.

R O'R: Just like the IRA liked ambushing and killing them and other British Army soldiers, whether armed or unarmed.

IRA vol: Do you want this interview, or not?

R O'R: Of course.

IRA vol: Then don't equate us with the SAS.

R O'R: Okay. So, on the night of the 'op'. What happened?

IRA vol: Our safe house was about three and a half miles away from where the ambush was to take place.

R O'R: What type of rifles?

IRA vol: It doesn't matter. Let's just say they fired straight. I'm not gonna tell you where the target was either 'cause that's none of your business. So, we made it to the area where we planned to hit these UDR people. And about three fields away from the road, the one the UDR people patrolled, I motioned to the other two volunteers, indicating we should get down on our bellies from there on in. We crawled into an area that gave us the best view of the overall ambush site. I was on point and took the lead. I was in a ditch behind a hedge and there was this breeze-block garage to my right, on the other side of the hedge. No big deal, right? Most bungalows and houses have breeze-block garages. And then I heard voices, English voices, coming from the garage.

R O'R: They must have been loud?

IRA vol: No, they weren't, but they were clearly English.

R O'R: And how did that affect your operation?

IRA vol: I waved my adjutant up and put a finger to my lips, telling him to be very quiet. Then, when he was beside me, I pointed to the garage. We both listened to the whispered English voices.

R O'R: Why did you risk bringing him up?

IRA vol: 'Cause I didn't want to be accused later of losing my balls and inventing the voices to get out of the op.

R O'R: And what were the SAS saying?

IRA vol: You couldn't actually make them out, except for one word … 'fucking'. We caught that over and over again. The English always pronounce their 'ings'. Then we both realised the SAS were in position to ambush us and we knew there'd be other SAS men in and around the kill zone, so we were in a dodgy position.

R O'R: The ambushers were in danger of being ambushed?

IRA vol: You could say that.

R O'R: What did you do?

IRA vol: We'd no choice. We backed out on our bellies.

R O'R: And what thoughts were running through your head as you made your way back over the fields?

IRA vol: Our runback wasn't back to our starting point … it wasn't that far away, actually … but I think we all had the same thought. The adjutant asked me how the fuck the Brits knew we were carrying out the operation on that night.

R O'R: And what did you say?

IRA vol: I'll never forget it: I told him we'd a Gypo Nolan in our midst.

R O'R: A Gypo Nolan?

IRA vol: Yeah. A tout. An informer. At least one, probably two.

PREFACE

I knew Freddie Scappaticci. Fortunately, I didn't know him well. I first encountered him in the early 1970s when he and I had been interned without trial in the cages of Long Kesh prison. He was housed in Cage 5 and I was in Cage 3. Occasionally, as we walked around the perimeters of our respective cages, we would have nodded to each other.

Like many from 'The Troubles' generation, Freddie and I were both politically baptised in the communal violence that erupted in Belfast in August 1969. That baptism came after almost three years of a civil rights campaign during which political activists in the north of Ireland had marched in demand of equal citizenship and the right to one-man-one-vote, an end to gerrymandering in overwhelmingly Catholic constituencies, better housing and fairer employment opportunities. For their endeavours, they were beaten off the streets and country roads by the state's paramilitary police force, the 'B Specials', and the Royal Ulster Constabulary (RUC).

On the balmy summer's night of 15 August 1969, I sat in the rear bedroom of our two-up-two-down home in Peel Street, just off the Falls Road, with my seventy-six-year-old grandfather, John Collins, and my father, Harry. While my grandfather sat on the bed, clutching his rosary beads, praying furiously under his breath, my father stood guard at the bedroom door, armed with a lump hammer. Behind him, I held a hurling stick.

Just before midnight, a fierce gun battle broke out and, approximately 150 yards from our house, whole Catholic streets in the Divis area were being burned to the ground by loyalists, backed up by heavily armed B Specials. Entire families, many with young children, had to flee their homes with nothing more than the clothes on their backs after petrol bombs were thrown through their windows. The next day, the pattern was repeated, with more street burnings in Catholic areas of Belfast.

On the evening that the guns came out, I was an impressionable fifteen-year-old schoolboy, while Scappaticci was a twenty-three-year-old, married bricklayer. Like many young men and women, I was incandescent with rage that our neighbours were burned out of their homes for no reason other than that they were Catholics. And so, when a new, militant Provisional IRA emerged from the ashes of the torched homes and broken lives, I felt compelled to join up, as did Freddie Scappaticci and hundreds of other young people who saw in the Provisionals an organisation that was willing to defend our local communities from attack and to fight for Irish freedom. It seemed the natural thing to do.

Initially, Scappaticci was a model IRA volunteer. Having interviewed former IRA volunteers from the Markets area of Belfast where he lived, it struck me that he was a natural leader, one who could not only get things done but who had a fine eye for detail. It was not long before he came to the notice of his superior officers and was promoted to Officer Commanding (OC), Markets. Unfortunately for him, Scappaticci also came to the notice of the police and, when internment was introduced on 9 August 1971, he was one of the first IRA leaders to be arrested and locked up without charge. He was released from internment in January 1974, and re-interned in August 1974. His enthusiasm for the cause appears to have waned, and although he did eventually rejoin the IRA after his release in 1975, things had changed; some time in the next few years he became a British agent.

It was this role that makes Scappaticci such a hugely important historical figure in the conflict that engulfed Ireland and Great Britain for almost thirty years. The part he played in the war and subsequent peace merits thorough examination, and that is the aim of this book. Far from castigating him, a writer could be forgiven for saying that Scappaticci was a catalyst for peace, that his activities, and the intelligence he provided, helped bring the IRA to the peace table. Dr Anthony McIntyre, a former IRA volunteer, had these insightful comments to make about Scappaticci: 'The organisation's weaknesses and strengths, the unquestioning or critical approaches to leadership ... would all have been known to [Scappaticci]. He damaged the IRA irreparably and helped pave the way for its defeat ... a seriously compromised IRA campaign would reinforce a peace lobby within republicanism. Arguably, this is where the role of [Scappaticci] became crucial.'[1]

Moreover, if he was the point man for the British military when it came to intelligence-gathering, he clearly wasn't alone. While interviewing former IRA volunteers for this book, I repeatedly encountered strong suspicions that a certain comrade, much more senior than Scappaticci, might also have been in the pocket of British Intelligence. For fear of being hauled before the courts in their old age, most of those former IRA volunteers insisted on remaining anonymous and assumed aliases.

From a different perspective, such was the power and fear Freddie Scappaticci exerted over sections of the nationalist community that –

almost two decades after he was outed as an informer – some civilian contributors to the book, people who grew up with him, even some who drank with him, followed the same path as former IRA volunteers and insisted that their identities be withheld.

Scappaticci's role as the British agent known as 'Stakeknife' led to the establishment of Operation Kenova, a government-sponsored investigation into his activities when he was a member of the IRA's Internal Security Unit (ISU). Sources from the political sphere, the legal profession and the media have told this author that detectives from Operation Kenova revealed that Scappaticci informed his British Army Intelligence handlers – in advance – about all the interrogations and murders in which he and the IRA's ISU were involved. Just how many murders can never be stated with certainty, but a former Director of Public Prosecutions for Northern Ireland is on record as saying that Operation Kenova detectives forwarded files to him alleging that Scappaticci had been involved in eighteen.

Such evidence inevitably raises the question of why the British intelligence services allowed multiple murders of their own citizens to occur when they could so easily have prevented them. Who were the shady figures in the Tasking and Co-ordinating Groups (TCGs), the Intelligence spooks who evaluated Stakeknife's information and, time and again, made decisions to allow the IRA's ISU to execute suspected informers in order to protect the identity of Scappaticci and other agents? How have they been able to stay under the media radar for so long?

There are no hard-and-fast answers to these questions because most of those who profess to know the truth have a vested interest in sculpting the narrative. Indeed, I'm not even sure that Freddie Scappaticci knew the full truth. And, even if he had tried to shed light on these highly secretive matters, which he steadfastly refused to do, who could believe him, given that he was a notorious liar who never admitted to working for British Army Intelligence, let alone showed an ounce of remorse or sympathy for his victims? In contrast, the late Frankie Mulhern, whose son Joseph was executed by the ISU in 1993, forgave the IRA volunteer who shot dead his child. If Frankie had been expecting a magnanimous response from Scappaticci, he must have been disappointed. Indeed, the only people Scappaticci did not disappoint were his British spymasters.

This book deals with the war of whispers in Ireland, Stakeknife's war. It is a war which, to date, has been told largely from a British Intelligence perspective, with British spymasters and agent handlers rushing to pen graphic accounts of how they outwitted the IRA – with some justification. For the first time, IRA volunteers give accounts of their encounters with the British, Scappaticci and the ISU. Theirs is not a feel-good story, but it is one that must be heard.

1

A MERCURIAL VOLUNTEER

'Be careful who you trust; the devil was once an angel.'

Anonymous

Empty stomachs drive roving eyes that can see across the tallest mountain and widest ocean. Rarely was this more evident than in the middle to latter part of the nineteenth century, when hunger was the constant companion of the peasant class throughout Europe. On the Italian peninsula, in 1848, Giuseppe Garibaldi returned from exile in South America and kick-started a revolt that lasted, intermittently, until 1862, when the insurrectionists created the United Kingdom of Italy. But revolution does not always deliver the land the milk and honey that its exponents might envisage, and never was this more evident than in Italy: 'Life was always a struggle for the *casalezze* [people who lived in the village of Casalattico in central Italy],' Dr Tony Rosato said. 'But it wasn't until Garibaldi united Italy in 1862 and thereafter that there was total economic chaos.' Dr Rosato continued, 'People weren't eating. Starvation or emigration? Not much of a choice.'[1]

Italian émigrés proved to be a dexterous lot. They were industrious, entrepreneurial and hard-working. It is estimated that 80 per cent of the Italian families who emigrated to the north of Ireland came from Casalattico. Why there? Dr Rosato said, 'If you look west, you've got the United Kingdom. You've got to remember, the UK was the engine of the Industrial Revolution, and it was seen as the place to be if you wanted a decent standard of living, and nowhere was this prosperity more evident than in Belfast.'[2]

The first recorded entry of Italian migrants to Belfast dates to 1876. Historian Jonathan Bardon wrote of the burgeoning city: 'By 1891 Belfast was the biggest city in Ireland. Its industrial and commercial progress was without parallel, and the Lagan valley formed the vital and closely integrated western corner of an area encompassing the manufacturing regions of Scotland and the north of England, then one of the most advanced economic regions on earth and the industrial heartland of an expanding empire.'[3]

It is therefore no great surprise that the émigrés opted to live in Belfast. But Belfast, also known internationally as 'Linenopolis' because of its association with linen production, was a dangerous place in which to reside in the latter half of the nineteenth century – especially if you were a Catholic, as was invariably the case with the Italians. There were intermittent riots in the 1850s, 1864, 1872 and 1886, and at the heart of these riots was a virulent strain of sectarianism that was promulgated by figures like the Rev. Hugh 'Roaring' Hanna and the Rev. Thomas Drew, who finished a Twelfth of July sermon in 1857 to members of a Protestant Orange Lodge with words that could only inflame his susceptible audience: 'The cells of the Pope's prisons were paved with the calcined bones of men and cemented with human gore and human hair … The Word of God makes all plain; puts to eternal shame the practices of persecutors and stigmatises with enduring reprobation the arrogant pretences of the Popes and the outrageous dogmata of their blood-stained religion.'[4]

Running parallel with this heady brew of sectarian hatred was a fear of losing social privilege and well-paid jobs due to an influx of Catholics and nationalists from rural Ireland: 'By mid-century, Protestants already monopolised the skilled jobs in the engineering and building industries, and the few in the mills. They were the fitters, boilermakers, carpenters, and bricklayers: the artisan élite of the town. As shipbuilding developed, they took most of the skilled jobs there too. A third or more of Protestant male workers made up this "labour aristocracy". Their wages were on a par with those of skilled workers in Britain – but were three times higher than the wages of Belfast mill workers. Shipyard workers were particularly well paid. Most lived on the Shankill [a Protestant area] – built in the 1870s and regarded then as the town's healthiest working-class area – or increasingly, across the river in Ballymacarrett. Few shipyard workers were Catholic: Sir Edward Harland said in 1887 that only 225 of his 3,000 operatives were Catholics.'[5]

Not all Italians who emigrated to Belfast in the 1870s were poor. Some were tradespeople who put a high premium on their skills as paviours, asphalters and mosaic-workers. Others were highly talented craftspeople who made a living at sculpting, creating mostly religious statues for the emerging Catholic churches that were springing up throughout the city to cater for the influx of new parishioners. Many Italian immigrants gravitated towards trading in food, especially the selling of fish and chips or ice cream, while some Italian women went to work in the numerous linen mills.

Amongst the *casalezze* who eventually emigrated to Belfast were Bernardo Scappaticci and his wife, Maria Celesta Elisabetta Magliocco. The couple had two daughters and three sons. Their second son, Donato, was born on 13 January 1919. It was Donato, or 'Danny', as he was later affectionately called in the Markets area of Belfast, who was the father of Frederick Scappaticci, the man whom General Sir John Wilsey described as 'the military's most valuable asset'.[6] Like most of the newly arrived Italians, the Scappaticci family were industrious and independent, successfully making and selling ice cream for a living. They lived at 92a Royal Avenue, alongside the then Avenue cinema, where Danny worked in his father's ice-cream parlour.[7] It was a good time to be an Italian ice-cream seller – especially if your place of business was beside one of the biggest cinemas in Belfast.

Danny Scappaticci, a precocious young man, eventually took over the family business and expanded it, putting several ice-cream vans on the road. In 1941, he married Mary Murray and they set up residence in Joy Street, in the Markets area of Belfast.[8] The Scappaticcis had five children, the third-eldest of whom, Frederick, or 'Freddie', was born on 12 January 1946.

As a child growing up in working-class, inner-city Belfast, Freddie would have been aware of the thin lines of demarcation that existed between Catholic and Protestant areas. But the last thing on his mind would have been the simmering political tensions within Northern Irish society, or the profound alienation felt by many within his own community. Neither could he ever have imagined he would play such an important role in the thirty-year conflict that was hovering in the distance and which was about to engulf the whole of Ireland in a bloody shroud. The fact that some people had multiple votes, while others had none, would have been lost on him. And the sectarian discrepancy in housing allocation would also have been unfamiliar to him. Moreover, had Freddie heard the term 'gerrymander' it's safe to assume that he would have thought 'Gerry' was a First Division footballer. Like all kids in pre-Troubles Belfast, there would have been more important things happening in his life: hanging out with friends, schooling, listening to the Beatles or the Rolling Stones on Radio Caroline, learning street-craft. But, above all else, football was Freddie's first love.

The former Markets resident Seán Flynn remembers Freddie as 'a life-long friend'.[9] Flynn, who became a republican leader at the advent of the Troubles, also recalls his warm friendship with Freddie's younger brother, Bernard. He speaks with considerable affection about Freddie: 'When we were kids, we played football matches in the street that lasted from morning to night. And then we played Under 14 for Ormeau United. Freddie was left-back on the team. He was tough, a ferocious tackler.' Sitting in his garden on an overcast morning, Flynn stares ahead, as if long-gone pals are leaning on the garden's red-brick wall staring back at him, waiting on his next word, daring him to say the things that dare not be said. 'Most of our team were shot dead in the Troubles. And the guy who ran the team was deaf and dumb, and so was his son. The son played in the team. We'd some good players on that team, but Freddie was the best.'[10]

In 1962, Scappaticci caught the eye of the former Manchester United and Irish International Johnny Carey, who recommended that he should go for a trial to First Division team Nottingham Forest. Three weeks later, Freddie returned to Belfast. Flynn recalled, 'He went over to Nottingham Forest, and they sent him back, said he was ... said he had to lose weight, let's put it like that. He was stocky, y'see, and he'd a bit of weight on him. He never went back, like, and they never asked for him again, but he was some player.' Flynn also recalled that the Scappaticcis always seemed to have money, and he put this down to Danny's hard work. 'The Scappaticcis had a TV before anyone else in the district. That was a big thing back then. And I remember, you couldn't move in their living room; there must have been twenty fellas packed in, and we were all watching the 1963 European Cup final, or was it the 1962 final? It doesn't really matter; it was brilliant anyway. And when it was over, we all went and played football in the Ormeau Park, even 'oul Danny, Freddie's da.'[11]

Besides his football ability, Freddie was also gifted, or damned, with a volcanic temper. Given his diminutive size, he would have needed to know who the best street fighters were and, more importantly, how to avoid getting into scraps with them. Moreover, as he got older, he would also have had to learn to bridle his tongue, which would not have come easy to a young man who was inclined to punch first and rationalise later. This tendency to resort to violence inevitably earned him the respect and disrespect of those on the street. It also brought him to the attention of the police.

By the time he was eighteen years old, the mercurial Freddie was no stranger to the law. On 25 February 1964, the apprentice bricklayer found himself in the dock of the magistrate's court for participating in a street fight, along with William McMullan (18), Samuel Bell (17) and Alan Morton (19). As Bell and Morton hailed from the Protestant Shankill Road, and McMullan and Scappaticci from the Catholic Markets area, it is safe to say that this fracas had a sectarian flavour to it.

Head Constable Robert Finlay told the court that a fight had begun on the evening of 8 February 1964 when two sets of youths met in the city centre. A chase followed, and this ended in the Markets area. The police officer continued: 'Constable Samuel Davidson got out of a police car and William McMullan crashed into him and he fell, breaking his leg.'[12]

The head constable then told the court how a Constable McAuley saw Samuel Bell fall to the ground in Cromac Street, whereupon William McMullan kicked Bell on the body and face. A contemporaneous newspaper report says, 'The chase through several city centre streets was led by Scappaticci, a member of a Belfast football club.'[13] If the head constable's account is accurate, then it appears that Freddie and McMullan had chased the two Protestant youths into Cromac Street. The newspaper reported that, in mitigation, 'The court was told that Scappaticci had had a month's trial for Nottingham Forest, and West Ham and West Bromwich Albion were said to be interested in him.' Scappaticci was fined £10 for his involvement in the affair.

A former IRA volunteer, 'Frankie Garland', who emphasised he was a 'past' friend of Scappaticci, did not remember the fracas with Bell and Morton, but he was not surprised that it occurred: 'The Markets is really a part of the city centre, so it was natural we'd have run into "Orangies" [Protestants]. They used to hunt down "Taigs" [Catholics] and if they found one of us, they used to get us to say the "Our Father" [the Lord's Prayer]. If the Catholic didn't finish the prayer with, "For thine is the kingdom, the power and the glory", they knew he was a Taig and beat him up.'[14] Garland went on to say, 'Here's the thing you've gotta remember about Scap: when he was your mate, he was your mate ... he'd have faced Goliath for you.'[15] The former volunteer also served with Freddie in the IRA and he had nothing but admiration for him: 'After he became OC of the Markets, oh, about 1970, he never asked a volunteer to do what he wasn't prepared to do himself. I know for a fact he went out on bloweys [bombing missions in Belfast City Centre]. He had balls to burn.'[16]

Evidently, Freddie Scappaticci was a complicated man who was liked and despised in equal measure. 'Marian McMullan', a neighbour who grew up with him in Joy Street, commented, 'The Troubles had just started, right? He'd been burnt out of his house in Pine Street in Donegal Pass [an adjacent Protestant area]. What happened was, a petrol bomb was thrown though his [Pine Street] living-room window in 1969, while his family were watching TV. One of the kids was nearly burned alive. Then he moved to the Markets.

'Cards on the table? He was a fucking bully. He was married at the time, and he had the place terrorised. People were afraid of him because they knew he was a top 'RA man. He was married to Sheila Cunningham, and he regularly beat the crap out of her. And he sometimes tooled up when he was going into a fight. He beat a fella over the head in Rutland Street with a brick in a sock.'[17] When asked if Scappaticci had any redeeming features, his former neighbour replied, 'He was a good worker, I'll give him that.'[18]

Twenty-year-old Scappaticci had married local girl Sheila Cunningham in St Malachy's Church, Belfast, on 4 October 1966. Despite the anarchic life that Frederick would come to lead, the marriage lasted until Sheila's death in 2017.

Although he had fond memories of childhood escapades with Freddie, Seán Flynn recalls an occasion when he ended up involved in a fight with his friend: 'It was early '71, before internment came in, I'm not sure exactly what month, but the Troubles had started, and we were all in the Black Bull Bar in Cromac Street when Freddie started punching Pat Dalton. Pat's dead now. Now, in a fair dig, everybody knew Pat would've slaughtered Freddie. But Freddie got stuck into Pat, and Pat didn't lift his hands 'cause he was shit-scared of Scap 'cause the wee man was the top Provo in the Markets. So, I grabbed Freddie out of the way, and me and him went at it. I was a leading member of the Official IRA in the Markets at that time, so I didn't give a fuck who or what he was. No matter. It was quickly broken up. But that didn't stop us from being friends; we still talked for years afterwards.'[19]

'Jean Lennon' is another former Markets resident who was less than fulsome in her praise of Scappaticci, when she was interviewed in 2021: 'He was like … like a wee ball walking towards you, the shoulders swinging in that wee Barbour jacket. You'd have been frightened of him and he knew it; he was a bully. Even now, and me and you are talking, I don't want my name mentioned in this book. I'm still afraid of Freddie Scappaticci.'[20] After being assured that her name would not appear in print, she said, 'I knew his wife, Sheila, dead well. I knew her all my life, and she was a different kettle of fish. Sheila was pure gold. She'd never have met you without giving a compliment and he'd have just stood there, shuffling his feet, like every man does when his wife is standing gabbling. Sheila was a lovely person, and he murdered her – he beat her black and blue, he did.'[21]

'Kathy McDermott', also from the Markets, shared the view that Scappaticci was to be treated with caution: 'Freddie and Sheila had six kids: Liz, Teresa, Eamonn, Paul, Danny and Maria. There's a twenty-year gap between his first-born, Liz, and Maria, his last-born. Now, Freddie's dad, 'oul Danny, was an ice-cream man and he was always good to us kids, gave us plenty of ice cream. And Danny was well-respected in the district, but he could be abrupt. Freddie was respected too – but for a different reason: he put the fear of God into you. And I heard Scap's mummy, Mary, was a lady, a real gentle woman. Scap's wife, Sheila, was a lady too. She was one of the Cunninghams. And Sheila had lots of mental-health problems, like, she used to have breakdowns. She had motor neurone disease. But she stuck with him to the very end, even when he went away to England after he was outed as a tout. Sheila would have gone over to him every other weekend.'[22]

It is clear from these accounts that Scappaticci the Younger was given to violence long before the advent of the Troubles. Virtually everyone spoken to from that community used the word 'bully' when describing him. Frankie Garland described him very succinctly: 'Scap stood out of the crowd. He didn't drink, well, not heavily. Even on a Friday night when everyone was in the club, he'd have had one, maybe two pints, but that was it. You see, he had an overpowering presence about him that bordered on intimidation. I always saw that.'[23] That presence was about to be put to good use by the IRA.

2

BELFAST BURNING

'Catholics breed like rabbits and multiply like vermin.'

Reverend Ian Paisley at a loyalist rally in 1969

The world into which Freddie Scappaticci was born was one where unionist politicians selfishly guarded their electorate's most-favoured status by treating their Catholic neighbours as second-class citizens. But for some more extreme unionists, like the Reverend Ian Paisley, betrayal was in the air. Paisley pointed an accusing finger at the moderate unionist, the then prime minister of Northern Ireland, Captain Terence O'Neill, and condemned him as a 'Lundy', someone who had betrayed the Protestant and unionist cause by meeting with the Irish taoiseach [premier], Seán Lemass, whom O'Neill had invited to Stormont parliamentary buildings on 14 January 1965. Paisley, a religious zealot in the 'Roaring Hanna' tradition, who co-founded the Free Presbyterian Church in 1951, drove up to Stormont the following day in a car with an Ulster flag trailing from a window and placards which read, 'No Mass', 'No Lemass', 'Down with the Lundy's' and 'IRA murderer welcomed in Stormont'.[1]

The journalist and author Max Hastings had a caustic view of Paisley: '[B]eyond any shadow of a doubt, no single man in Northern Ireland bears a greater share of the blame for all the horror that took place than Ian Paisley, leader of the Protestant extremists'.[2] Virulently anti-Catholic, Paisley conducted his orchestra of sectarian bigots with great aplomb and by the early 1960s he was dipping his toes into local politics. In 1964, he precipitated three nights of serious rioting in the Catholic Falls Road area by calling upon Protestants to meet in their thousands at Belfast City Hall and thereafter to march on Divis Street to remove an Irish tricolour from the offices of a local republican election candidate, Billy McMillen. Fearing a Protestant invasion of the Falls and the serious resistance that such a vista would have provoked, the police, using pickaxes and crowbars, forcibly removed the tricolour for Paisley, thus provoking the nationalist community. The demagogue's blackmailing tactic, with its inherent threat of violence and civil unrest, had won the day.

Two years later, on 6 June 1966, he was once more stirring up inter-communal tensions. On this occasion, aided by a heavy police escort, Paisley led 1,000 supporters in a march to Belfast City Hall and then to the Presbyterian headquarters in nearby Howard Street. In protest at the Paisleyites marching through their area, 200 Markets residents blocked the Albert Bridge, whereupon the police drew their batons and beat the protesters off the road, thus opening a pathway for the Paisleyites to cross nearby Cromac Square. Freddie Scappaticci's footballing friend Seán Flynn, who had stood on the bridge and protested against the march, said, 'Here was Protestant supremacy in the flesh. Pure sectarianism. It was a case of, fuck youse, we'll walk wherever we want.'[3]

In the aftermath of the march, serious rioting occurred in the Markets district, with four policemen and a twelve-year-old girl being injured, and ten people being arrested. Later, a triumphant Paisley said, 'This is the first Protestant parade through the Markets area in thirty years. It is quite a victory.'[4] One of the ten people arrested was Seán Flynn, by then a merchant seaman. Flynn, after securing bail, fled to Southampton, England, where he shipped out to sea. In the meantime, the first of Flynn's co-accused, Kathleen McKnight, was sentenced to one month's imprisonment for riotous behaviour because of the protest. Except for Flynn, all of the accused who turned up in court shared her fate – and all appealed. At the appeal court, their sentences were increased to six months. In his absence, the court fined Flynn £50, a considerable sum in those days, which was paid after a collection was made in the Markets area.

Yet, despite the cleric's gargantuan endeavours to ignite a sectarian firestorm on the streets, the pre-1969 era could be said to have been relatively peaceful, especially when set alongside the three decades of political violence that was to engulf the north of Ireland from that year until the signing of the Good Friday Agreement in 1998.

One of the reasons why things were so calm on the streets was the IRA leadership's refusal to be goaded into retaliatory action by Paisley's provocations. Irksome as he no doubt would have been to many republicans, Paisley was nothing more than a distraction to the IRA leadership that emerged from the collapse of the 1950s' border campaign, which had been a dismal failure and was unceremoniously abandoned on 26 February 1962. What materialised from that fiasco was a new swathe of republican revolutionaries, led by Chief of Staff Cathal Goulding, who were convinced that the rattle of the Thompson machine gun was the death rattle of Irish republicanism. The unity of the Catholic and Protestant working class was the new mantra.

This would have made perfect sense had class politics been the dominant feature of societal division – but in a Northern Ireland where unionist hegemony was absolute, religious affiliation was the ultimate arbiter of political policy. Not that many people gave much thought to politics. Much more important for the youth of the 1960s was whether the Beatles or the Stones were at number one in the charts, and whether Engelbert Humperdinck was the main act in the Plaza dance hall. Who cared about who was scoffing prawn vol-au-vents up in Stormont?

The birth of the Northern Ireland Civil Rights Association (NICRA) in January 1966 seemed to offer liberalising republicans the possibility of bringing about peaceful societal change. The NICRA was a broad front of middle-class nationalists, liberal unionists, communists, trade unionists and Irish republicans, who were committed to dragging Northern Ireland into the twentieth century by confronting state discrimination against the nationalist minority. Tellingly, what was not on the agenda at those civil rights meetings was a united Ireland. Reform was the big word: let's have equality of citizenship, let's take religion out of politics, let's make Northern Ireland work for everyone.

The first chairperson of the NICRA was Betty Sinclair, a communist and the secretary of the Belfast and District Trade Union Council. However, while Goulding and the republican movement embraced the civil rights movement and were delighted by this appointment, to traditional republicans the idea of reformism was the stuff that horses leave behind after a good feed of grass.

Veteran republican Billy McKee, who was Belfast OC under Goulding from 1961 to 1963, explained some of the problems with Goulding's strategy, as he saw them: 'And it [working-class unity] was a good idea all right, but not in Northern Ireland. I could not join the Orange Order. When they would ask me, "Was I a Catholic?" – out. To get into the Masons, you could be in a hundred years, and you'd never get in on their leadership. You had no chance of taking over that. The trade unions – there were different branches in the trade union – and to get in there would have been all right, but they were mostly left-wing people. So why would I want to get in there? They [the Goulding faction] were going out to disband the gun.'[5]

To the 1960s' Goulding IRA leadership, the Billy McKees of this world had become *de trop* – better for all if they would quietly shuffle off the stage and slip out the back door of the theatre. But that was wishful thinking – like the Goulding leadership, dissidents like McKee believed the fight for Irish freedom was a lifelong commitment and they rejected Goulding's conciliatory approach, being convinced that Britain would only leave Ireland if forced to do so through armed struggle. When the inevitable split came in 1969, it was not surprising that McKee became Belfast OC of the newly formed Provisional IRA.

In August 1969, backed up by gun-toting RUC officers and the B Specials, Protestant hard men petrol-bombed dozens of Catholic homes and properties. Entire streets looked like they had been blitzed by Heinkel bombers. Dr Tony Rosato recalled standing at the front of his family home in Deerpark Road, in north Belfast, on 15 August and feeling the intense heat from houses that were burning in the Ardoyne area, which was at least half a mile away.[6]

While the Ardoyne was ablaze, over in west Belfast, police snipers had taken up positions on high buildings and were opening fire with .303 rifles on anyone who moved in the Divis or Falls areas, while other officers patrolled the streets in Shoreland armoured cars, opening fire with .30 calibre Browning machine guns. Four Catholics were killed, including a nine-year-old boy, Daniel Rooney, who was shot in his bed when a machine-gunner raked Divis Tower with fire. A twenty-year-old

British Army soldier, Hugh McCabe, was home on leave when he was shot dead by the police outside Divis Tower. In Divis Street, a Protestant, Herbert Roy (26), was shot dead by republican gunmen.

Fra McCann, a young man who would soon become a member of the republican movement, described the carnage that was unfolding around him: 'All that I seen was loyalists coming down with RUC and B Specials attacking ... at the front of Divis Flats, St Comgall's School, and you look at the front of it, the walls are still riddled with bullet holes ... from 1969 to 1970. I stood on the stoop and watched women trying to carry their children with loyalist mobs running after them – couldn't even get their belongings out of the houses and the whole houses were burnt down around them. And RUC men and B Specials actively took a part in it.'[7]

While the causes that led to the catastrophe of 1969 have been debated *ad nauseum*, and are often disputed, there is little doubt that the 'not-an-inch' attitude of the Unionist government towards the minority nationalist community was the real trigger behind the violence. What is certain is that the events on the streets of Belfast on 15–16 August 1969 were a disaster for the IRA, which had been lamentably ill-prepared for the armed police and loyalist onslaught on the Catholic community. People were angry and they expressed their anger – for instance on a wall across the road from Peel Street, which ran off the Falls Road, where someone daubed, 'IRA = I Ran Away'.

As the months passed, young men and women who hitherto had little interest in politics were drawn to both the IRAs, but Freddie Scappaticci, by this time twenty-three years old, did not rush out to join the ranks of either. Instead, immediately after the violent assaults on Catholic areas, Scappaticci took his place amongst the many vigilantes who patrolled the streets of the Markets area at night. Meanwhile, his friend

Seán Flynn did join the IRA that August. He found the Markets unit to be a small, ineffectual outfit with virtually no guns: 'Before the Troubles, there was only a few IRA members in the Markets area: the McKnight brothers, Bobby and Seán, Billy Weir, Jim Hargey, Jim Webb, and Joe McCann. But after the loyalist street burnings and the RUC murders in August '69, there was an influx of people joining the 'RA. I joined. Freddie didn't, well, not that I remember, not immediately anyway. He was a vigilante. Scap and most of the vigilantes turned Provo [Provisional IRA]. Jim Webb was the first OC of the Provos in the Markets and Joe McCann was OC of the Officials. There was fifty-four of us in the company by the time I was made Joe's adjutant [second-in-command]. Me and Freddie was on opposite sides, although to be fair, there was never any Provie/Sticky friction in the Markets in those early days.'[8]

New recruits flocked to the Provisionals because they appeared to be more militant than the Official IRA, who were perceived to have failed the Catholic population during the communal tumult that occurred in 1969. Despite the largely peaceful co-existence that marked relations between the differing organisations in the Markets area, the presence of two competing IRAs could be a recipe for strife, and derogatory terms of identity were hurled at the opposition, with the Official IRA being delineated as 'Stickies' because they wore a sticky-back Easter lily to commemorate the 1916 Rising, and the Officials calling the Provisionals 'Pinheads' because they wore a pin in their Easter lily.

While most of the vigilantes joined the Provisional IRA, most of the pre-Troubles IRA stayed with the Official IRA. This meant there was a dearth of experienced volunteers in the Provisionals and this, in turn, led to natural-born leaders, like Scappaticci, rising rapidly through the ranks. Anthony McIntyre, who was only twelve years old when the Troubles broke out in 1969, would go on to join the Provisional IRA at the age of sixteen and spend eighteen years in prison for murder, where he would obtain a first-class honours degree through the Open University; upon release he completed a doctorate through Queen's University Belfast. McIntyre knew of Scappaticci from an early age: 'I didn't know him before the Troubles at all, but everybody knew Freddie Scap after '69. His was a big name in the Markets from the very start, just like Jim Bryson [an IRA leader from the Ballymurphy area who was eventually shot dead in a British Army ambush]. That was one of the things about the Troubles – lots of people, who otherwise would have been unremarkable, could become personalities and celebrities very quickly. Scap was one of those people; he was recognised as a staunch republican, a diehard, if you want. And there was a certain added dimension to his character, the Italian-sounding name added to his mystique. You know, Scappaticci, it sounded like somebody out of *The Godfather*. Even when you didn't know him personally, you knew of him. He was OC of the Markets before internment and was on … the battalion staff. You can't take that away from him … he was well thought of back then.'[9]

One person who did not think well of him was former Markets resident Marian McMullan. She recalled one night in early 1971 when 'the 'RA were all standing at "Provie Corner" in the Markets and I saw Scap coming down, the leather coat on, and I saw … it looked like a machine gun protruding out of his coat, and he comes over to these 'RA men, and they're all standing there, real heavy 'RA men, guys that had killed people, and I saw his finger going mad; he was pointing in their faces, laying down the law and then he turned and walked away, and he turned back again, and the finger was pointing again.

'I later found out one of his sons had driven a stolen car into a garden wall and all the talk was the 'RA were considering knee-capping him. I also found out that he told them, "If you touch my son, I'll blow you all away. I'll fuckin' stiff the lot of you." And they all just stood there, with their heads down, and Freddie walked away. What did I think of him after that incident? He scared the shit out of me. I'd never seen the likes of that before.'[10]

However, despite this hard-man image and a rivalry between the Official and Provisional IRA in relation to fighting the British, during Scappaticci's time as Provisional IRA OC of the Markets area his unit did not come up to the mark in IRA terms – they did not shoot dead one British soldier. This contrasts with the Official IRA, which, on 22 May 1971, ambushed a mobile patrol of the Royal Green Jackets and shot dead the patrol's leader, Corporal Robert Bankier, a twenty-four-year-old married man with two children. Joe McCann, who led that ambush, was later shot dead by members of the Parachute Regiment in Joy Street on 15 April 1972.

Despite his unit not having killed any British soldiers, Scappaticci was far from idle in terms of operations. Indeed, because the Markets was geographically already in the city centre, his unit gained a reputation in the IRA for carrying out numerous bombing attacks on commercial properties. The success of the Provisional IRA's campaign would soon lead the British government to introduce internment without trial in an effort to nullify the organisation, but this would prove to be a disastrous move.

3

NO JUSTICE, NO PEACE

'Those who make peaceful revolution impossible will make violent revolution inevitable.'

John F. Kennedy, 13 March 1962

It was the Year of the Stuttering Revolution: 1970. The first fatalities of the Provisional IRA's campaign to free Ireland from British rule were three of its own volunteers and two daughters of one of them. Thomas McCool, Thomas Carlin and Joe Coyle perished on 26 June 1970 while assembling a bomb in McCool's home. Also killed were McCool's schoolgirl daughters, Bernadette (9) and Carol (4).[1] As Derry wept, a series of unforeseen events, which began the following day, saw the Provisional IRA emerge as the praetorian guard of the Catholic community.

On 27 June, three Protestants – Alexander Gould (18), Daniel Loughlins (32) and William Kincaid (28) – were shot dead by the Provisional IRA during rioting in the Ardoyne area of north Belfast.

Later that night, an intense gun battle took place around St Matthew's Catholic church in the Short Strand area of east Belfast and two more Protestants, James McCurrie (34) and Robert 'Ginger' Neill (38), were similarly killed by the Provisionals. Also shot dead was IRA volunteer Henry McIlhone, while Billy McKee, who is said to have led the Provisional IRA unit defending St Matthew's, was badly wounded in an exchange of fire with loyalists.[2] Loyalist spokespersons dispute that McCurrie and Neill were gunmen, but what is beyond question is that the Provisionals came out of these confrontations confident in the knowledge that they were being lauded in nationalist areas as defenders against perceived Protestant aggression. The Provos had nailed their colours to the mast. Billy McKee would later say that after that nobody wrote 'IRA = I Ran Away' on the walls any more.

Six days later, on 3 July 1970, the British Army flexed its muscles by imposing a curfew on the Lower Falls area of Belfast. Over the next two days, the army shot dead four innocent men, one of whom was a young Polish reporter. It was the Crown forces' turn to demonstrate that their capacity to kill more than matched that of the Provisional IRA.

On 12 August 1970, Constables Samuel Donaldson and Robert Millar were the first RUC officers to be killed by the Provisional IRA during the Troubles, when a car that they were towing exploded after being booby-trapped. It would be the following year before the first alleged informer was shot dead by the IRA, on 27 January 1971. John Kavanagh (28), a married roof tiler with two children, lived in the Catholic Kashmir Road area of Belfast. Kavanagh was shot in the back of the head from no more than twelve inches away. He was the first of many alleged informers who would be slain at the hands of the IRA.[3]

As the body count in the fledging Troubles began to mount up, the introduction of internment without trial polluted the air. The draconian measure had been introduced in 1956 by the then Stormont Home Affairs minister, Brian Faulkner, to effectively guillotine the IRA's 1950s' campaign. Now Faulkner was Prime Minister of Northern Ireland, and he was convinced that a similar outcome would be forthcoming should internment be introduced once more. Rumours of its advent had been circulating in IRA meetings for weeks before its actual implementation – volunteers had been told on several occasions to stay out of their houses, only to find that the warnings were false alarms.

On 8 August 1971, the night before 'Operation Demetrius' took place, the Provisional IRA OC Markets, Freddie Scappaticci, ordered his volunteers to stay out of their own homes because internment was expected to be put into operation the following morning. Many volunteers obeyed the order, but not Freddie. At 4.30 a.m. on 9 August, the Scappaticci front door was kicked in and the house was invaded by screaming British soldiers. The little man with the jet-black hair and fiery disposition was unceremoniously trailed out and taken to an interrogation centre, along with 342 other IRA and civil rights suspects.

A commander should never ignore his own orders, and, in Scappaticci's case, it would prove to be a costly mistake. He was driven to Girdwood Army Barracks in north Belfast, which lies adjacent to Crumlin Road Gaol. Like his fellow prisoners, whilst being transported to the barracks he was subjected to a severe beating by soldiers who thrashed him with their rifle butts, batons and boots. But to a scrapper like Freddie, taking a general beating in the back of a British transporter would have been like having smoke blown in his face. Unfortunately, for him and his fellow arrestees there was more than smoke awaiting them at the end of the journey: 'Whilst in Girdwood, they were forced to run a gauntlet outside. This consisted of broken glass and rough stones. The prisoners were made to run this barefoot, while being flailed from both sides with batons.'[4]

Whether or not Scappaticci had time during his arrest to admonish himself for not following his own order, he might have drawn some comfort later from the knowledge that others had fared much worse than he, with one prisoner outlining his experiences at the hands of the British Army: 'I was [hooded and] brought out and a rope was tied around me under my armpits. This was attached to a helicopter and the helicopter suddenly arose, taking me with it, hanging underneath it. I don't know how high it went up. I was finding it difficult to breathe. Then the helicopter came down again and when I was about fifteen feet or so above the ground, I was suddenly dropped to the ground.'[5] There is no record that Scappaticci was subjected to similar treatment. Indeed, his ill-treatment was relatively mild when compared with that of some of his comrades, especially those who became known as 'The Hooded Men'. These were fourteen individuals from across Northern Ireland who were hooded and tortured for over a week. They were only released into the custody of the prison wardens in Crumlin Road Gaol after a writ of habeas corpus was filed.

When it came to who to arrest in the internment round-ups, the RUC's Special Branch had primacy, but their files were outdated and, consequently, most of those detained were former IRA men from the 1940s and 1950s, many of whom were old-age pensioners who had long ago hung up their Sam Browne belts and broad black brimmer hats. Accordingly, 116 suspects were released within forty-eight hours. Freddie Scappaticci was not one of them.

Things would improve for the security forces on the intelligence front in the weeks and months after the introduction of internment, as the harsh, often brutal, interrogation of suspects led to enhanced intelligence return, which accordingly led to more accurate targeting of IRA personnel.

The 9 August 1971 internees were initially held in Crumlin Road Gaol while the government rushed to make ready an internment camp at Long Kesh, a former Royal Air Force (RAF) base outside the town of Lisburn, County Antrim. By the end of November, all internees had been transferred to Long Kesh, with Scappaticci incarcerated in Compound Two, known to the prisoners as 'Cage 2'. As the numbers of internees increased, Scappaticci was moved to Cages 4 and 5 respectively, where he made his mark, noticeably for his irascible attitude, which prompted one fellow-internee, Micky Donnelly from Derry, to remark, 'Freddie Scap was short-tempered and quick to throw a punch … If he'd been a foot taller, he would have been a dangerous bully, but as it was, he usually had one or two with him when he did throw his weight about, and he didn't do much damage.'[6]

One Derry IRA volunteer who was interned with Scappaticci recalled, 'I was in Cage 5 with him, around '73. I'd been on the run for a year and a half. I was very lucky, a year and a half in the area was good going. I didn't go outside the area. I can't remember if Scap was on the cage staff, he might have been a hut OC or something. Now, Scap was an aggressive wee boy. My first impression of him was he was a scrapper, but even at that, he was different. A lot of Belfast people were gobshites, big mouths who got themselves a bad name. Freddie wasn't one of them. I got to know him through being in the cage and playing football. He wasn't a gobshite; he kept his mouth shut. I actually liked him. It seems he could be a nasty wee fucker, but he was never, ever nasty with me.'[7]

For Scappaticci, as for all internees, life was excruciatingly mono-tonous. In many ways, it was the hardest time that a prisoner could endure because, unlike someone serving a sentence from the court, those who were interned had no release date and were subject to the arbitrary decision-making of the governing authorities, who in turn were regulated, in the main, by public opinion and the level of violence that was emanating from the IRA campaign. Consequently, if the IRA had the upper hand in their war with the British, the prospect of the internees being released was drastically diminished – and at times it appeared that the IRA did have the upper hand.

The banner headline of the first edition of the republican newspaper *An Phoblacht* boasted: '1972: A Year of Decision'.[8] In the accompanying article, an optimistic assessment was given of how the IRA's war with the British was going: 'England is on its knees; Stormont is finished ...'[9] In one respect, the article was accurate: the Northern Ireland parliament, Stormont, *was* finished and, on 24 March 1972, British Prime Minister Ted Heath announced that the political institution, which had been the bastion of unionist domination in Northern Ireland since 1921, was to be suspended. However, while the fall of Stormont represented a win for the IRA, it was a pyrrhic victory because, contrary to republican propaganda, the British were not on their knees. Instead, they were recalibrating their approach to an unbalanced political dynamic. The defeat of the IRA was still the primary objective, but they had come to the realisation that this could only be brought about with the IRA's alienation from its nationalist support base.

It was time to ask themselves how that divorce could be achieved. In strategic terms, the causes of discontentment needed to be addressed, so internment without trial had to be ended and nationalists had to be given equal citizenship and representation within any future Northern Irish political institutions. In essence, this meant that a nationalist/ unionist power-sharing executive had to be the cornerstone of any political settlement. This was a panacea that the Social Democratic and Labour Party (SDLP) had been advocating for since its inception in August 1970.

Accordingly, in December 1973, the British government proposed that a power-sharing Stormont regime should be convened, with the executive role being shared by those willing to compromise – specifically, the SDLP, Ulster Unionist Party (UUP) and the middle-of-the-road Alliance Party. This looked good from a nationalist perspective. Far from the days when they were just seeking civil rights, nationalists, along with unionists, now had their hands on the steering wheel of power and the IRA were on the ropes, with victory appearing to be further away than ever.

Such a transformed political landscape barely affected Freddie Scappaticci's stalwart republican outlook, and the evidence for this emerged when his name appeared on one of a series of lists drawn up by the British authorities in 1973. Signed by a Captain E.P.G. Springfield, 'List B' was headed: 'Republicans who have recanted but still will not sign the oath', and it contained the names of internees whom the British said they were considering releasing, including Scappaticci. What is evident about this list is that Captain Springfield was guessing who might, and might not, recant their republicanism and thus qualify for release. The hard reality is that the document was a contradiction in terms, because if these republicans *had* recanted their IRA involvement, as Springfield said, why would they not sign a document declaring that they would have no further involvement with the IRA upon release?

This author has contacted several internees named in List B, and each said that they were never approached by the British authorities and asked to renounce their commitment to the IRA. That is not to say that other republicans may not have been offered an opportunity to repudiate their membership of the IRA and secure release. However, there is no evidence that any of the men on List B ever indicated to the British that they would renounce their republicanism. What is important here is that if, like the others on the list, Scappaticci did turn down this get-out-of-jail card, it would be telling because it would show that he was still a committed and principled IRA volunteer and was untainted at this stage with the mark of informer.

The names on List B were:

John Davey, OC, Bellaghy Unit, IRA, 9 August '71

Fred Scappaticci, OC, B Coy, 3 BN, IRA, 9 August '71

Gerry McKerr, OC/EO [executive officer], Armagh/1 town, PIRA, 9 August '71

Patrick McNally, Adj, Armagh, PIRA, 9 August '71

Owen Farley, OC, C Coy, 1 BN, PIRA, 5 Sept '71

John Gabriel Young, Vol, G Coy, 1 BN, PIRA, 7 Oct '71

Kevin Hannaway, TO [training officer], Belfast Brigade, PIRA, 9 August '71

Sean Watson, OC, B Coy, 1 BN, PIRA, 9 August '71

Paddy McDonald, TO/IO [intelligence officer], B Coy, 1 BN, PIRA, 9 August '71

John O'Rawe, OC, 1 BN, PIRA, 9 August '71

Gerry McGuire, EO, 1 BN/OC B Coy, 1 BN, 9 August '71 (leader of the Provisionals in the Maze)

Sean Murphy, TO/IO, 1 BN, PIRA, 9 August, '71

Joseph O'Neill, Vol, D Coy, 3 BN, PIRA, 20 October '71

Daniel Canning, OC, Derry City Coy, PIRA, 17 September '71

Michael Donnelly, OC, Derry City Coy, PIRA, 9 August '71

Sean O'Hare, Vol, Derry City Coy, PIRA, 9 August '71.[10]

At the bottom of the document, a circumspect Captain Springfield hedged his bets: 'These lists probably contain a number of detainees who are worthy of consideration for release. However, there are indications that the Provisionals are using the opportunity [of internment] to put forward a number of top officers who would once again become active on release.'[11] Scappaticci did not recant his republican beliefs, but in the end this decision mattered little; although he did not know it at the time, freedom still beckoned.

4

MAKING MONEY

'They were just drunks by now. Incompetents. They didn't know what they were doing half the time. Scap and his lot hadn't been on ops for years. They knew nothing.'

Gerry 'Whitey' Bradley,
IRA ASU commander[1]

Freddie Scappaticci was released from internment in January 1974 and immediately reported back to the IRA. By this time, Anthony McIntyre was a sixteen-year-old IRA volunteer, and he recalls meeting Scappaticci in a drinking club in the Markets. 'He was a wee small guy, but people used to look up to him because of the name, former internee and all that; his height didn't matter.'[2] McIntyre soon found himself arrested and charged with IRA membership. Being too young to be sent to Crumlin Road Gaol, he was remanded into the custody of the De La Salle Brothers in St Patrick's Boys Home on Belfast's Glen Road. Later, in and around March/April 1974, he absconded from the home, waved off from the correctional site by the same Brothers whose responsibility it was to keep him in custody.

Having 'escaped' from custody, McIntyre went on the run and was taken to a house in Mountpottinger Road in the Short Strand area of Belfast where he was visited by IRA leaders Freddie Scappaticci, now a battalion officer, and Jimmy Davidson, who was OC of the Markets and Short Strand IRA Company. The escapee was given five pounds existence money and thereafter visited weekly by Scappaticci, who always brought a fiver with him.

After several weeks, McIntyre moved back to the Ormeau Road/ Markets area, where, he says, 'I had operational dealings with Scap.'[3] McIntyre did not know what rank Scappaticci held, other than that he was higher up in the command structure than any of the local officers in the Markets/Short Strand IRA Company. The Markets and Short Strand, two areas separated by the River Lagan, had originally been separate IRA companies but they had merged to become one unit in 1973.

A former IRA battalion commander, 'Diarmuid O'Toole', spoke of the early 1970s as a time of considerable organisational fluidity in the Belfast IRA, with staff officers changing, sometimes on a weekly basis, due to individuals being interned or sentenced before the courts. In July 1973, for example, things took a decided turn for the worse for the IRA in Belfast when the Belfast Brigade quartermaster-turned-informer Eamon Molloy passed on the location of an upcoming brigade staff meeting to British Intelligence. As a result, on 19 July, the brigade operations officer, Brendan 'The Dark' Hughes (so called because of his dark features), and staff officer Tom Cahill, as well as Gerry Adams, arrived at a house in the Iveagh district of the Falls Road, whereupon they were promptly arrested and dragged off to Springfield Road RUC

Barracks. They were soon joined by another brigade officer, Owen Coogan. Several hours after the arrests, and again on information supplied by Molloy, the entire third battalion staff was arrested at a house in the Ardoyne.

It was obvious to all that an informer was in their midst, but he/she was hard to pin down. Eventually, after a process of elimination, the informer was identified as Molloy. He was arrested by the IRA in May 1975 and made a full confession regarding his involvement with the security forces, owning up to handing over important information to the security forces from 1972, including fingering dozens of IRA personnel and revealing the locations of a huge arsenal of weapons. Molloy was killed with a bullet in the back of his head and then 'disappeared', a euphemism for a victim being buried in a secret grave in the Irish Republic.[4]

O'Toole offered that Scappaticci was Belfast Brigade OC for a very short time following his release from internment in 1974. 'He became OC after Big John. It was around the time of those 1,000lb car bombs outside the likes of the Grand Central Hotel, in Royal Avenue. My recollection was that he was a brigade squirrel [an intelligence officer], then he was definitely brigade OC. Here's the way it went: Ivor [Bell] was OC after [the previous OC] and The Dark were scooped in July '73. Then Ivor was arrested in January '74, and he was followed for a short period by Seán Convery. Just before Ivor's arrest [8 December 1973], The Dark had escaped from Long Kesh, and he took over as OC from Convery until he was rearrested on 10 May 1974. Then we had Big John, and then Scap.'[5]

Scappaticci's time in charge did not last long. He was recaptured that August and his arrest was newsworthy enough to make the front page of the *Belfast Telegraph* on 16 August, the triumphant headline proclaiming, 'Troops capture "Top IRA Officer"'. The article pointed out that he 'is understood to have been one of the "top ten" on the Army's wanted list in the 3 Brigade area', and that 'he had an Italian-sounding name'.[6] Frederick Scappaticci, diehard IRA volunteer, yielded no information to his police interrogators and was once again interned without trial in Long Kesh, whereupon he found that the days were just as long and monotonous as ever.

Nevertheless, by 1975 an intermediary called Brendan Duddy, a businessman from Derry, had become involved in contact between the IRA Army Council and the British government, and the prospect of a ceasefire was being discussed between the warring parties. The resulting ceasefire did not immediately bring about the end of internment, but it did herald the start of an undeclared non-aggression pact between the IRA and the British Army. For IRA prisoners in Long Kesh, it was a period when bowed heads met in whispered conclaves, not least because the prisoners could see that a massive building programme was under way in the northern part of the prison. Yet, word was reaching the most senior republican captives in the prison that Ruairí Ó Brádaigh and Billy McKee were engaged in secret talks with representatives of the British government in Derry, and that the British were indicating that they wanted to withdraw from Ireland and needed the help of the IRA. Many republicans were bewildered and anxious, yet hopeful that the national leadership could produce a positive outcome.

However, while there was no Alan Turing in the republican movement, prisoners Gerry Adams, Ivor Bell and Brendan 'The Dark' Hughes were working their way through the enigma that was the British position and, no matter which way they looked at it, Perfidious Albion's chocolates seemed to be laced with poison. Both Adams and Bell had been part of a republican delegation that was flown to London in 1972 to speak to British government ministers and officials, and the talks had broken down precisely because the British were not prepared to give a date for withdrawal from Ireland. Not unreasonably, the three men were asking themselves a series of biting questions: Why didn't the British indicate in 1972 that they were intent on leaving if they had had their fill of Ireland? What had prompted them to change their minds on such a fundamental issue as withdrawal? And what was all the building about in the northern part of the prison?

It was only with the passage of time that it became evident that the British were intent on criminalising the republican struggle by denying political status to future republican prisoners, whilst simultaneously portraying the IRA as a mafia-type gang. Meanwhile, they were buying time by hinting that they wanted the help of the republican movement to withdraw from Ireland, even as they were building a new prison called 'The Maze' in the northern part of Long Kesh. For the British criminalisation plan to succeed though, internment had to end because, intrinsically, internees – being people incarcerated without charge – were political prisoners. Accordingly, all remaining internees were released on 5 December 1975. Freddie Scappaticci was at large again.

Mighty things were expected of Scappaticci upon his release. One young IRA volunteer recalled: 'I remember the talk of Scap getting out and Big Jimmy [Davidson] and all were there, and people were talking about, you know, is he coming back, and he didn't seem to be coming back. I think he began to get frowned upon because people had been waiting on him to report back and he hadn't reported back.'

When he had been released back in January 1974, Scappaticci had reported back to the IRA within twenty-four hours. Now, on his second discharge from internment, people were wondering if Scap was going to report back at all. Was he contemplating walking away from the struggle? Was he now convinced that it was a waste of time and life?

Wrestling with the Irish-Italian's reluctance to re-immerse himself in the IRA's armed struggle, some reasoned he was taking time to evaluate his life, to determine what was best for his family and himself. After all, internment had lasted four years and four months and he had spent three years and eight months of that time locked up in Long Kesh, never knowing when he would be released, not providing for his wife and children, and receiving only a meagre stipend from the republican movement. And what did a future in the IRA promise other than the strangling prospect of going back to prison, or even winding up being shot dead by loyalists or British soldiers? Yet, if he did not return to active service, his standing in the republican community would plummet and, for a man with a massive ego, this would have been the psychological equivalent of committing hari-kari. Like many IRA volunteers who had spent time in prison and no longer wanted to be considered for operations, Scappaticci may well have been looking for a middle way, a means whereby he could remain in the IRA and be held in the vaulted esteem to which he had become accustomed without the worry of being murdered by loyalists, or of once again finding himself in the suffocating confines of a prison cell.

Scappaticci's first task was to make provision for his family's welfare and he made sure that, in the years after his release from internment, they wanted for nothing. To his credit, Scappaticci liked to put in a day's work and so, after he was released from Long Kesh, he went to work on Belfast's building sites, where it did not take long for him to find out that there was a get-rich-quick tax scheme that exempted the owner of a '715' tax booklet from paying weekly tax. Each 715 booklet contained 25–50 vouchers – virtual blank cheques – and could be renewed once all the vouchers were used. The scheme operated as follows: every week the building contractor would pay the total site wages due to his workers, inclusive of tax, to the holder of the 715 voucher and receive a voucher for same in return, which the contractor could show to the taxman at the end of year. From the money received from the contractor, the holder of the 715 would then pay the building-site subcontractors, minus their tax. The subcontractors also received a 715 voucher that they could show the taxman at the end of the year to say they had paid their tax. The overall idea was that, at the end of the financial year, the person whose name was on the 715 vouchers would be responsible for paying over the accredited tax revenue to the taxman. However, it was often the case that the original owner of the 715 would 'sell' his booklet to the highest bidder in the knowledge that when the day of reckoning came with the taxman, he would declare himself bankrupt and put his lack of funds down to him being an alcoholic or a gambler. Sometimes the owner would declare to the taxman that he had 'lost' his booklet.

Scappaticci started buying 715 booklets and 'taxing' construction workers. The building trade in Northern Ireland was booming in the mid-1970s and, if the 715-holder had 200 construction workers on his books, he could potentially draw more than £5,000 per week without setting foot on a building site. As a supplement, the single weekly voucher could be 'beefed up' by 'putting on' other builders, from other building sites, and, as the limit on a single voucher was £500,000, the potential earning power for the owner of the voucher was astronomical.

In no time at all, the money was rolling in for Scappaticci.[7] Clan Scappaticci was getting larger and consequently he built a double-storey extension onto his home in Farnham Street in the Lower Ormeau area, creating a larger living room, kitchen and extra en suite bedrooms. The family had not been on many holidays during his years of imprisonment, so he also brought them to Lido di Jesolo, a beach resort in the province of Venice, Italy, as well as on trips to France, Bulgaria and Florida – and even on a skiing holiday, which virtually no one in working-class Belfast would have contemplated in the mid-1970s. If there was a new technological gadget, such as a large television screen, his was the first family in the Markets to get it. Scappaticci changed his car every year, and the replacement vehicle had to be brand new. He was football mad and was a Manchester City season ticketholder. The family also moved house twice between the mid-1970s and the 1980s. When they moved into new homes in Twinbrook, and in Riverdale, in the Andersonstown area, Scappaticci completely gutted the properties and undertook major renovations to both dwellings. In his Riverdale house he installed a bar and a full-size snooker table.

On top of the money he was getting from the illegal tax scam, Scappaticci continued to carry out building work. One man, 'Barney McHugh', who worked for him as a bricklayer, said he was getting 'three fortunes'.[8] Barney explained how Scappaticci was tied into the scam with members of the Official IRA from the Markets area, who were the scheme's primary architects. Barney held mixed views of his former boss. While the two had been on friendly terms, Barney thought him 'stingy' when it came to dolling out the wages on payday: 'There wasn't always an argument, but if he could cut you up for a few bob, he'd do it. I resented that because, you know, it wasn't as if he needed the money.'[9] That said, Barney recalled that Scappaticci wasn't hard to work for and never brought up politics whilst working. Neither did he loose-talk. Equally, he never gave any indication he was in the IRA, even though everyone knew his history.

By the end of 1976 Freddie was back in the IRA, operating as a Belfast Brigade intelligence officer. In this capacity, he was debriefing volunteers who were released from interrogation centres. Diarmuid O'Toole said, 'I'm not exactly sure who talent-spotted Scap, but even then he was recognised as a top man when it came to debriefing the volunteers who were being released from Castlereagh [an RUC interrogation centre].'[10]

For the IRA, these were difficult times. They were emerging from a ceasefire that had proved disastrous. While Scappaticci was busy building up his lucrative tax scam, the doublespeak of the British government negotiators who had been communicating with Ruairí Ó Brádaigh and Billy McKee was finally deciphered, and in the opening months of 1976 the IRA ceasefire broke down. The end of the ceasefire would bring about a period of intense security-force activity, during which hundreds of insurgents were brutalised by police interrogators. Central to the new British approach was a well-concealed programme called 'criminalisation/Ulsterisation/normalisation', the aim of which was to put as many insurrectionists as possible into the newly built H-Block complexes of the Maze prison. British propagandists were declaring to the world that the IRA were a bunch of hoodlums and godfathers and, therefore, their struggle for Irish freedom was a conspiracy that had to be dealt with through the courts, which was the 'criminalisation' aspect of the policy. As the H-Blocks were filling up with IRA and Irish National Liberation Army (INLA) prisoners, whole regiments of the British Army were being withdrawn from the North and replaced with freshly recruited local police officers and members of the local militia, the UDR. From this came the term 'Ulsterisation', which then led automatically to the advent of 'normalisation'.

An integral facet of the 'criminalisation' policy was another little-known concept called 'noble cause corruption'. This term is a euphemism for the procurement and acceptance of corrupt evidence, which usually amounted to suspects being coerced into making statements of admission whereby they would admit their involvement in IRA, INLA or loyalist paramilitary groups. These statements could then be presented to the courts as *prima facie* evidence. The concept behind the process was that a noble cause (in this case, the conviction of persons whom the authorities presumed to be guilty of 'terrorist crimes') could only be served by the corruption of the judicial system, because in the normal course of events only a fool would make an incriminating statement that would see him or her spend many years in prison. The term was first introduced in 1992 by Sir John Woodcock, HM Chief Inspector of Constabulary, but the concept had been around for much longer according to Tory MP Sir Ivan Laurence QC, who said that during the 1960s and 1970s, 'the police made things up in a large proportion of cases. I defended villains, including the Krays. And they were always being verballed [being attributed false verbal statements of confession], sometimes planted.'[11] Charles Pollard, chief of the Thames Valley police force, reinforced Laurence's assertion: 'Everybody knew it happened like that, judges, magistrates, the whole criminal system had a sort of conspiracy.'[12] In Northern Ireland, there were two limbs to the noble-cause-corruption programme: the extraction of confessions from suspects by dint of torture or brutality, and the blanket acceptance of those confessions in the High Court.

To maximise the possibility of convictions, and for the forced confessions to stand up in court, the system needed to be rigged in favour of the police accusers. In other words, suspects needed to be tried in the Diplock court system. These were courts that came about after a recommendation from Lord Diplock in December 1972, when he suggested that jury trials be set aside and that a single judge officiate over trials involving 'scheduled' offences, a synonym for 'terrorism'. Given that in the early days of the Troubles, 90 per cent of the judges were avowedly unionist, some being former Unionist politicians, this was a formula guaranteed to produce a wealth of convictions.

What aided and abetted this perversion of justice was the fact that this was the era before the Police and Criminal Evidence Act 1984 (PACE), and so there was no visual or audio record of police interrogations that could be presented to the courts. That left the judges with a simple choice: to accept police officers' contentions that suspects habitually brutalised themselves in their cells, or to believe the accused when they asserted that police ill-treatment had resulted in their making a confession. Put another way, judges were faced with a decision to take either the word of a police officer or that of a 'suspected terrorist'. The judges invariably ignored defendants' claims of having been brutalised into making confessions and usually handed down the harshest sentences possible. Thus was the noble cause served.

Having been sentenced by the courts, prisoners were faced with the final limb of the criminalisation/Ulsterisation/normalisation strategy when the British declared that, after 1 March 1976, all freshly sentenced prisoners would be housed in the Maze, the site that had previously piqued the interest of Gerry Adams, Ivor Bell and Brendan Hughes. Government spokespersons also stated that those prisoners sentenced after this date would not be able to avail themselves of the 'Special Category Status' that Adams, Bell, Hughes and other republican and loyalist prisoners had experienced in the Cages from 1972. This meant that all sentenced prisoners, whether republican or loyalist, would have to wear the prison uniform, dubbed 'The Monkey Suit' by republicans, and present themselves for prison work every day. The sprint to the finishing line was on as far as the British were concerned. But even the most intricate of plans can fall apart, especially when confronted with the obstinacy of patriotism.

The Secretary of State for Northern Ireland at this time was a Yorkshireman called Roy Mason, who regularly described republican leaders as 'godfathers'. He also boasted in the *Daily Express*, 'We are squeezing the terrorists like rolling up a toothpaste tube.' In relation to this latter statement, Mason was not lying.

As the IRA's ranks began to be depleted and the jails to fill up, there was a realisation within that organisation that a dramatic change had to occur, and a more centralised counter-intelligence unit had to be developed if total defeat were to be avoided. This concept had its origins in Long Kesh in the mid-1970s, when Bell, Hughes and other republican leaders began debriefing IRA members arriving in the prison to discover what the authorities knew or wanted to know about the IRA. As a result, a new leadership was put in place in the IRA after February 1977, and it brought into being the ISU in the autumn of 1978.[13] It was as a member of this unit that Scappaticci's name would become infamous within IRA circles.

5

NUTTING-SQUAD RULES

'He's not in your face so he's not in your mind, but Scap knows everything because he's knocking around with guys who know everything.'

Gerry Brannigan, leading republican

The new unit was known as 'IS', or 'Internal Security', in IRA circles, although as time went on the press would dub it the 'Nutting Squad' because, soon after its formation, the bodies of suspected informers began to be found in back-street alleyways and on remote border roads. Most of the victims had two bullet holes in the back of their heads, the second bullet making sure of the kill. Given its strategic importance, infiltration of the ISU would become a major priority for British Intelligence.

The remit of the new unit was to plug any holes in the organisation's security by vetting all new recruits, debriefing all volunteers who were being released from police custody, implementing anti-interrogation techniques and getting to the bottom of any operations that had gone awry. This meant that those in the ISU would have known the identities of all new recruits, the nature of the RUC Special Branch's questions and volunteers' responses to those questions while in an interrogation centre, and who specifically had been out on an operation that had backfired. In time, Internal Security would have the power of veto over all operations in the Belfast area, which effectively gave them control of the IRA in the city.

Those selected to join the ISU were all seasoned volunteers, men in their thirties and forties who had been in prison and were well versed in the tactics of police interrogators. This would-be *corps d'élite* were mostly drawn from the Lower Falls' 'D' Company, a unit that had fought pitched battles with the British Army in the early 1970s. The head of the ISU was an ex 'D' Company man called John Joe Magee. A portly, middle-aged man with receding, once-ginger hair, Magee, at first glance, looked like an old soak, but he had been a member of the Special Boat Service (SBS), a special-forces unit of the Royal Marines. The former SBS soldier was a soft-spoken, contemplative man but a hard drinker, and yet, inexplicably, he was trusted by the IRA leadership to head up this most influential of departments.

In 1978, Freddie Scappaticci was appointed second-in-command to Magee. This job was tailor-made for the Markets man, because in the ISU his status as a major IRA figure would be enhanced, while at the same time he would avoid having to take part in dangerous operations that could lead to him either returning to prison or being killed. Moreover, he would be exercising life-and-death control over those volunteers unfortunate enough to come to the ISU's attention. Tellingly, unlike his fellow tout-catchers, Scappaticci was not a heavy drinker, which endeared him to the IRA leadership.

Over the next fifteen years, Scappaticci would prove to be a persua-
sive inquisitor, often promising those under suspicion of being British
stool pigeons that the IRA would set them free if they just gave up the
details of their informing activities, but, as Scappaticci remarked, that
was a lie 'and everybody being what they are, everybody has a breaking point, y'know, and they think they're going home – but they don't.'[1]
Whether or not the ISU's victims had all been informers – and many
of the victims' families dispute this claim – there is a chilling vulgarity
about Scappaticci's remark: the victims did not go home because he,
and those he so willingly commanded, made it their business to break
them and then oversee their executions.

It was not only the victims' families who loathed the ISU; there
were also IRA volunteers who despised them. 'Daithi Harkin', a former
Derry Brigade officer, recalled, 'I got on all right with him [Scappaticci],
probably because I didn't have any great dealings with him. He was IS
and I only came across him what … a half a dozen times when dealing
with problems in Derry.'[2] When asked what Scappaticci was like on
the occasions that he met him, the volunteer observed, 'He was fairly
professional, to pay him his dues. He would have come up to Derry,
done what he had to do, and got out as quickly as possible. But he was
a bullshitter.'[3] The former volunteer went on to explain this contempt
for Scappaticci: 'Y'see, he could talk a good operation, he knew how
ops worked, but I don't think I ran into him too many times out on
ops. This guy would be a super soldier now, aye, he would be. Dead
bodies behind him all the time. Aye, Scap was good when there was
nobody on the other side fuckin' shooting back at him, when some
poor fucker was hooded an' tied up, an' on his knees in some remote
bog, and all he had to do was to put a couple of bullets in the back of
the guy's head.

'The reason he was in IS was to hide … see at the very start, when it was formed, it was formed for older volunteers who hadn't it in them anymore to do active service. So, they [the IRA leadership] wanted somewhere to put them, somewhere to hide them, and basically that's where they went. I wanted fuck all to do with IS because the only time we seen them was when there was a fuckin' problem, so if I didn't see them, I was doing all right.'[4]

Another IRA man who had little respect for those in the ISU was Gerry 'Whitey' Bradley, who, along with journalist Brian Feeney, published *Insider: Gerry Bradley's Life in the IRA*. Bradley was known by the RUC and British Army to be an active service unit OC, someone they believed had been involved in the deaths of multiple security-force personnel. On one occasion, he was arrested and brought to Castlereagh holding centre and, during his detention, his police interrogators mentioned operations that had not come off or had been in the planning stage. Upon release, Bradley was debriefed by Freddie Scappaticci in Jamaica Street in the Ardoyne district.

'Something's going on,' Bradley told Scappaticci. 'How do they know about ops that never happened? I'm not doing any more until it's sorted out.'

Scappaticci replied, 'Look, there's a big inquiry going on.'[5]

Bradley was not one to pull his punches and he was scathing in his assessment of the ISU: 'They were complete incompetents, drunks, wasters. Some people confuse them with the "Nutting Squad". They wouldn't have had the balls. They did the beatings, torturing, but not the killing. They spent their days in the pub at the bottom of Clonard Street. They did their interrogations in a house near the pub so they didn't have to walk too far.'[6] The killings to which Bradley is referring were those carried out by IRA operatives who were not directly attached to the ISU, but, despite his contemptuous remarks, there is no doubt the ISU carried out its own fair share of executions.

Bradley himself had once been arrested by Internal Security and brought to the house near the pub in Clonard Street, where he was tied up in a darkened room: 'I reared up at them because I could smell the drink on them while they were doing interrogations. They were just drunks by now. Scap and his lot hadn't been on ops for years. They knew nothing. I told them I was expecting them. They said, "How did you know?" I said Paddy McDade told me. "Oh," they said, "he wasn't supposed to tell anyone." Pathetic!'[7]

The ISU was troubled by Bradley's active service unit, and he outlined why: 'Me and Paddy McD were organising to whack a Peeler [police officer] in the Short Strand. A Peeler opened the barrier at Mountpottinger Barracks every day. We were going to use a .303. We had a house overlooking where he would be. Paddy Murray was from the Short Strand, Beechfield Street. He was the main organiser. I was going to do the shoot. You couldn't miss. The house we had was so close you could have thrown the rifle out the window and hit him.'[8] The operation was 'on' three times, but it never got the final go-ahead because the Belfast Brigade quartermaster, Larry Marley, suspected that Paddy Murray was an informer.

After being summoned to an ISU inquiry in west Belfast on 14 August 1986, Murray casually told his interviewers that he had informed his Special Branch handler where the meeting was being held. Blind panic and a stampede to the back door of the house followed. Bradley claims that Murray was moved to a safer house. 'No blindfold now. Not tied up. Now can you believe this? Internal Security know he's a Brit agent. They know he told his handler. Yet they brought him to another safe house. No weapons, no security. Is he carrying a homer [electronic homing device]?'[9]

Murray would go on to reveal that he had pushed for the Short Strand operation to go ahead three times because on each of those occasions the SAS, an elite unit of the British Army, had been waiting to kill McDade and Bradley. For his betrayal, Murray was found shot dead in an alleyway off Dunmore Street in west Belfast on 15 August 1986. The IRA let it be known that he had received £10,000 from RUC Special Branch in the eight years he had been informing. Reflecting on Murray's death, Bradley says, 'The Brits sacrificed him. They knew he was going to Internal Security. He told them – but he'd served his purpose. They let him die. I believe, to protect somebody else. Scap? Magee? Who knows? Why did he not run? I think he was too embarrassed and ashamed by what he'd done over the years … he wanted to be killed. Anyway, where was there to run to?'[10]

Some informers were able to hide their treachery better than others. While Paddy Murray seemed to want to admit his treachery, Freddie Scappaticci would turn out to be the opposite. But what prompted Scappaticci to turn on the organisation which held him in such high esteem?

In his book, *The Ulster Tales: A Tribute to Those Who Served 1969–2000*, General Sir John Wilsey, Commanding Officer of the 1st Battalion, Devonshire and Dorset Regiment from 1979 to 1982, has some observations on the potential motivation of informers. He suggests that some become ideologically disenchanted with their organisation and wish to harm or destroy it. Others seek revenge against an individual or individuals within the organisation for a perceived slight. Some informers are seduced by an offer of big money. Tellingly, Wilsey wrote, 'The principal motivation was often to take part in a clandestine enterprise; those living dull, humdrum lives in drab surroundings found the notion of pitting their wits secretly against others irresistible.'[11]

However, author Stephen Grey, an investigative reporter who specialises in intelligence matters, identified some of the more venal reasons that led to such decisions: 'In general, the FRU look for the usual diseases – greed, jealousy, anger, lust, envy – as motivating factors for recruiting prospects. In order to avoid being tricked, they liked traits or weaknesses that could be corroborated. An IRA member was sleeping with another man's wife? That could be verified. And the target would inevitably be jealous and angry – ripe for an approach.' Interestingly, Grey claims that the 'FRU also came to reject any form of volunteer or "walk-in", a luxury that most secret services could not afford. Walk-ins are absolutely the worse kind of agent. You have absolutely no reason to know who they are. It was often a test [by the enemy] to find out what we knew or see how we worked, or to feed us false information.'[12]

The 'FRU' to which Grey refers is the Force Research Unit. It was created in 1978 and it was the brainchild of General Sir James Glover, who had been Commander-in-Chief Land Forces (Northern Ireland) from 1979 to 1980. Its primary purpose was 'recruiting, developing, and controlling the Army's "human intelligence" assets in Britain's secret war on the IRA.'[13] The FRU was operational from 1980 until 1995 and is said to have been responsible for running over 100 agents, including Freddie Scappaticci.

One improbable reason why Scappaticci might have gone over to the British side is that he had become disillusioned with the struggle and wanted to save lives. When this possibility was put to a former IRA Belfast Brigade adjutant, he remarked, 'It's possible, but how do you save lives by shooting people in the back of the head?'[14] So what did prompt his conversion to the other team?

A story has been circulating for some time that Scappaticci was a 'walk-in', that he simply strolled into a police station and offered his services to the security forces. But why? What could have compelled him to take such a drastic course of action? Some journalists say that Scappaticci had been beaten up by his brothers-in-law and fellow-IRA men Jimmy and Brian Davidson because he was having an affair with another IRA man's wife, and that his pride had been hurt to the point where he wanted revenge. But revenge against whom? It wasn't the IRA who called for him to be beaten up, if, indeed, such an assault ever occurred. Moreover, as Stephen Grey has noted, such walk-ins were generally not trusted, yet Scappaticci became one of the top informers for the British forces.

John Ware, an influential BBC journalist who made 'The Spy in the IRA', the ground-breaking 2017 *Panorama* documentary about Scappaticci, has spoken to the faceless men of the British security services, who told him that Scappaticci changed sides after he was arrested by the RUC over a fraudulent tax exemption scheme (the 715 scheme) he had been involved in since his release from internment. By 1980, this scheme had put Freddie Scappaticci firmly in the taxman's crosshairs. The street fighter was not the type to show worry or fear, but in the back of his mind he must surely have been aware that one person from the Markets area, who had worked the same scheme, had been sentenced to eight years' imprisonment for fraud, and another from west Belfast to five years'. For a man who had already spent almost four years of his life in an internment camp, the prospect of a return to prison must have presented a harrowing prospect.

If this version of events is to be believed, when confronted with the prospect of being locked up for up to five years, Scappaticci opted to co-operate with the security forces. According to Ware, who spoke to FRU operatives, Scappaticci believed the RUC to be a sectarian force, so, after two months, he went to work for military intelligence. 'Barney',

Scappaticci's former employee, is unsure of the date of his boss's arrest, but he recalled that his boss *was* arrested by police on suspicion of involvement in tax fraud. However, this is not proof that Scappaticci had only been turned in 1980 because, like all well-known IRA volunteers, he would regularly have been arrested and 'screened' by the security forces since his release from internment.

A more likely account of Scappaticci's recruitment comes from General Sir John Wilsey, who, in *The Ulster Tales*, is adamant that Sergeant Peter Jones converted the Irishman in 1977. Jones had enlisted in the Devonshire and Dorset Regiment on 10 June 1960, although his journey to becoming a soldier was more unorthodox than most. Most teenagers do stupid things and, in that year, the sixteen-year-old PJ stole cigarettes from a beach kiosk, was caught and handed over to the police. At worst he would probably have received a police caution and a small fine, but he had a colossus defending him in the person of his mother, a lady with a penchant for firmness. Standing in front of the magistrates, she informed them in no uncertain terms that it was her intention to bring her son around to the army recruiting office the next day and force him to enlist. The magistrates were duly impressed and her son was discharged without a stain on his character. Mrs Jones was as good as her word.

If we are to believe his commander, Jones had struck up a friendship with the Irishman 'before his Devon and Dorset colleagues completed their six-month tour and returned to Germany'.[15] The Devon and Dorsets completed two tours of duty in Northern Ireland between January 1977 and May 1979, and after the first tour, from January to May 1977, they rejoined the 12th Mechanised Brigade in Osnabrück, West Germany. So, if Wilsey is to be believed, Scappaticci may well have been informing from 1977.

Wilsey lauds Jones' character, saying that he had 'a twinkle in his eye, a casual and unhurried manner, and a wry disrespect for authority; his whole personality attracts those who enjoy mystery and intrigue. Certainly, PJ's new republican friend [Scappaticci], himself unconventional, was attracted from the outset by this rebellious streak.'[16] He describes how Jones hooked Scappaticci: 'Like a skilled and patient fisherman, PJ read the water well. He bided his time, until, intuitively, he judged the moment right to cast his fly. He then hooked and landed his fish. This fish represented the Security Forces' biggest intelligence breakthrough at the time and, arguably, the Army's most significant contribution to the whole campaign.'[17]

According to Wilsey, Jones frequented 'the republican pubs and clubs in Belfast, such as Dubarry's'[18] and 'over time, succeeded in forging a drinking companionship with one of the many engaging characters [Scappaticci] in the clubs and bars of Belfast frequented by republicans'.[19] The companionship that Wilsey claims Jones forged with Scappaticci in places like Dubarry's is seemingly the bond that led Jones to persuade Scappaticci to turn informer. However, Wilsey must not have had occasion to frequent Dubarry's himself, or he would have realised instinctively that it was not a haunt in which republicans would have congregated, given that it was in the centre of Belfast, which always had a heavy security-force presence. Moreover, Dubarry's was close to the docks area and was recognised as a watering hole where sailors and soldiers picked up prostitutes.

When General Wilsey's anecdote about Scappaticci's conversion to the away team was put to Freddie's former IRA comrade Tommy Gorman, he replied, 'That's unadulterated bollocks. Scap wasn't a heavy drinker; he barely touched the stuff. And to say he brought this British intelligence officer ... Jones. To say he brought Jones into republican clubs, and they whooped it up and got steaming drunk and nobody raised an eyelid, is ... that's nonsense. Any boyo who walked into a republican club with a thick Co. Devon accent would have had a gun stuck in his ear and he'd have been frog-marched out of the club and interrogated – even if he was with Scap.'[20]

None of the many republicans who contributed to this book have any recollection of Peter Jones. In fact, many laughed when it was put to them that Jones had been feted in republican clubs in Belfast in the 1970s. I wanted to talk to this enigmatic man, to hear his side of the story, and so, in 2021, I made an approach to him through a friendly journalist, who met Jones in a café in London on my behalf. As well as asking him to facilitate an interview with me, the journalist handed him a letter I had written to Scappaticci requesting an interview. Jones accepted the letter but reflected that were he to agree to meet me, MI5 would probably ask him to try to recruit me, and that, as a result, it would be better for all that no meeting took place. Jones, a fledging screenwriter, surely had a sense of humour.

John Ware had other possible scenarios relating to Scappaticci's conversion, one of which is that he was 'open to blackmail because of his notorious interest in pornography, including watching videos in his two-up, two-down house in Farnham Street, off Belfast's Ormeau Road'.[21] While it is no secret that Scappaticci did have 'cupboards' full of porn movies, that may not have been enough to get him to work for the British.

More pointedly, Ware says that several IRA volunteers told him Scappaticci had an unhealthy interest in pre-teen girls. An IRA interviewee for this book augmented Ware's thesis: 'I think Scap was turned because of a lust for young children. I can tell you stuff when I see you but it's not for print [we were on a video conference].' The source went on to say, 'he was reported to the RUC for having abused a child in west Belfast, but they never acted upon it. Another thing: I had a friend who was travelling with him one time. They were driving down a street in a lorry and some kids were swinging on a lamp and they had short skirts on and Scap made a very lewd remark about the kids. My mate says it was paedophilic. It always stuck with him.'[22]

If a charge of having sexually assaulted a minor had been preferred against him – and he has not been found guilty in a court of law for such an offence – Scappaticci's reputation in the IRA and the community would have been shredded. Indeed, it is doubtful if the IRA man would have been allowed to return home, in which case the life that he had so carefully nurtured would be over. In all probability, he would have had to remove himself and his family from Belfast. Never mind booze-ups in republican clubs, or being hypnotised by captivating British Army intelligence officers, this accusation would go a long way to explaining Scappaticci's bizarre behaviour.

Whatever the truth is about his recruitment, what is incontrovertible is that Freddie Scappaticci, aka 'Stakeknife', alleged to be the most important IRA informer ever to fall into the hands of the British Army, was run by a team that operated from the 'Rat Hole', a series of fenced-off, secure portacabins in Thiepval Barracks, the British Army's headquarters in Northern Ireland. Peter Jones would become one of these handlers when he later joined the FRU. It was from these portacabins that the FRU collated data and facts on the IRA from agents like Scappaticci. What is also clear is that Scappaticci was an effective and valuable informer. One man who knew him well was Gerry Brannigan, once a leading republican in Belfast, who said of Scappaticci, 'He's not in your face, so he's not in your mind, but Scap knows everything because he is knocking around with guys who know everything.

I daresay people would've been loose talking to him. He was Northern Command. He was devious rather than clever; a clever guy would have cultivated an amicable facade, but not Scap. He could be nasty. In my view, he had dissociative identity disorder, or DID. That's a convoluted way of saying he could hear alternative voices in his head telling him to do different things.

'I also believe that his handlers had told him he was under no threat, that they had his back,' Branigan continued. 'This strategy of using local people to carry the fight to the IRA came from British Army tactician, Brigadier Frank Kitson. Kitson had written a book called *Low Intensity Operations* and in it he advocated the use of undercover operations … pass-by shootings of suspects, and the bombings of places of succour for the insurgent, stuff like that. He was very important in those early days to the British Army, a guy who knew the importance of "seeding" people. This is where individuals were put into the likes of Sinn Féin to create a persona. The consequences of that are you're noticed, and you might be tested, and if you come through, you might be incorporated into the army, where, again, you build up trust by your willingness to go out on ops, to get arms dumps, etc., and if you're seen to be good, you get promotion to a position of influence. Don't forget, the Brits were psychologically profiling volunteers, looking for insecurity and opportunities to turn volunteers into assets, and then once they're assets they own them. The subtlety of this process is important because at its core is persuasion through seduction and, by that, I mean, the more you rise in the ranks, the more respect you get from other volunteers.'[23]

Their new asset was vulnerable, however. In 1982, Markets resident Marian McMullan was working in the kitchens of the five-star Culloden Hotel in Holywood, County Down, and one morning, at 5.45, she was walking through the car park to go to work when someone caught her eye. 'Is that Freddie Scap?' she asked herself. 'At this time in the morning?' She continued to stare. It *was* Freddie and he was engrossed in conversation with two men who had long hair. She found it unusual that he would be having a meeting in a car park that early in the morning. 'They looked like Branch men,' she said of the two men who were conferring with him. 'I'm from the Markets, I know what Special Branch look like. These two looked like ordinary men, but they weren't. One had an anorak on and the other had a three-quarter-length coat. I just knew they were Branch men. After work, I told my partner, who was in the 'RA, that they were Branch men and he told me to wise up. But they were Branch men, nobody will tell me different.'

When asked if he had seen her, she said, 'I walked right past him in the car park. He saw me, alright, I know he saw me.' As it happens, he *did* see her, and he remembered seeing her. Eleven years later, on 26 August 1993, Scappaticci met journalists Clive Entwistle, Frank Thorne and Sylvia Jones in the same hotel car park and revealed IRA secrets to them. At that meeting, he remarked that he was uncomfortable with the venue because, 'You never know who might be working in this hotel.'[24] It was lucky for Scappaticci that McMullan's partner, a top IRA operative, didn't believe her, or his story might have been very different.

6

THE RISE OF THE TASKING AND CO-ORDINATING GROUP

'Good God! An informer is the great danger. Every man's hand is against me. I must make an example of this fellow.'

Liam O'Flaherty (The Informer)[1]

Historically, in Ireland, there is no greater crime than being a traitor for the Crown and yet, the bitter reality is that Irish rebels have always suffered the plague of the informer. The FRU agents who handled Scappaticci were simply the latest in a long line of British operators in Ireland who used informers to infiltrate what were perceived as rebel organisations, a line that goes back at least as far as 1798, when leading Dublin barrister Thomas Magan QC was the informer responsible for the capture and death of Lord Edward FitzGerald, the United Irishmen leader in Dublin and the man who led the city's rebellion. Likewise, in 1803, Leonard McNally, Dublin barrister, informed on Robert Emmet, and, in 1883, James Carey and Michael Kavanagh of The Invincibles turned Queen's evidence.

Michael Collins, the IRA's leader during the 1919–21 War of Independence, detested informers, viewing the deed of killing them as 'cleaning our own house until the last traitor Irishman had been identified and fittingly dealt with'.[2] Once the Anglo-Irish Treaty had been signed in 1921, cementing the partition of Ireland, the RUC's Special Branch acted as the primary intelligence-gathering agency in the fight against IRA insurgents.

The Branch's *modus operandi*[3] was to arrest and intern as many IRA suspects as possible as soon as they had any indication that the organisation was planning something. Crucial to a successful drive against the IRA was knowing who the players were, where they lived and what intrigues they were plotting. Then, with their intelligence in place, the RUC would swoop in, arrest the plotters and imprison them. Billy McKee and many of the men who would go on to form and lead the Provisional IRA, for instance, never fired a shot during the IRA's 1950s' campaign because the identities of the Belfast and northern IRA commands were known to Special Branch, who rounded up the insurrectionists within hours of the IRA's 'Operation Harvest' being launched.

The Provisional IRA was more of a mystery to British intelligence gatherers than its predecessor because, while its leaders quickly became known to them, there was little or no intelligence on the rank and file, most of whom had been in their teens when they had joined the IRA after the eruption of 1969. The British had no idea who the various battalion or company staffs were, who was carrying out the shootings and bombings, how weaponry was getting into Ireland and who was supplying it, or which locals were providing the Provisionals with space to meet or to hide weapons.

However, as internment proceeded, reports began flooding into newspaper offices of suspects who had been picked up being systematically brutalised by police and British Army interrogators. The names of rank-and-file IRA personnel who had not come to the security forces' attention began to be uttered by broken and battered men in interrogation rooms. This led to Special Branch building up a more comprehensive picture of the opposition – and, consequently, internment prisons filled up. Yet, even with enhanced intelligence, Special Branch often got it wrong, interning many people who had no political association with the IRA.

In response, IRA intelligence officers in the prisons smuggled out communications telling their comrades on the outside the names of those in whom the Special Branch had expressed an interest. Suddenly the undergraduate, who thought his student card was a stay-out-of-jail pass, was on a wanted list; no longer could he go to university or college and, moreover, staying at home was an invitation to a Grand Long Kesh Internment Ball. The scholar's only option was to go on the run. The woman who provided a room to the IRA so that a training officer could give a gun lecture was also on the security forces' radar; her front door would be kicked in at 5 in the morning. And the family man who had secreted a gun under the floorboards slept fitfully, unable to escape the fear that he had been compromised.

For their part, British Army intelligence officers never stopped coming up with new ways to gather intelligence and take the fight to the IRA. One approach was the formation of shadowy counter-insurgency groups, one of which was called the Military Reconnaissance Force (MRF). This unit endeavoured to use IRA tactics on the IRA by engaging in drive-by shootings of unsuspecting volunteers, gathering intelligence in republican strongholds by masquerading as a mobile laundry business and cultivating 'turned' IRA men – known ironically as 'Freds' – into potential British assassins. The MRF operation lasted fourteen months and collapsed when the IRA learned from a 'Fred' that the force was running a massage parlour, an ice-cream business and the laundry operation in Belfast. In a concerted operation in west Belfast on 2 October 1972, volunteers killed an MRF soldier who was hiding in the converted roof space of the laundry van. They also shot up the massage parlour and visited the ice-cream parlour, but it had already been vacated.

Undaunted by this disruption to their counter-insurgency operation, the British simply changed the initials of their undercover terror group from MRF to SRU (Special Reconnaissance Unit) and continued with their undercover activities.

Why are the MRF and SRU so important? Because they were precursors to the FRU, whose intelligence officers ran Freddie Scappaticci and a host of other informers. It is worth considering how the FRU was so successful against the IRA. An interesting comparison can be made between the FRU and 'The Cairo Gang', an elite British Intelligence undercover unit used by the British in the War of Independence. However, while Michael Collins knew enough about the identities and movements of his opponents to arrange the assassination of many of them in Dublin on Bloody Sunday, 21 November 1920, the FRU ran rings around the IRA in the 1970s and 1980s. That was not because the Provisional IRA were stupid, but rather because the British had learned from the folly of allowing spies with English accents and foreign habits to live in local, sometimes hostile, communities. As well as that, Collins had useful contacts inside the British forces, such as Eamon Broy, who worked as a clerk within the Special Branch's 'G' Division in Dublin Castle, while the Provisional IRA only ever had one RUC reservist who was attached to Intelligence working for them, and he was quickly identified. Thus, while the Provisional IRA were cut from the same cloth as Collins when it came to executing traitors, they did not have his Intelligence contacts and that seriously inhibited their ability to locate informers. Nobody knew of Freddie Scappaticci's treachery. Nobody.

It is indisputable that the Provisional IRA underestimated the forces arrayed against them. Many former republican activists believed that if they had grown up with and known someone all their lives, then that person could never become an informer. Even more naively, most IRA people thought that the ultimate test of loyalty was killing or executing someone for the cause: this was seen as commitment *par excellence*. The fatal flaw in this thinking was the erroneous, if unspoken, belief that the security forces occupied the high moral ground and would never allow one of their informers to willingly take a life. But at least one informer did.

One of those in the ISU who had real-time experience of Scappaticci was Newry man Peter Keeley, aka 'Kevin Fulton', a young Royal Irish Ranger soldier. Keeley had been recruited by British Military Intelligence before successfully infiltrating the ISU in the mid-1980s after he had cultivated a relationship with a leading IRA bomb-maker. There he met John Joe Magee and Freddie Scappaticci, whom he called 'Michael' in his book *Double Agent: My Secret Life Undercover in the IRA*.

Keeley writes of a conversation he had with 'Bob' and 'Pete', his MI5 and FRU handlers, about the prospect of having to shoot an alleged informer:

"'You want to stop an atrocity?" said Bob. "Well, it's only by getting in with these people that you can even become party to operations on this scale."

"'But what if I have to execute someone?" I replied. "I mean, surely this is overstepping the mark."

"'No, look," said Bob, "we've managed to get other people into positions like this. Use your common sense. If it isn't you putting the bullet into the tout's head, it'll be someone else. At least you know that somewhere down the line it'll pay off for us. If you don't do it, someone else will. There's no point trying to save any of these people anyhow. They're only IRA scum after all."

"'Another dead IRA person gets shot," says Pete, "so what? Another dead Provie is hardly bad news for anyone, is it? And it's the ultimate cover for you. Who'd ever suspect that someone executing informers is an agent?'"[4]

Very few did.

Keeley went on to recall his encounters with Scappaticci, saying that 'he was small in stature, yet his reputation within the IRA was legendary'. Insightfully, Keeley recounts how Scappaticci 'seemed interested only in someone's guilt. "Michael" thought nothing of promising an amnesty to an informant during a court of inquiry, only to renege on that deal once the accused had confessed. It seemed the lowest of tricks.'[5]

Eamon Collins, a customs officer from Newry, was also a member of the ISU and an informer, and he writes of having the same conversation with Scappaticci and Magee in his book *Killing Rage*: 'One time I sat in a house with them to await the arrival of some men who had just been released from police custody. The woman of the house made us tea. John Joe and Scap started reminiscing about past experiences. I asked them whether I would personally be expected to shoot informers. Scap, his mouth full, said that when the time arrived, I would have to do it. I asked whether they always told people that they were going to be shot. Scap said it depended on the circumstances. He turned to John

Joe and started joking about one informer who had confessed after being offered an amnesty. Scap told the man he would take him home, reassuring him that he had nothing to worry about. Scap told him to keep the blindfold on for security reasons as they walked away from the car.

"'It was funny," he said, "watching the bastard stumbling and falling, asking me as he felt his way along railings and walls, 'Is this my home now?' and I'd say, 'No, not yet, walk on a bit further ...'"

"'And then you shot the fucker in the back of the head," said John Joe, and both of them burst out laughing."[6]

Collins wrote of how he came to know Magee and Scappaticci well, describing how he had watched the latter vet five potential recruits in a dark room in Newry: 'Scap asked them all the same questions: had they had any previous connection with the republican movement? Did they attend republican marches, events, or funerals? Did they drink in well-known republican pubs? Had they ever sung rebel songs publicly? Were they known in their areas as IRA supporters? Had they ever been arrested? Did they have a criminal record? If so, what for? If they answered yes to any question, then Scap would ask follow-up questions: when, where and with whom did they attend this march, event, or funeral? The most significant question was: why did they want to join the IRA?'[7]

After the recruits passed their grilling, Scappaticci would tell them to keep their heads low and to avoid making themselves known to the security forces. It was good advice, which no doubt the IRA novices appreciated; they probably thought that Scap was a moral man, someone worthy of the utmost respect. Little did the would-be IRA men know that Scappaticci, who would have been given their names in advance, would already have told the security forces all about them.

In Freddie Scappaticci, the British had the perfect spy quite simply because, to those who did not really know him, he appeared to be the perfect IRA volunteer: he was, on the outside, a conscientious family man (even though he was a porn addict who had extra-marital affairs); he had temperate ways; he had a means to explain where he got the money he so lavishly spent (the 715 tax-exemption scam); he was meticulous in his IRA 'work', and he never had any compunction about recommending that someone be executed whenever John Joe Magee and he deemed that person guilty of treachery. The hypocrisy of Scappaticci is that no one was more guilty of treachery than himself.

Year after year, Scappaticci was involved in killing, dispatching his victims in the isolated country lanes and back alleyways of Ireland. And all the while he was reporting back to his FRU handlers – Colin Parr, Peter Jones, David Moyles, Ronnie Anderson – and their cohorts, who were reporting back to the TCGs, who, in turn, ruminated over whether to let a potential victim live or die.

The TCG was a body made up, primarily, of intelligence chiefs from the RUC's E4 Special Branch, MI5 and the FRU. It was formed in Castlereagh on 1 May 1978, and sprouted branches in the RUC's Gough Barracks in Armagh in 1979, and in Strand Road Barracks in Derry soon afterwards. The mastermind behind the group's formation was Sir Maurice Oldfield, the former chief of MI6, and his remit was to ensure closer co-operation between the various branches of the security forces by ensuring all intelligence was channelled through the relevant TCG, which would then decide whether or not a situation needed security-force intervention. The TCGs worked as collators of ongoing intelligence operations in each of the E Division's (Special Branch) areas. They were enablers for the Special Branch, security services and military, although all operations, both covert and overt, had to be cleared by

Special Branch. Besides actioning operations, the TCGs made sure that those on active duty did not compromise each other by, for example, engaging in blue-on-blue shootouts.

For the TCGs to function coherently and efficiently, they had to familiarise themselves with all facets of security-force intelligence-gathering in all parts of Ireland. This meant that they had to be fully cognisant of and approve the FRU's and Special Branch's odious undercover activities, which included supplying intelligence to loyalist death squads who murdered hundreds of innocent Catholics during the Troubles. The prominent defence and human rights lawyer Pat Finucane was one of those assassinated by loyalists acting on intelligence provided by the FRU agent Brian Nelson, a leading member of the Ulster Defence Association (UDA). Finucane's assassination on 12 February 1989 was always going to be highly controversial and, almost inevitably, led to an inquiry by the UK's top policeman, Sir John Stevens, which commenced in 1999. In 2003, *The Guardian* reflected on Stevens' report: 'The conflict in Northern Ireland was needlessly intensified and prolonged by the "disastrous" activities of a core of army and police officers [the TCGs] who colluded with terrorists responsible for dozens of murders ...'[8]

The role of the TCGs was further explained in the MacLean Report on the killing of Loyalist Volunteer Force (LVF) leader Billy Wright in 1997: 'The main function of the TCG was to coordinate all security force operations within the region, involving both long-term intelligence-gathering operations, and live action operations which might arise on a day-to-day basis. The decision to undertake an operation involved weighing up priorities and deciding how best to use available sources.'[9]

Warranted though it may be, 'weighing up priorities and deciding how best to use available sources' is intriguing phraseology and opens up some appalling vistas, the most pernicious of which is that the keeping of an informer in place sometimes trumped the saving of life. With this cancerous ethos at the heart of policy, the TCGs did not seem to have any trouble turning a blind eye to Scappaticci's involvement in the serial murder of British citizens. Indeed, it must have been quite an arresting occasion when a decision had to be taken as to whether an agent being held by the IRA should be allowed to die to protect another agent's identity. One may well wonder how the decision had been taken. Was it a collective TCG decision or did the head of Special Branch have the honour? What did the decision-makers feel after the unfortunate had been dispatched?

All of this begs the question of whether there was always unanimity within the TCG when a report came in that the nutting squad had arrested someone and was holding the suspect in a named location – and that, in all likelihood, that person would soon be shot dead. There must have been a discussion around the TCG table about possible security-force intervention, which would have centred around whether the suspected agent was valuable enough to be allowed to live, or whether the identity of Scappaticci was more important and needed to be protected, even at the cost of another's life. Since Barra McGrory QC SC, who served as Director of Public Prosecutions for Northern Ireland from 2011 to 2017, claims there is evidence which indicates that Scappaticci was involved in 'eighteen murders', it seems the TCGs did not have any trouble turning a blind eye to him facilitating the deaths of others if it meant he was able to continue being an important British asset.

7

STIFF ALL TOUTS

'When devils with the blackest sins put on,
They do suggest at first with heavenly shows.'

William Shakespeare, Othello

From its establishment in late 1978, the ISU set about its task of weeding out informers in the ranks with a ruthlessness that put the fear of God into even the most hardened of IRA volunteers. Only about twenty strong, the unit became the *bête noire* of the IRA volunteer because its members zealously grilled everyone who came out of the interrogation centres and if they as much as got a hint that something was amiss or that someone was not being totally truthful with them, they thought nothing of taking that person away for a deeper 'debrief', which sometimes meant torture.

The very first victim of the nutting squad was IRA volunteer Michael Kearney in 1979, a twenty-year-old from the Lenadoon area of West Belfast. Kearney had been under security-force surveillance after being compromised by an undercover British agent, who informed his handlers that Kearney had delivered forty-two bombs and other devices to a lock-up garage in the Short Strand area of east Belfast. The young IRA volunteer was subsequently arrested by the security forces and then released. He was then arrested by members of the ISU and held for seventeen days, during which time he was tortured.

On 15 May 2022, Michael's brother, Seamus, alleged during a radio interview with presenter James English that he was sent for by a solicitor in Belfast city centre who told him: 'We've uncovered files from the British and they were involved in the execution of your brother. They set him up. They had infiltrated the Internal Security Unit through other people, including, but not only, Stakeknife. So Stakeknife was there when your brother was executed, that he was a double agent working for the Force Research Unit, and your brother was set up in Castlereagh [police and interrogation centre] through the FRU and the ISU, which had been infiltrated. So the ISU of the IRA, which had arrested Michael and took him across the border, were working for the British and they executed him.'[1]

In an article on The Pensive Quill website, Seamus wrote, 'While in Dundalk from Monday, June 25th to July 12th, 1979, Michael was interrogated by Stakeknife and at least two other senior members of Internal Security, one of which [sic] is now deceased ... Stakeknife, as an observer for the British, reported back to his handler on exactly the situation and identified the people involved in Michael's interrogation within the house in Dundalk.'[2]

Determined to right a terrible wrong, Seamus went on to say, '[Stakeknife's] handler, as is standard practice, wrote out a Contact Form which was handed into the Task Coordinating Group (TCG), and stored at Castlereagh. Despite the RUC destroying all Contact

Forms in later years, mainly due to the Stevens Inquiry, etc. – to erase a paper trail back to them – a Master copy, or the Miser [MISR], as it is internally called, was produced by MI5 and held in Whitehall Headquarters in London. Michael Kearney's master copy has been retrieved by Operation Kenova, identifying all those involved in his interrogation and eventual execution.'[3]

Seamus Kearney's testimony is hugely significant and revelatory because, if the Kenova investigators really did have an MISR stating that Freddie Scappaticci had told his handlers the location and names of those interrogating Michael Kearney while this was still going on, and if the handlers had indeed passed it on to the TCG, and if that body didn't lift a finger to save Kearney's life, then the TCG may justifiably be open to the accusation that they aided and abetted murder. In reality, it appears that they simply sat it out. They may have watched the clock and counted down the minutes until Kearney was killed. Perhaps they believed that they had a valid reason for not acting – he was an IRA man and *not* an informer, after all. Conceivably, it could be suggested that someone forgot to put the call in to the Irish police, but it's hard to believe this could have gone unremembered over the course of seventeen days. Had the Irish police been made aware of what was happening in their jurisdiction, they could have acted to save Michael's life and arrested those interrogating him.

On one of the few occasions that the TCG did intervene, they put in a call to the Irish police to save a condemned man, James Young, a forty-one-year-old married man who was later found shot dead on a border road near Crossmaglen on 13 February 1984.

While his family denied that he was an informer, the IRA claimed responsibility for his death, saying in a statement, published after his execution, that 'during his service to the police Young gave details of a planned coordinated bombing strike in County Down, leading to its abandonment.[4] The IRA also claimed that Young had passed on details of an IRA training camp in 1983, and disclosed the movement of weapons.

Seamus Kearney maintains that it was Northern Command who brought in the ISU to interrogate Young in south Armagh, and that within three days the accused 'confessed that he was an agent, working for special Branch and British military intelligence.'[5] Having broken Young, Scappaticci and John Joe Magee went back to Belfast. At some stage in the process, Scappaticci passed on to his handler the details of James Young's arrest, including his then whereabouts. Scappaticci's handler then filled in an SB50 form, which contained the intelligence given by Scappaticci, and it was passed on to the TCG, who informed the Irish police. Acting on the tip-off, the gardaí cordoned off a cul de sac, but hit the wrong house, thus giving the IRA the opportunity to escape out the back door with the unfortunate Young. Then, with everyone else gone, two unarmed IRA men decided to simply walk out of the front door of the house in which Young had been held, and as they were getting into their car, a garda said to them, 'You have a cheek defending anyone at a court martial.'[6] Once away from the scene, the IRA men asked themselves the logical question: How did that garda know someone was being court-martialled?

The South Armagh IRA pointed the finger of blame at Freddie Scappaticci, who had aroused their suspicions during Young's interrogation when he asked questions about IRA operations and personnel that had nothing to do with the suspect's arrest. Consequently, the South Armagh IRA sent word to the Belfast IRA that Scappaticci was not to be trusted. The Belfast IRA ignored the protestations and Scappaticci was kept in place.

This would not be the last time the TCG would play God. Indeed, intervention became the exception rather than the rule when it came to saving a person's life.

One man who would have been on the receiving end of an ISU deep debrief was thirty-three-year-old father of four Peter Valente, an IRA member from Stanhope Drive in the Unity Flats area of Belfast. As the leading ISU officer in the city, Scappaticci would have been a central figure in Valente's interrogation and eventual execution in November 1980.

A key player in the journey that led to Valente's death in a Belfast alleyway is 'Officer A', a full-time reservist attached to Intelligence, who was allegedly feeding information on his police colleagues to the top north Belfast IRA commander, Martin Meehan, in the spring of 1979.[7] The renowned author of *The Dirty War*, Martin Dillon, commented, 'I am reliably informed that Meehan was filmed entering the upper end of the waterworks at its Cavehill Road entrance and Officer A [the RUC informer] from the Antrim Road exit. Officer A was walking his dog and they appeared to meet casually at a point between the disused reservoirs.'[8] Subsequently, Officer A was arrested by police on 26 October 1980 and found to be in possession of the names, addresses and vehicle-registration numbers of members of Special Branch. Confronted with the film of his meeting with Meehan, he confessed to working for the IRA after receiving large sums of money.

Officer A's betrayal represented a serious conundrum for the Branch. How could they publicly admit that they had been penetrated by the IRA? Had this fact made its way into the media, it would have eroded any confidence that existed in the RUC and, inevitably, would have led to a massive internal inquiry to determine the bona fides of each individual officer in the force. Embarrassing questions would have been asked and someone's head would have rolled. For Special Branch, the

only way out of the situation was to keep the compromised officer out
of jail by offering him his freedom provided he fully co-operated with
his superiors. Officer A accepted and, with a pardon from the attorney
general in his back pocket, he was allowed to leave Northern Ireland.

Dillon conjectures that Special Branch blackmailed Valente into
working for them by threatening that Officer A would give evidence
against him. But what evidence could he have given? Without a taped
recording in which Valente implicated himself in IRA activity, Officer
A's evidence would have had no value. It seems more plausible that
Valente was a state agent *before* Officer A's double-dealing came to
the attention of the RUC. This is alluded to in Mark Urban's book *Big
Boys Rules*, where it was recorded that it was Valente who tipped off
the Special Branch about Officer A's meeting with Meehan. Whichever
story is correct, Valente's time was running out.

On 10 November 1980, an IRA volunteer was having a romantic
liaison with another man's wife in a country hotel, when he saw Valente
speaking to a man he knew to be Special Branch. Valente, realising he
had been spotted, tried to bluff his way out of his predicament, saying
he was casing the hotel in the hope it could be blown up at some time
in the future. But the other man's suspicions would not be allayed; loyal
IRA men do not have illicit meetings with Special Branch officers in
isolated country hotels. When he got back to Belfast, the IRA man
reported what he had witnessed to ASU commander Whitey Bradley,
who did not hesitate to report the incident to the Belfast Brigade, which
set the ISU on Valente.

On 12 November, Valente disappeared, arrested by the nutting
squad. During his interrogation, he alluded to other IRA men being
informers – men who, until named by him, had been held in the
highest regard. The Belfast IRA was punch-drunk with the scale of

what Valente had revealed. Forty-eight hours later, he was executed in an alleyway in the Protestant Highfield estate. The location was specifically chosen because Valente had a brother on the blanket protest in the H-Blocks of Long Kesh and, being a high-profile supporter of the protesting prisoners, the IRA thought it might be damaging if it were to emerge that they had assassinated him – hence, their attempt to give the impression loyalists had killed him. While there seems a certain rationale to leaving Valente's body in a loyalist area, this was contradicted by the fact that, when found, there was new, crisp £20 note in his hand, indicating that he had taken British money to inform on his IRA comrades.

Bradley recalled that, after he had reported Valente to the Belfast Brigade, 'The next thing I heard, Valente was lifted and whacked [shot dead]. He told his interrogators, "I'm not a tout; I'm a British agent." When they came to take him out to be shot, he said, "OK, come on, let's go."'[9]

Michael Kearney's and Peter Valente's murders were only the beginning: Scappaticci and the ISU were just warming up. On 20 January 1981, they were homing in on another target. Relying on information conveyed by Valente during his interrogation, twenty-four-year-old IRA volunteer Maurice Gilvarry was next in their sights. Gilvarry, known as 'Isaac' to his friends, was said to be a confident young man, someone who was remembered by IRA volunteers as a committed republican before he was labelled an informer and executed.

In the IRA, a good operator rarely stays incognito for too long, and Gilvarry was seen as a good operator and thus considered trustworthy by his contemporaries. In one operation, on the evening of 3 February 1980, he killed sixty-year-old retired prison officer Patrick Mackin and his wife, fifty-eight-year-old Violet, who were watching television in their Oldpark Road home when Gilvarry burst through their living-room door.

Gilvarry later admitted to his ISU interrogators that he had informed the Branch about the operation after it took place, but it is unclear if he identified himself as the killer. If he had, the Branch overlooked his admission of guilt to keep him in place in the IRA. That would not have been too unusual. The two IRA volunteers who accompanied Gilvarry on the job, whose identities Gilvarry would have made known to Special Branch, were never charged.

When arrested by the ISU, Gilvarry was taken to an underground bunker in south Armagh, an area frequently used by Scappaticci and the ISU to carry out interrogations, where he was allegedly tortured. Broken by his interrogators, he admitted to having been an informer from 1976. His body was found lying on a country roadside near Jonesboro on 20 January 1981. It later emerged that he had fed information to his Special Branch handlers which led to the SAS executions of three IRA volunteers – Dinny Brown (28), Jim Mulvenna (28) and Jackie Mailey (31) – at 'Price's Fields', on the Ballysillan Road, Belfast, on 21 June 1980. The three unarmed IRA men were intent on torching a Post Office depot when they were riddled by the SAS, who fired 171 bullets in the ambush. The details of their deaths are no less gruesome than those of the Mackins.

Geraldine Keenan, sister of Dinny Brown, said in 2000, 'They were shown no mercy whatsoever. The three of them were unarmed, one was carrying unprimed petrol bombs. The post office was unoccupied so there was no threat to life, and they could have been arrested. In the inquest papers, it is said the SAS went over to two of them, and they were still moving on the ground – this is after having been initially shot – and they finished them off. If that's not murder – what is?'[10] An innocent passer-by, William Hanna, was also killed by the SAS in a case of mistaken identity, yet none of the soldiers were ever charged with the four killings or brought before a court of law to explain why they did not take the IRA men alive. It did not seem to matter that they had fired 171 bullets into their victims.

And the killings went on. At 3 a.m. on a rainy morning in August 1986, Paddy Murray was shot dead in a dark Dunmore Street alleyway. Murray did not deny to the ISU that he worked for Special Branch when he came to meet them in a house on the Falls Road. The Short Strand man went further, telling the ISU that he had informed his Special Branch handler he was meeting with them and the location where their encounter was to take place. It would be slipshod if Murray's handler did not pass the details of the meeting on to the Belfast TCG. But even if the TCG was unaware that Murray had been summoned to meet the IRA's ISU, Special Branch knew what was happening in real time. Did the Branch initiate surveillance on the ISU meeting house? Did they fit Murray with a bugging device, which would have been standard procedure? Did they consider surrounding the house and making a security-force intervention to save Murray's life? Did it cross their minds that they had a moral imperative to preserve their agent's life? The answer to all these questions can be found in the Dunmore Street alleyway. Clearly, in the cut and thrust of the intelligence-gathering business, Special Branch took no action to save Murray's life because he had been uncovered by the IRA and was arguably of no more use to them.

The question then arises: who *really* oversaw IRA executions? In the IRA's *Green Book*, the effective text of rules and regulations for membership, it is written, 'In the case of the death penalty, sentence must be ratified by the A/C [Army Council].'[11] As a result, it was widely accepted that an Army Council member had to be on site to pass a sentence of death on a suspected informer. But what is now materialising out of the misty veils of the past is the vista of the TCGs as the supreme authority when it came to who, amongst their agents, should live and who should die. The spooks' greatest trick was to let the IRA Army Council think that they were in control of the agent's destiny, when, all along, the TCGs were deliberating and cogitating over the heads of the republican militarists. For example, the execution of Michael Kearney, an avowed enemy of the state, at the hands of the IRA, sculpted by the TCGs, may well have been considered a successful operation.

Consistent with Seamus Kearney's contention that the TCGs stood idly by while his brother was executed is an observation made by leading human rights lawyer Kevin Winters of KRW Law: 'As I understand it, there is a potential assertion that every single case that is the subject of the Kenova investigation, in every single killing, that those deaths were preventable had there been some form of state intervention and that's a pretty stark assertion to make.'[12] Commenting further on the roles of the TCGs, the British intelligence services, the IRA's ISU and Chief Constable Jon Boutcher's Kenova investigation into the activities of Stakeknife, Winters had this to say: 'Boutcher has told us, privately, that when he comes to do his public-facing report on Scappaticci, he'll be making it very clear that all the lives that were taken could have been saved. *The state had the capacity to prevent the taking of life in all cases involving the nutting squad* [author's italics].'

Winters' information regarding Scappaticci's relationship with his handlers is backed up by BBC journalist John Ware: 'Culling agents was, of course, one of the [nutting] squad's key tasks, so Scappaticci's British army handlers could have been in absolutely no doubt that he was involved in the murder of his fellow agent — time and time again.'[13]

These claims are backed up by 'William', a prominent journalist, and 'Feargus', a politician, both of whom were informed, at separate meetings, by members of the Kenova team that the state had had the power to save the lives of virtually all of those eventually executed by the nutting squad. This revelation is a staggering indictment of the TCGs, one of such magnitude that I considered it needed re-affirming, so I approached all three interviewees again and asked them if Scappaticci had told his handlers about every one of those arrested and killed by the ISU. They each replied that this was what they were led to believe.[14]

In the same year that one of the ISU's victims, Maurice Gilvarry, met his death, Ian Hurst, a working-class man from Leeds, who was to emerge as a critical part of the Scappaticci story, first arrived in the north of Ireland. Initially, Hurst had wanted to become a member of the Parachute Regiment, but, after ten weeks on the para course, he decided instead to join the Intelligence Corps. Towards the end of 1981, he was sent to Headquarters, Northern Ireland (HQNI), where he was attached to 121 Intelligence Section. In 1982, Hurst applied for, and was accepted into, the FRU, whereupon he was sent to FRU North (Derry).

Hurst is the man who outed Freddie Scappaticci as Stakeknife in an interview with *Sunday Times* journalist Liam Clarke on 8 August 1999, and is co-author of the book *Stakeknife: Britain's Secret Agents in Ireland*, an exposé of the roles of Scappaticci and the FRU in the Troubles. He explains his motivation for writing the book: 'It is with the intention of speaking out for the sake of a better future that I am revealing things I came across in my work within intelligence-gathering. Certain activities of the FRU have sickened me. I want them aired in public. I feel this is right and necessary.'[15]

When writing, he must surely have realised he would become engaged in a battle for the truth, with former colleagues doing all in their power to denigrate his testimony, which has been severely challenged. The common criticism is that he 'to a substantial degree, exaggerated the importance of his role at HQNI and his level of knowledge and access to intelligence'.[16] However, he speaks with a lucidity and flow that sounds unrehearsed and convincing.

In an interview with reporter Suzanne Breen in 2006, Hurst recalled how each FRU operative had 'eight agents and co-handled another four. Informers were collected by van at an agreed location. They would be interviewed inside the vehicle … which consisted of a sofa and kettle … or at the handler's [undercover] home.' In another interview, on 9 April 2021, he said that the first time he became aware of Freddie Scappaticci was a 'fluke', an accident. This was before Hurst even joined the FRU. During a night shift at HQNI, when he was providing what he termed effectively an 'on-call service for agents', there was a phone call from the Donegal Pass Police Station. Hurst explained how the service worked: 'We had to support – in HQNI there is an operations officer, I think on the 4th floor, and he may want to access documents in close-hour and so we had to support them, and we also looked after telephones for MI5 and the Rat Hole [the HQ of the FRU].'

On this particular night, someone used his phone call to alert the service. 'The RUC officer said a Frederico Scappaticci had been arrested for drink-driving on the Lower Ormeau Road and had requested him to phone this number.' As a result, the person working with Hurst that evening, Sam Southam, contacted Colin Parr, commanding officer of the FRU. Apparently 'all hell broke loose, with officers coming back on duty. The C.O. collected the Ops Officer, and they went to Donegal Pass to sort the mess out. The next day, Sam and I were told [by FRU ops officer Anthony J. Greenfield] to forget about what had happened the night before.'[17]

Authenticating Hurst's account of his peripheral encounter with Scappaticci in 1981 is virtually impossible, because no drink-driving charge would have been preferred against the informer and it is unlikely that any police record of the incident still exists. However, during the Smithwick Inquiry of 2011–13, one of Scappaticci's main handlers, Major David Moyles, was asked about it. All that Moyles would say on the matter was to confirm that the Rat Hole was 'the unit that dealt with the agent called "Stakeknife", and that he personally handled 'Stakeknife'.[18] Hurst has also spoken of how Peter Jones, David Moyles and 'others' would have had assistants and would have alternated their spell 'in theatre', each serving two and a half years at a time, 'so you have continuity of people he [Scappaticci] can trust'.[19]

In his book, Hurst alleges that FRU sources told him how Scappaticci's information helped the security forces to counter IRA kidnappings in the Irish Republic. One of those kidnapped was the supermarket magnate Ben Dunne Jnr, who was taken hostage by the South Armagh IRA in 1981 while travelling north to open a new store. After a six-day ordeal, Dunne was released when £1m was allegedly paid to the IRA.

Don Tidey, another supermarket executive, was kidnapped on 4 November 1983 by the IRA near his Dublin home. After being held for twenty-three days, a joint Garda–Irish Army search team found Tidey and four IRA men in a dug-out in Ballinamore forest, County Leitrim. A gun battle ensued, during which trainee Garda officer Gary Sheehan (23) and Private Patrick Kelly (35) were shot dead. Tidey was rescued. It's not known what information Scappaticci gave his British handlers, but perhaps he was able to reveal the location of the dug-out.

If we accept Hurst's assertions that Scappaticci passed on information about these kidnappings, the question then arises: how would Scappaticci have known about these? In the late 1970s–early 1980s, the ISU would not have been privy to plans for unlaunched IRA operations, especially in the border and Dublin areas. The answer could be as simple as someone loose-talking to him. But these kidnappings would have been General Headquarters (GHQ) operations; would have been carried out on a strictly need-to-know basis; and, even if Scappaticci were sitting in on GHQ meetings, which he was not at that stage, the minutiae of these kidnappings would not have been discussed in open session. So, either someone from IRA GHQ operations department was surreptitiously telling Scappaticci about the kidnappings, or someone at GHQ level, more senior in rank than he, was the British agent who provided the security services with this intelligence. The latter seems more plausible. Besides, Scappaticci was rather busy in his nutting-squad role.

From the IRA's perspective, there was no inkling that Scappaticci and the recently formed ISU were anything other than a resounding success, as the inquisitors weeded out, one by one, those they claimed to be touts. Basking in the radiance of the nutting squad's perceived achievements, Scappaticci's reputation was growing exponentially. He already knew most of the Belfast leadership from his internment days and thereafter, and he was now ingratiating himself with the rest of the national IRA leadership, who regarded him as a highly resourceful and valuable volunteer. He was certainly valued, not least by the FRU.

8

HIDING IN PLAIN SIGHT

'It is forbidden to kill; therefore all murderers are punished unless they kill in large numbers and to the sound of trumpets.'

Voltaire

Patrick Trainor was not an IRA man. He was a twenty-eight-year-old married man with three children from west Belfast who was abducted and tortured by the ISU, before being shot dead on waste ground on Belfast's Glen Road on 22 February 1981. Eileen Hughes, Patrick's sister, recalled, 'My mother was in hysterics. Another brother went to identify him. He said Paddy was covered in cigarette burns. He was shot to cover up for someone else.'[1]

The IRA released a statement alleging that Patrick had been an informer who worked for the British for five years and they allowed his brother to listen to a 'confession' from the condemned man. Confessions in such instances should not be construed as actual guilt, however. It was common practice for the ISU to tape-record confessions from suspects broken under interrogation, but that does not necessarily mean that the suspects were informers – only that they would do whatever was necessary to stop the torture.

The hard reality was that, according to the Trainor family, Scappaticci had worked his magic on Patrick Trainor by promising him an amnesty if he confessed – after he had been used as an ashtray by other ISU interrogators. Trainor was a slight man, someone who would not have been tough enough to withstand a heavy beating – and certainly not a burning – so the promise of a way out of his immediate predicament would have been too much for him to resist.

In 2015, the Trainor family called for an independent investigation into the activities of Scappaticci and rejected claims that Patrick was an informer. Eileen has led the fight to clear his name: 'We know he [Scappaticci] did it and he used my brother as a scapegoat. Paddy was definitely sacrificed to protect someone higher up.'[2] She later said, 'I would like to see Scappaticci charged. I used to know him; my best friend used to go out with him. His father sold ice cream around the area. I blame the police and the government. They knew these kids were getting shot to cover up for Stakeknife.'[3]

What makes this unfortunate man's killing so cruel is that Scappaticci boasted about dispatching him, telling whoever wanted to hear how he had been the poor wretch's executioner. No doubt seduced by a sense of invulnerability that comes with knowing the governing authorities are prepared to let you get away with murder, Scappaticci joked with Eamon Collins and John Joe Magee about how he had made Patrick Trainor keep on the blindfold for security reasons, before shooting him dead. Collins recorded this conversation in his 1997 book *Killing Rage*, published five years before Scappaticci was outed as Stakeknife. Moreover, Collins said that out of all the

IRA people he met while in the organisation, he liked Scappaticci the most. Unlikely though it may seem, in the manic world of the IRA, one man's rat is another man's lion. And, lest there be any doubt, some IRA volunteers did like Freddie Scappaticci, although others dreaded laying eyes on him.

On 27 June 1981, the nutting squad was on the prowl again. This time the body of IRA volunteer Vincent Robinson, a twenty-nine-year-old father of two, was left in a garbage chute at the Saint Jude's block of the Divis flats. According to IRA sources, Robinson had been shot dead by Scappaticci. In the wake of his death, Freddie Scappaticci visited Robinson's sister, Meg, and her then husband, both of whom were republican activists. 'Looking Scappaticci in the eye, she [Meg] asked him if her brother had been tortured before death. Looking Meg Robinson in the eye, Scappaticci said, "No".[4] However, at the inquest into Robinson's death, it was revealed that he had been struck at least five times with a rod-like instrument, akin to an iron bar, before being executed.

Robinson had come to the attention of the IRA and been handed over to the ISU after being identified some time earlier as a state agent by Maurice Gilvarry. The IRA released a statement saying that he had been a Special Branch informer and had given away a 300lb explosives dump. Robinson's family denied that he was an informer, as did the RUC.

The human rights activist Father Denis Faul was a fierce critic of the security forces, tirelessly confronting them in the media whenever they brutalised IRA suspects in custody. He was also an outspoken opponent of the IRA's campaign of violence. Father Faul's view of the IRA statement was that it was 'as full of holes as a net. Vincent Robinson was not murdered because he was an informer, because he was not. The accusation concerning the bomb is patently false. So why was he murdered? Was someone else covering up their own activities? He devoted himself to the republican cause for many years and suffered much at the hands of British agents. None of them treated him as badly as his comrades.'[5]

What was absent in the IRA's pursuit of informers was an understanding of the advances that the British had made in technical surveillance. If an arms dump was lifted by the British, the first thought that struck IRA leaders was that an informer had given it away, as was the case with Vincent Robinson. It never crossed their mind that the car parked up the street had surveillance cameras in its headlights; or that most streets had tiny cameras attached to the top of telephone poles that could detect all the movement down below; or that MI5 could enter a house, place listening devices and cameras everywhere, and get out again without the owner of the house having any clue that his or her property had been bugged. Despite all this, however, Detective Superintendent Ian Phoenix, head of E4A, the RUC's spearhead anti-terrorist unit, was still of the view that 'informers remain the most powerful tool that the police have against illegal organisations, allowing them to anticipate crimes'.[6]

Even as Scappaticci and the nutting squad were seeking out new victims in the late 1970s and early 1980s, republican leader Gerry Adams had arrived at the conclusion that the IRA were incapable of winning the war against the British and that the only way forward for the republican movement was to engage in constitutional politics in both Irish jurisdictions. At the time, within the IRA this thinking amounted to treason, because the reason why the Provisional IRA had broken from the Official IRA in 1970 was precisely because the Officials wanted to pursue constitutional politics.

Adams' assessment was based, to a degree, on war-weariness and the reality that, even though the struggle had been going on for ten years, the British had shown no inclination to leave Ireland. Coupled with this was a view that ever since a successful IRA operation had killed eighteen British soldiers at Narrow Water, near Warrenpoint, in 1979, the British were once again in the military ascendancy.

Then came the 1981 hunger strike. On 1 March, the IRA prison leader, Bobby Sands, went on hunger strike to attain political status for his fellow-Blanketmen and to further the IRA's armed struggle. Frank Hughes, Raymond McCreesh and Patsy O'Hara soon joined Sands on the fast. After being elected MP for Fermanagh/South Tyrone on 9 April, Sands died on 5 May, followed by a further nine hunger strikers. IRA volunteers on the outside were itching to take on the British Army, but their leadership held them back, judging, correctly, that they were militarily too weak to engage the might of the British in open warfare.

In the meantime, Adams and the coterie of republicans who surrounded him were looking to take advantage of the huge support for the prisoners that was being expressed at the ballot box and on the streets. They believed it was time to build a relatively obscure political party, Sinn Féin, into a radical vehicle for Irish freedom. But there was a downside: if the republican movement were to abandon armed struggle completely and embrace constitutional politics, it would have to accept the principle of consent, which stated that there could only be a united Ireland when voted for exclusively by the people of Northern Ireland (a gerrymandered state that had been established on the back of a sectarian headcount, which had been specifically designed to ensure a perennial unionist majority).

For the British, it must have seemed that Adams was no longer the Devil incarnate. Indeed, they may well have regarded him as an asset – someone who needed to be safeguarded from the possibility of loyalist assassination and protected from the fanaticism of more diehard republicans – but also someone who needed to be surrounded with agents who could report back his every movement and thought. One MI5 agent was already so close to Adams he could have told them which toothpaste he used; others burrowed their way into his trusted inner circle. One was his main driver; another was Freddie Scappaticci, whom Adams would have consulted in relation to the security status of people who gravitated towards him and his inner circle of confidants.

Besides sucking up to Adams, Scappaticci and his Belfast ISU were nothing if not industrious. On 27 September 1981, IRA volunteer Anthony Braniff, a father of three from the Ardoyne, was found shot dead in a back alley off Odessa Street in the Falls Road area. This would not be the last tragedy suffered by the Braniff family. In 1989, Anthony's father, David, was assassinated by loyalist gunmen in his Alliance Avenue home in Belfast as he knelt with his wife and daughter saying the Rosary.

Twenty-two years after Braniff's killing, the republican newspaper *An Phoblacht*, in its 25 September 2003 edition, published an IRA statement saying, 'On 27 September 1981, Anthony Braniff, a Volunteer in the IRA, was executed in Belfast. Our investigation has found no evidence to support the claims made at the time that Anthony Braniff "was responsible for passing information concerning the location of arms dumps and the movement of volunteers" and that "he met his Special Branch contacts regularly … while receiving, in return, sums of money". Tellingly, while Braniff was exonerated, no public IRA apology was made and no reason given as to why he had been persuaded to admit to being a police informer or to having given up arms dumps and the movement of volunteers in the first place. Despite this, a grateful Braniff family welcomed the IRA statement.

The transformation of republican politics was best summed up at Sinn Fein's Ard-Fheis (convention) on 31 October 1981 by the party's Director of Publicity, Danny Morrison: 'Who here really believes we can win the war through the ballot box? But will anyone object if, with the ballot box in one hand, and an Armalite in the other, we take power in Ireland?' Few delegates at the time appreciated the inherent contradiction in Morrison's appeal: Armalites do not fit into ballot boxes. Whether or not the Adams leadership grasped that fact – and it is highly probable they did – others definitely did.

There were delegates, such as the Sinn Féin president, Ruairí Ó Brádaigh, who had deep suspicions that Adams and his inner circle were intent on leading the republican movement out of armed struggle and into constitutional politics, a prospect that was repugnant to the traditionalists. In British military and intelligence circles, the prospect of the republican movement embracing electoral politics must have been an empirical moment, inasmuch as they had fought this army of Irish rebels and forced them to consider going down the road of constitutional politics. For MI5 officers like 'Bob', who had been Peter Keeley's handler, Adams, and those who wanted to reform the republican movement, were the way forward: '"The crucial dynamic" lay in how the political people faced down the military people. It was the political people who went straight to the [British] Army. They betrayed military operations. Not all of this was due to self-initiative. In fact, many of those had been agents of influence.'[7] Bob may well be telling the truth but, then again, he was in the business of shaping perceptions, and selling falsehoods was an integral part of his tradecraft. Another vendor of falsehoods was Freddie Scappaticci, who sold the IRA leadership an image of himself as the perfect volunteer when, all the while, he was working to destroy them as an effective fighting force.

9

THE IRA'S *GREEN BOOK*: LIFE OR DEATH?

'God is on everybody's side ... And in the last analysis, he is on the side of those with plenty of money and large armies.'

Jean Anouilh, French dramatist

Freddie Scappaticci was a cautious man by nature. Every morning, before getting into his car, he checked underneath it for booby traps. He changed his car regularly. He varied his movements and timetable. If you were talking to him, his darting eyes clocked every passing car. He had steel drop-bars on his front and back doors.

In Farnham Street, he was particularly vulnerable because there was a Protestant district across the road and loyalists had left pipe bombs on the windowsills of other republicans in his street. Scappaticci would have been acutely aware that, even with his security-force pals' protection, he would be a juicy target for the loyalists. So, in 1982, he moved his family to Glasvey Drive in the Twinbrook area of west Belfast.

Unlike his former residence, Twinbrook had no immediate loyalist neighbours and he was just one of many republicans. For Scappaticci, it was business as usual. He went to work on building sites every day and attended to his IRA activities in his spare time. At other times, he taught his children to swim in Lisburn leisure centre and played five-a-side football with the local IRA men in Andersonstown leisure centre. One young republican recalled Scappaticci exhorting him to leave the IRA, saying, 'the struggle is going nowhere, and it'd be better if you got on with your life'.[1] The informer went on to tell the republican youth that he would prefer it if the volunteers made another life for themselves rather than end up in a prison cell or dead. Here was another side to Scappaticci, a compassionate side, a side that hadn't been openly demonstrated before. Clearly, he had reached the conclusion that the IRA campaign was doomed to failure, and he was trying to dissuade this volunteer from making the same mistakes he had made. Noble though that appeal might have been, Scappaticci was not inclined to practise what he preached.

A man called Collins made the mistake of publicly calling the area in Twinbrook in which Scappaticci lived 'Provie Corner'. Scappaticci did not like that and decided that Collins had to pay for his transgression. He knocked on Collins' door and, when it was answered, the informer battered the older man multiple times over the head with a sock containing a brick. Only when Collins collapsed did Scappaticci walk away.[2]

He also stubbornly continued to ensure that people perished at his and the ISU's hands. The success of the ISU would have been measured by the IRA Army Council in the number of British informers the unit found and shot dead. In 1981, they kept themselves busy, executing four alleged informers in Belfast: the aforementioned Gilvarry, Trainor, Robinson and Braniff.

At the start of the following year, another apparent victim was twenty-nine-year-old father of four John Torbett, who was shot in his home in Horn Drive on 2 January and died of his wounds on 19 January. The IRA had previously given Torbett seventy-two hours to leave Northern Ireland and said in a statement he had refused to comply with their instructions. They also said that "'an intelligence unit" [ISU] accused him of agreeing to pass on information to the RUC'.[3] Fr Faul once again condemned the IRA, saying, 'The IRA had no right to enforce exclusion orders against their fellow-Irishmen. They are imitating the worst excesses of the British Prevention of Terrorism Act'.[4]

The ISU's area of influence extended throughout the Northern Command area, and, on 6 March 1982, Seamus Morgan, a former election worker for Bobby Sands and father of four, was found shot dead on a roadside outside the village of Forkhill in south Armagh. The dead man's wife said that nineteen days before his death he had been released from police custody and had gone to stay in County Monaghan. A police witness told the coroner at Morgan's inquest that he had not been an informer.[5] Another killing carried out at that time by the ISU, besides James Young, was that of Brian McNally.

Eamon Collins went into some detail about McNally's interrogations at the hands of both the RUC and IRA, indicating that, after being released from RUC custody on suspicion of having driven a motorcycle whose pillion passenger had shot a UDR soldier, McNally told the IRA that the police had subjected him to 'a horrendous catalogue of assaults and abuse'.[6] During a local IRA debriefing in Dundalk, he reported that he had not broken under interrogation. But he still had to be debriefed by the nutting squad, which looked upon the organisation's *Green Book* as its bible.

The *Green Book* was first introduced to all volunteers in 1977. It deals with how best to handle interrogations, as well as the tactics used by RUC interrogators to get their suspects to reveal what they know regarding the IRA and about specific operations. Being 'green-booked' – verbally lectured on the details of the book – was important for IRA volunteers because it removed the excuse that they did not know what to expect when arrested. It also added to the prospect of IRA volunteers being punished if they did break under interrogation and did not report the fact to their IRA superior officers when released from custody.

When McNally returned to Dundalk for a second debrief, he was arrested by the ISU and very quickly admitted that he had lied when he said he had not broken in Gough Barracks and that the police had tried to get him to set up a prominent IRA man for assassination. Eamon Collins ruefully said, 'He was not very intelligent, and I doubted he could have ever worked out a way to extricate himself from his peril. The police who had threatened and manipulated this vulnerable young man were no less reprehensible than the people who murdered him.'[7]

Another ISU killing that took place outside of Belfast was that of Damien McCrory, a twenty-year-old man with learning disabilities who was shot twice in the head and whose body was found in the Drumrallagh estate in Strabane, west Tyrone, on 7 October 1985. The IRA said that McCrory had informed the RUC about three IRA volunteers – Charles Breslin and the two Devine brothers – who were killed by members of the SAS while they were walking across a field with automatic weapons after an ambush they had planned had been called off. In an extraordinary development, the family of one of those who was executed spoke out for McCrory, saying that he was not an informer. The Breslin family identified a man called Declan 'Beano'

Casey as the real informer, noting that Casey and his family had been spirited out of Strabane by the security forces. Casey would later deny this charge.

As the 1980s progressed and the ISU's victims continued to be found scattered around country roadsides and Belfast's back alleys, there were conflicting agendas at play within republicanism. Shortly after the 1982 election, a Redemptorist priest, Fr Alex Reid, initiated one-on-one talks with the vice-president of Sinn Féin, Gerry Adams, in the hope that, ultimately, an alternative to the IRA's armed struggle could be found.[8] These talks were kept hidden from the IRA volunteers and the Army Council because Adams was unsure if he would have received their approval. Moreover, Adams must surely have been aware that what would not be on offer was a united Ireland – yet this was the pumping heart of the armed struggle. So he concealed his hand and patiently bided his time, keeping the ASUs and the hard men in ignorance of what he was involved in behind the scenes. This was a dangerous stratagem, as Ed Moloney observed: 'Had they [the volunteers and Army Council] thought that the political path down which Adams had taken them would lead into negotiations that threatened to dilute dearly held republican beliefs, most would have seen it as treachery.'[9] The IRA's penalty for treachery was execution.

What had not been taken off the drawing board by the peace talks was the loyalist targeting of Adams. Despite British intelligence services having key players in position within the loyalist paramilitary leadership, Adams was still at the top of the hit lists for the UVF and the UDA, both of which regarded him as 'Chief of Staff of the IRA'. The reality was that Adams was not the IRA's chief of staff, but he was widely viewed by loyalists as the public face of the IRA. So, by this time, he had surrounded himself with bodyguards: IRA men whom he trusted to take a bullet for him. Some would, but, in a sign of the times, at least one of his supposed bullet-stoppers, a former republican prisoner and trusted driver from the Turf Lodge district of Belfast, would flee Ireland after having been discovered to be a security-force spy.

Despite his bodyguards, Adams was almost killed when, on 14 March 1984, as he and four other republicans were leaving Belfast magistrates' court (where they had been answering charges of obstruction), a UDA hit squad pulled up alongside their car and opened fire. Adams was shot in the neck and shoulder, Seán Keenan in the face, Joe Keenan in the body and hands, and Kevin Rooney in the body. The bullets missed the driver, Bob Murray, who spirited his passengers off to hospital. All survived the attack, and the loyalist gunmen were arrested minutes after they opened fire by an off-duty policeman and three plain-clothes military police officers who happened to be in the vicinity.

Interestingly, according to former FRU staff sergeant Ian Hurst, 'Undercover members of the security forces watched the entire incident. They allowed the attack to take place, but when the shooting ceased, they swooped on the three loyalists within seconds.'[10] Hurst says that two FRU agents in the UDA leadership had pre-warned their handlers of the attack and told them that the weapons to be used were stored in a shed in the Rathcoole area. Hurst alleges that his FRU colleagues 'jarked' (tampered with) the weapons, thus reducing the charge in the bullets to minimise their impact. This may have been considered enough to ensure Adams would not be badly hurt, but a bullet in his head could still have been fatal. So did the TCGs know about this proposed murder bid on Adams and his party? It seems likely. But if so, why didn't the Belfast TCG have the police arrest the loyalist gunmen before their attack on Adams and his comrades?

Hurst's unconvincing explanation is that the FRU wanted to protect the cover of their top UDA agent, Brian Nelson, but if Adams had been killed, any chance of a peace process would have died with him and it may have taken years before another credible process could have been put in place.

Like Adams, Freddie Scappaticci had a hankering for a long life, but, unlike Adams, he could not surround himself with bodyguards – so his plan was to be popular or, if he couldn't be popular, at least be feared.

'Matthew O'Cleary', a former Northern Command staff officer, recalled Scappaticci on one of his visits to Derry: 'It was pre-'87 and two IS guys came down to Derry for some reason. And one of them stayed in Big Kevin Daly's house that night, but Scap stayed in my sister's house in the Brandywell. And he says to me, "Any chance of going to the dogs [greyhound racing]?" So he went to the dogs. And he stayed in the house that night and they left the next day. And, do you see when they left ... the four end houses in the square that my sister lived in were raided by the Brits. Scap must have touted that he stayed in an end house in that street, and they raided all four end houses. All he knew was he stayed in an end house. He actually went to the dogs on his own that night.'[11]

'Mark Gallagher', a second former Northern Command officer, also remembered Scappaticci: 'I came out of Castlereagh one time and was dark-roomed [made to sit facing the wall in a darkened room] and he said to me, "You can't see my face. You have to turn your back to me." And it was away up the country. And do you know what I says to him? "How do you know if a man's lying if you're looking at the back of his head? Don't be stupid," I says. "Fuckin' face me." He didn't.'[12] It is a measure of Gallagher's sense of worth that he felt he could be curt with

Freddie Scappaticci … most IRA volunteers would have been glad if they never set eyes on him.

10

FRANK HEGARTY'S IRA SPONSOR

'Hegarty was an affront. He [Martin McGuinness] took it very personally. Before Hegarty was shot, I knew about it. A friend of mine was to interrogate Hegarty, but McGuinness, [A] and [F], interrogated him. McGuinness ordered his shooting.'

Freddie Scappaticci, The Cook Report

On top of his role in the ISU, throughout his period as a British agent, Scappaticci oversaw IRA civil administration in Belfast. This meant that he sat in an office in a Sinn Féin centre in Belfast along with Diarmuid O'Toole and decided who was going to be knee-capped and who was going to be spared and given a second chance. Often, the issue boiled down to the pleas of relatives. O'Toole seemed genuinely shocked at his former friend's betrayal: 'Scap? A tout? I couldn't believe it. Nobody could. I worked with him on civil administration three, four times a week for years – and he was a lot tougher than I was when it came to listening to the crying mothers.

'I knew he was in the ISU. He was one of the IRA's top squirrels [intelligence officers], if not the best there was. He was in the loop with all intelligence matters; it was his job, as number two to John Joe [Magee], to know everything that was going down. So, if a suspect tout was picked up anywhere in the Northern Command area, it was usually Scap who was sent for to question him or her, so it wouldn't have been unusual for him to be in Derry, or south Armagh, or Monaghan: his job took him all over the place. And this gave him access to almost all the OCs and staffs in the Northern Command area.'[1]

Martin McGuinness and Freddie Scappaticci were once pals according to O'Toole. 'Why wouldn't they be good friends? They were both senior IRA men, both would've had to meet on a regular basis to discuss army business, so it was in their mutual interest to get along. As I recollect, theirs was more than just a business relationship, they were genuinely close. Martin sometimes stopped over in Freddie's house when he was visiting Belfast on Northern Command business, and he also had dinner with the Scappaticci family. I haven't a clue why they fell out, but fall out they most definitely did. I mean … look at how Freddie gutted [disparaged] Martin to the Cook reporters.'[2]

O'Toole is referring to a secret interview that an irate Scappaticci gave to reporters on 26 August 1993, during which he said, 'McGuinness? Oh, I know him very well. I know him about twenty years, you know.' He went on to say, 'He is ruthless. I can say that unequivocally. He has the final say on an informer, whether that person lives or dies.'[3] Scappaticci was being disingenuous here, because he knew only too well that, in the cases where he was involved at least, it was the TCGs who made the final decision on who lived and who died. But what had prompted Scappaticci to turn so publicly on his erstwhile friend? O'Toole offered that perhaps Scappaticci was furious because McGuinness had subverted his role in the Frank Hegarty affair by excluding the Belfast ISU team from the suspected informer's interrogation.

Forty-five-year-old Hegarty had been an Official IRA OC in Derry's Rosemount area in the 1970s but had been dismissed because the Stickies had suspected he was an informer. He had joined the Provos in the 1980s and by 1985 was assistant to the Northern Command's quartermaster (QMNC), a role that was particularly significant at that time as IRA GHQ appeared to be formulating plans for a major escalation. The idea behind the big push was later described by some commentators as a 'Tet Offensive', a term that had come to describe the January 1968 North Vietnamese Army attacks on southern Vietnamese towns and cities. While undoubtedly ambitious, the plan was that the IRA would endeavour to annex territory in rural areas and, in a similar manner to what had been happening in south Armagh, make it impossible for the British writ to run there.

The first part of the plot was to import hundreds of tonnes of arms from Libya into Ireland. This was successfully accomplished when four Libyan arms shipments landed in Irish inlets between September 1985 and July 1886. Included in the shipments were over 1,000 AK-47 rifles, one tonne of Semtex explosives, twelve SAM-7 missiles, and heavy machine guns. The success of the importation depended on secrecy, with only two men from the south Armagh and north Louth areas knowing all the details of the arms shipments. These arms were then distributed and secreted in dumps across Ireland, but much of the matériel was hidden in the northern part of the country, where the war was being fought, and was under the control of the QMNC and his new assistant, Frank Hegarty.

For the British, the introduction by the IRA of such a large amount of weaponry was a war-changing development and they rightly assessed that it was critical they knew where the arms dumps were hidden. However, the only way of finding out where the dumps were was to have an informer at the distribution point – in the QMNC's department. This was easier said than done because the then QMNC was a tough, no-nonsense volunteer with a long pedigree in armed struggle – someone who could neither be bought nor compromised. Hegarty, or 'Agent 3018', was not cast from the same mould.

Matthew O'Cleary and Mark Gallagher were former Provisional IRA senior officers from the city and county of Derry. Mark recalled hearing of Hegarty during the early 1970s. 'We'd an op out in Rosemount and the unit came back to me and said that Franco had compromised their op,' O'Cleary said. 'So I found out he was in Hughes' bar and I went down to confront him. And I went in and loudly asked: "Is Franco here?" No one opened their mouths. And I says, "You tell Hegarty … he has to get in touch with me."'[4]

When asked how Frank originally got into the Provisionals, despite his history with the Official IRA, Matthew said, 'I can fill you in there. The first time he was in the 'RA, in the mid-seventies, there was a fella called "Joe". And him and Franco were two buddies, and Franco got into the 'RA through Joe. And then Joe went off the rails and it was you [Mark] and I dismissed him [Frank]. He was knocking about with a girl and the Derry Brigade had her down as a tout. So I went to Ivor [Bell], he was OC Northern Command at that time, and told him about this girl, and he said: "Tell that boy if he wants to screw women he'd better make sure they're not touts." I told Franco the craic, but he ignored the order, and then me and you saw him in the car with her –'

Mark intervenes: 'That's right. He was driving towards us, and he ducked her head down as we passed him in a car.'

After seeing him in the car, Matthew went to Frank and said, '"You're gone." And I took the keys of the [IRA] car off him. And that was him gone.'

When asked, neither of the Northern Command officers knew if Hegarty had been cleared by the ISU before being allowed to rejoin the IRA. Matthew said, 'I never heard of IS vetting him. Did you?'

'No,' Mark replied.

'And see, until he gave away all that gear [arms], he was never a suspect,' Matthew said.

Mark disagreed, recalling, 'No, you're wrong. Franco *was* a suspect. I remember meeting you and "John Scullion" [another senior Derry IRA man] in Lifford dogs one night and John called him a tout right to his face.'

According to Mark, who was the QMNC at the time, McGuinness had originally chosen Hegarty to take over in his position as he wanted Mark to go on operations on the Continent. So Hegarty became privy to the locations of all the arms dumps. As Mark pointed out, 'He pretty much knew what I knew at the time. We supplied most of the west lands: Derry Brigade, west Tyrone, County Derry, south Derry; know what I mean? ... mid-Ulster, and I'd drop stuff off at Cavan and along the Fermanagh border to the different units.' What they didn't realise was that Hegarty had been a British informer before he joined the IRA.

'He was out this day and the Brits approached him and propositioned him and they gave him a phone and he took the money and that was it. He would hire a room in the Eglington Hotel and that was where he usually met his Brit contact. Fuckin' ... McGuinness came to me, and he says, "Take it from me that everything Franco knew, the Brits knew."'

Mark went on to complain that 'I wasn't at his interrogation. I don't think John Joe Magee or Scap were there either, but I can't be certain on that. Now, if anybody should have been there, it should have been them boys, but they weren't, and neither was I. I'm the fuckin' QMNC, I should have been there as of right, to hear what he told, to hear what fucking damage he'd done to my department. Nobody ever told me what damage he'd done. Can you believe that? Nobody ever thought to tell me what dumps he'd given away. McGuinness … he didn't want me there. And do you know why, Matthew? McGuinness landed up at my house looking you and I said I didn't know where you were. And he said he was going up to Rosemount and he didn't know that Franco was back in the 'RA a second time.'

Matthew: 'That's balls! *He* brought him back! *Him*. Not me, not you. *Him*. It was Martin who was sending you to Europe and pushing Franco into your job. All fucking roads lead to Martin.'[5]

If indeed all roads lead to Martin, then his credibility as a former republican leader and icon is severely punctured. Why? Because Ian Hurst and leading members of the contemporaneous IRA all say that McGuinness used his position to elevate Hegarty to the seminal role of assistant QMNC and planned to make him QMNC. Had that strategy come to fruition, had Hegarty been promoted, then British intelligence services would have had complete control over the IRA's northern arsenal. In this impressive grand coup, the British could have lifted hundreds of weapons whenever the notion took them and thus would have seized control of the IRA's capability to wage war. They could also have 'jarked' the weapons by putting minuscule tracking devices in them, allowing them to follow their journey throughout the country, whereupon they could then have set up ambushes to kill IRA personnel coming to collect the arms from dumps. Fortunately for the

IRA, Hegarty was discovered to be a British agent before the plan to elevate him to QMNC came to fruition.

In a later interview, Matthew made it clear that, while he thought McGuinness had handled the Hegarty affair badly, he was not alleging the IRA leader had been an informer. However, an alternative view was expressed by FRU officer Ian Hurst, who has always maintained that McGuinness *was* an informer. Hurst had been one of Hegarty's handlers, and had already met with him around twenty times over the course of six or seven months when he was told to steer Hegarty towards McGuinness by his boss, Captain John Tobias. 'The boss, who died in the Mull of Kintyre Chinook crash, says, "I want you to do something with Franco." And he says, "I want you to steer Franco towards Martin McGuinness ... I want you to get him to go and offer his services to Cable Street [the Sinn Féin headquarters in Derry]."'

Despite having serious doubts about this decision, Hurst and his partner, Frank Rimmer, 'had a meeting with Franco, and we tell Franco the score. Franco looks at us as if we'd two heads. He says, "What the fuck? Why would Martin McGuinness be interested in looking after me? There's linkage between him and me. They know about my past. They don't trust me. Why are you asking me to walk into the lion's den?"'

'They all knew he was a compromised agent. Even the Stickies knew he was an agent. This will sound amazing to you now, given what I've said ... Franco then goes and does exactly what we asked him to do – but with no expectation – and he is greeted by Martin McGuinness like a long-lost friend and given menial jobs for a period of time, and he was comfortable in the Sinn Féin headquarters in Cable Street. He then rises to the rank of assistant quartermaster northern command. That's a long way up the ladder and the only person who developed him in that role was his sponsor, Martin McGuinness.'[6]

IRA Commander Luke McCartney was as flabbergasted at Hegarty's return to the IRA as everyone else: 'I was shocked at the level of incompetence at command level. Fuckin' Franco Hegarty … as assistant quartermaster of northern command? Fuck me! Where was IS? All recruits were supposed to be rigorously cleared by IS … what happened here? Where was Scap and the rest of them boys when this was happening? I couldn't understand how he got back into the IRA – never mind him being made assistant QMNC. I went off my fucking head, I did; I went ballistic. I thought it was a joke. He [Hegarty] was a useless whore and I'm telling you straight: McGuinness had a fucking hand to play in it.'[7]

McCartney went on to complain, 'See, I think the only reason they kept me in place was because I was doing the fucking ops, me and a few people around me, and Martin McGuinness won the heart of the IRA on the basis of the work *we* were doing in Derry, not him. He wasn't risking his neck on the snipes and the ambushes. And we weren't losing people; we weren't getting our people shot. But while Martin wasn't doing any ops, he'd have claimed credit in the IRA for them. Then our ops started to be compromised – and at the highest level too. The highest level. It took me a while to get it right in my head, but see now, there are doubts.'

To illustrate this point, McCartney pointed to an operation during which the Derry Brigade had hoped to shoot dead twelve British soldiers who made the mistake of coming into a bar by the same entrance, at the same time, every Friday night. 'And I said, "Fuck me, will you look at this!" And then I thought, "We can do this." So I went to Martin and told him I needed six shorts [handguns]. "What's it for?" he asked, and I told him, and he asked, "When are youse doing that?" and I said as soon as we get the shorts. The Friday night that we went to do it, we were armed and in the bar. There were people out and about and reporting back to us. Next thing, we got word that dozens of Brits were coming into the bar, so we got rid of the shorts. Thirty-six Brits landed into the bar, not twelve. Then a Brit came over to me and said, "What are you [McCartney and George McBrearty, a volunteer who was shot dead on an operation by the SAS in 1981] doing here?" I told him we were having a drink.

'The next day the same Brit stopped us and said, "Which one of you cunts was gonna shoot me last night?" and I said, "The two of us; we were throwing up coins." Then I told him to fuck off.'[8]

McCartney reflected that in the thick of the action, or an ongoing conflict, there is rarely an opportunity to sit back and analyse what is happening in real time. 'I mean, take Scap, for example. Who saw him, y'know? He was nipping in and out of Derry, hoovering up volunteers' names and the details of failed ops; he was there, right in front of us, and we didn't see him. Like, we were emptying our guts out to Scap in dark rooms after coming out of the interrogation centres, and it never dawned on us he was "wrong" [an informer]. Why? Because, y'see ... when you're in the middle of it, when you're picking vols for ops, getting the gear in place, sorting out the runbacks, and all the other stuff, you never see it.'[9]

In a moment of lucidity, McCartney mirrored what others were saying, 'See, years ago, if someone had said to me that Scap was a dodgy boy, I'd have said, you're full of shit. Same thing with Martin. In fact, if somebody had told me Martin was a tout, I think I might have shot his accuser. Not so sure now. People are afraid to say anything about Martin McGuinness, but everybody is saying the same thing; they're not saying it loudly, but they're all saying it. All I'll say is: they [the British] had him on a fucking tape, and the registration number of a car, him helping put a bomb in the car, and then the bomb goes off in the middle of Shipquay Street, and McGuinness isn't charged. For fuck's sake! He's filmed showing kids guns! I mean, the tape disappears for over forty years, or 'til he's dead. Had that have been me, I'd have got twenty years, I'd have been sentenced and everything … how come he wasn't charged?'[10]

The tape to which McCartney is referring is of a programme called *The Secret Army*, which was produced and co-written by the American academic and author J. Bowyer Bell in 1972, and while McCartney is right in saying that McGuinness is caught bang-to-rights on camera being involved in a car-bombing and handling guns, things are not as clear-cut as the tape suggests.

The 2019 BBC documentary, *Spotlight on the Troubles: A Secret History*, shed some light on Bowyer Bell's explosive film. It shows, amongst other things, a segment relating to the Shipquay Street bombing in Derry on 21 March 1972. In this, four men are seen putting a 100lb car bomb with an alarm-clock timer in the trunk of a car with the vehicle registration 7337 UI, and McGuinness is seen walking alongside the men and looking intently at the bomb, which would later explode in Shipquay Street in Derry city centre, injuring twenty-six people. There follows a segment where McGuinness is showing a bullet to children and opening the chamber of a revolver. Placed alongside the IRA leader is a rifle.

What is important, from Luke McCartney's and other IRA peoples' perspective is that, despite what appears to be very damning evidence against McGuinness, he was never charged or brought before the courts, but then, neither were any of the other twenty or so IRA volunteers who were identifiable in the film. There are three potential explanations for this:

1. That British Intelligence, and thus the public prosecution service, were unaware of the film.

2. That British Intelligence were aware of it, but the public prosecution service did not believe they had a *prima facie* case to bring against McGuinness and the other IRA volunteers, although this was a time when IRA volunteers were being convicted on exceptionally weak evidence.

3. That British Intelligence did not make the public prosecution service aware of the recordings and instead banked the intelligence treasure trove so that they could use the film to blackmail McGuinness and those on show into becoming agents/informers for them at an appropriate date in the future.

The Bowyer Bell film's budget director and executive producer, Leon Gildin, notes, 'The "rushes" [the daily footage] were sent down to be developed in London. In London, British Intelligence, MI5 or MI6, I don't recall which, would review the material to see if they had captured anything that would be of interest to British Intelligence, or that British Intelligence did not want shown.' If this is true, then British Intelligence were aware of McGuinness' involvement in the Shipquay Street bombing and of him showing his revolver to children. If they were, then this would also mean that a decision would have had to be taken by British Intelligence not to prosecute McGuinness and the other identifiable IRA men, despite being given a golden opportunity to remove from the struggle some very committed IRA personnel. It seems likely, in the face of this evidence, that British Intelligence had a specific strategic interest in not seeking prosecutions.

Luke McCartney was also vexed about Frank Hegarty's elevation to the upper echelons of the Northern Command. He believed it was a monumental present to British Intelligence and, when asked how Hegarty had been able to skip a few ranks to become assistant QMNC, McCartney was forthright: 'This boy didn't skip a few ranks, somebody from up above threw him down a ladder. We always maintained that.'[11]

'John Scullion' – a former IRA commander for north Derry, north Antrim and south Down – agreed with McCartney's assessment that Martin McGuinness was the man who had thrown down the ladder for Frank Hegarty to climb to the QMNC floor: 'It [Hegarty's promotion] had to come from McGuinness. Everybody else was pullin' their hair out that he was back in the 'RA, never mind playing a leading role in the northern command's quartermaster department. I don't think he was the actual QM, but he was next to him in the command structure. And it had to come from McGuinness! No doubt about that. And McGuinness was a tout. I told him so in Maghera in 2004 when they called us all [the volunteers under John's command] to a house to thank us for our service and tell us to go about our business, that they no longer needed us. They basically told us to fuck off. I just came out with it in front of everybody and said to McGuinness, "You're nothing but a fucking tout" and I walked out of the house.'[12]

Scullion explained that sometimes what doesn't happen is just as important as what does. He had been in the IRA since he was fifteen years old and operated with men like Francis Hughes and Dominic McGlinchey. He was active in north Antrim, and north and south Derry, and recalls the following story about Hegarty and McGuinness. Scullion was staying in a house in Sliabh Snácht in Donegal and planning an operation with two other men when 'Franco Hegarty and John Davey landed in on us and Franco says to me, "Are you headin'?" And I says, "Shortly." And he says, "Well, I need to know what you're for doing." And I says, "Tune into Downtown [radio]." And he says, "No, no. Martin McGuinness wants to know what your ops are and when they're going down." And I turned around to the other two boys and said, "This isn't fuckin' right, boys. I don't like it." And the other two boys said, "If it's comin' from Martin McGuinness, we have to tell him." So, I did tell him and Davey and, about a week later, we headed out on one of the jobs I had in mind.'[13]

As outlined in the opening interview of this book, Scullion and his companions made their way to an isolated area where they planned to ambush three UDR men, crawling the last three fields on their stomachs. 'I was on point and took the lead. I was in a ditch behind a hedge and there was this breeze-block garage to my right, on the other side of the hedge. No big deal, right? Most bungalows and houses have breeze-block garages. And then I heard voices, English voices, coming from the garage. I waved my adjutant up and put a finger to my lips. Then, when he was beside me, I pointed to the garage. We both listened to whispered English voices. You couldn't actually make them out, except for one word … "fucking". We caught that one over and over again. The English always pronounce their "ings". Then we both realised the SAS were in position to ambush us and we knew there'd be other SAS in and around the kill zone, so we were in a dodgy position. We had no choice. We backed out on our bellies.'

On their way back to their run-back house, Scullion told his adjutant that they had a 'Gypo Nolan' in their midst. When asked what he meant by 'a Gypo', Scullion replied, 'A Gypo Nolan; an informer, a tout. At least one, probably, two.'[14]

The next day, in Letterkenny, Scullion and one of the volunteers who had been with him on the aborted operation met Hegarty and Davey in a safe house, whereupon the informer demanded to know why the operation had been called off. Scullion never missed his cue:

'The reason why it was called off is because one of youse two cunts is a tout! I don't know which one, but Franco, I think it's you.' Hegarty did not reply. Neither did Davey.

After Hegarty and Davey left, the volunteer who had been with Scullion on the operation said, '"You're in big trouble. They're gonna report you. Calling a volunteer, a tout. That's a head job." But never a word came back to me, and poor John Davey … he was shot dead in his own laneway by loyalists … well, so they say. I think he was done by a Brit undercover, probably the SAS. John knew too much, y'see. I also think he was asking questions. John Davey wasn't the tout. I've a funny feeling he was working things out and was getting too close to finding answers, and he was set up.'[15]

When asked how the ISU handled this major security breach, Scullion replied, 'The ISU were made aware of it – I made sure of that – but I never heard a peep from John Joe Magee or Freddie Scap, or anyone else for that matter. I remember … I thought it rare [strange] at the time, but if I wasn't being dark-roomed by IS, I wasn't going to complain. And I'll tell you another thing, Franco Hegarty wasn't questioned by IS either, even though there was strong evidence he was a tout. If we three had been wiped out that night by the SAS, there might have been an IRA court of inquiry, but we survived, so somebody buried any investigation. Now I wonder who would do that?'[16] This was staggering information and somewhat inexplicable because, in the normal course of events, such a foul-up would automatically have triggered an ISU inquiry, and usually an inquiry would have been led by Freddie Scappaticci.

When Hegarty was eventually arrested by the IRA, Luke McCartney insisted that Scappaticci was involved in his interrogation: 'See when they gripped [arrested] Hegarty and took him through interrogation, it would have been Scap …'[17] McCartney, of course, is speaking in the conditional tense when he says that Scappaticci *would have* been present during Hegarty's interrogation; he is not presenting a fact.

Ian Hurst, on the other hand, spoke as if he had direct knowledge of Scappaticci's role in Hegarty's interrogation, when he said, 'Scappaticci had been brought in by the IRA GHQ for this one, for this one was special.'[18] While a small suspicion remains that Freddie Scappaticci may have had a role in Hegarty's IRA arrest, the leading Derry IRA volunteers to whom I spoke were adamant that he did not shoot him dead. Ian Hurst, in an interview with me, took the opportunity to correct a misrepresentation in his book *Stakeknife*, where he had asserted, 'the man who actually pulled the trigger on the gun that killed Frank Hegarty was none other than Scappaticci himself. One FRU agent had killed another. Hegarty could have been saved, but somewhere a decision had been taken that it was better for him to die to help maintain Scappaticci's position. The gardaí could have rescued Hegarty if they had been given the details from the northern side, but that information was never passed on.'[19] On reflection, however, Hurst pulled back from his original position: 'When I say [Scappaticci] shot him, I mean in the sense that, he, essentially, although he was involved, it was the nutting squad. In a legal sense, if I instruct you to carry out a crime, then I am, in a sense, the criminal mind. The other person [the shooter] is the conduit who accepts the instruction, that is the end course. So, you can argue that the person who is the criminal mind is behind the murder. Freddie is the conduit to the person that actually pulls the trigger. I don't think in this instance that Freddie is the person who pulls the trigger, I don't know.'[20]

When asked if the FRU had had an observation post watching the location in which Hegarty was being held by the IRA, Hurst hesitated, saying that he did not know if the FRU knew the exact site, but they knew he was arrested by the IRA and was being held in County Donegal. If, indeed, the FRU were aware of the property in which Hegarty was being held, then the Derry TCG would also have known and, given that they did not try to save Hegarty's life, they would have had to take a decision to allow him to be executed – presumably to protect a more senior informer. This appears to be confirmed by something that Hurst said to this author: '[T]here was a desire within the FRU to go and get him and pull him out, but we were not allowed to do that because it served a useful purpose to have him as ... you know, a sacrificial lamb.'[21]

When pressed on who it was that stopped them pulling Hegarty out, Hurst said he did not know but that the decision would not have gone as high as Cabinet level: 'Essentially you have a body which brings together the various bodies and agencies [TCGs], and then you have an underbody [the operatives] that would decide how you develop cases.' On the reasoning behind the decision, Hurst said, 'We knew where he [Hegarty] was, that's true, and Mr Scappaticci can extrapolate on that, but the reason he wasn't pulled out, like Sandy Lynch was, was because they needed a sacrificial lamb to protect Martin McGuinness from the pressure he was under from the local IRA, and not only them, there were elements from within the very senior IRA who were suspicious of Martin McGuinness.' When asked if McGuinness was an agent, Hurst claims that he was with MI6 rather than with the FRU.

But, while Scappaticci admitted to having foreknowledge of Hegarty's arrest and his likely fate, he cast a shadow of doubt over both McCartney's and Hurst's claims that he had been present for Hegarty's interrogation when he gave his interview to journalists in 1993. '[McGuinness] gave the go-ahead for Frank Hegarty [to be shot dead], right? Well, I'll tell you what I know about it, right ... There were weapons caught in Donegal. It was 150 rifles caught. Hegarty was the one that gave the information on that. So, McGuinness got on the phone and says [to Hegarty, who was in hiding in Kent, England], "Come back. You'll be okay, blah, blah." Convinced him he'd be okay, convinced his mother. He [Hegarty] then came home and McGuinness was the instrument of him being taken away and shot [in May 1986]. I know it because, for a long time, I was at the heart of things. I'm no longer at the heart of things … haven't been for two or three years, but I know what I'm talking about.'[22] Scappaticci went on to say, 'Before Hegarty was shot, I knew about it. A friend of mine was to interrogate Hegarty, but McGuinness interrogated him.' If what Scappaticci says is true – and anything he offers should be treated with caution – then McGuinness usurped the role of the ISU for reasons best known to himself.

Even though Scappaticci says he had not been in the IRA 'for two or three years' (equating to him having parted company with the organisation sometime around 1991), he *did* know what he was talking about when it came to Martin McGuinness. They had been friends and he would have understood why McGuinness, right up to his demise in 2017, insisted he had left the IRA in 1974, when, in fact, he had gone on to be its chief of staff and Northern Command OC. Scappaticci would also have accepted that Hegarty had long been suspected as an informer, and that McGuinness' role in elevating him to the upper echelons of the IRA had damaged the latter reputationally. From his *Cook Report* interview, it appears that Scappaticci believed the only way the IRA commander could restore his bona fides was to engineer Hegarty's death.

Although he admitted that he had never met Scappaticci, many years after these events John Scullion was more philosophical than accusing when interviewed in 2021 by this author: 'Had I known what Scappaticci was up to, I'd have taken the greatest pleasure in nutting him but, when you get a wee bit older, you look back at these things and you realise that everything happens for a reason. Those UDR boys survived our op. We survived the SAS op. Scap survived the war. Isn't that something?'[23] When asked if he would nut Scappaticci if the opportunity came along today, Scullion just smiled.

On 25 May 1986, Frank Hegarty's body was found with bullet wounds to the head on the border road outside Castlederg, County Tyrone. His eyes had been taped up. In a press statement, the IRA admitted to the killing. Despite Hegarty's mother, Rose, insisting in the media that Martin McGuinness had persuaded her son to return to Derry from his exile in England with promises of safety, the Northern Command OC was never arrested or questioned by the police about his death. Politics may have played a part in McGuinness' non-arrest because it was a pivotal time in the evolution of the republican movement.

11

STAKEKNIFE TAKES CONTROL

'Could he with reason murmur at his case,
Himself sole author of his own disgrace?'

William Cowper, English poet

While Scappaticci and the nutting squad were busy hunting suspected
British agents and bringing about their executions, Gerry Adams had
been voted in as the new party president at the November 1983 Sinn
Féin Ard-Fheis, vanquishing the traditionalists led by the veteran
republican Ruairí Ó Brádaigh. What followed was not a revolution,
more a purging of a sacred credo. It was time to push on; to shed the
image of the *sans-culottes* and build a popular political party; to fight
and win elections; and, ultimately, to take seats in the Irish Dáil, or
parliament, and in a Northern Ireland assembly at Stormont. Most of
all, it was time to face the most biting reality of all: the war against the
British was unwinnable. It was time to make peace. That was a message
that many republicans – especially those in the IRA, and particularly

those in the ASUs – were not prepared to swallow. As it turned out, the road to peace was strewn with dead bodies – many of them ASU members, who were cut down in carefully constructed SAS ambushes.

With the leadership and the future political direction of Sinn Féin firmly in his hands, and with a majority of the IRA's Army Council in agreement with him, Adams opened up secret channels with Fianna Fáil leader Charles Haughey, John Hume of the SDLP and officials from the British government, with a view to ending the armed struggle. Adams was savvy enough to know that the first party to sue for peace in any conflict was always the party that would compromise the most. At any rate, he must have known from the outset of negotiations that when the guns fell silent, the state of Northern Ireland would still be a *de facto* part of the United Kingdom. Moreover, in the claustrophobic world of militant republicanism, Adams would have been aware that there were republicans who would not have given a second thought to executing him if they believed he was selling out the cause of the Irish Republic. Understandably then, he kept up the pretence that the waging of the armed struggle was still the fountainhead of republican policy when, in fact, he was dipping his toes in an altogether different pool.

What complicated matters for the republican peace corps was the successful importation of tonnes of arms from Colonel Gaddafi's Libya in the mid-1980s. As the effective leader of the republican movement, if not in name, then certainly in influence, Adams could hardly say to the IRA's ruling body that he did not want the guns brought into the country, so, instead, he persuaded the Army Council to agree that their use would be monitored by McGuinness.

All this chicanery, this charting of a peace strategy without the knowledge or specific approval of the rank-and-file IRA volunteers and without the prospect of a united Ireland, was always going to be a hard slog, and Adams knew this – hence, the secrecy surrounding his talks with the establishment. But pulling the wool over the eyes of the hardcore IRA ASUs was not always easy. Some, especially those in more militant areas like south Armagh, were distrustful of the Adams–McGuinness axis, believing, rightly, that they were not fully committed to the armed struggle. In real terms, a heresy was being laid bare: for the first time since the formation of the Provisional IRA in 1969, the well-being of Sinn Féin superseded the needs of the IRA and the armed struggle. Libyan guns or no Libyan guns, the march to peace would not be halted.

One man who had no idea what was happening was Belfast IRA leader and former hunger striker Brendan 'The Dark' Hughes, who, in December 1986, was released after serving twelve years in prison. On the first day of his release, Hughes reported back to the IRA. Unlike Adams, he was utterly convinced of the merits of physical-force republicanism. Not only was he a militant, he was an IRA prodigy: the man who had commanded the legendary 'D' Company in the Lower Falls during the early 1970s, when dozens of British soldiers were killed in combat. Because of his status, Hughes was immediately appointed as assistant to the GHQ Director of Intelligence, Pat Doherty, a portfolio that would have included keeping an eye on what the ISU was doing. Hughes recalled those days: 'At that time I didn't know what was going on but there was a rundown taking place in the IRA … in many places, especially Cork and Kerry, Pat Doherty was not trusted because he was seen as [one of those] intent on running the IRA down and … he was deeply mistrusted by the people. I didn't understand where the mistrust was coming from because I had just come out of jail.' Hughes would eventually arrive at the conclusion that 'the Army [IRA] was being run down purposely'.[1] Other veteran IRA activists, especially in east Tyrone, had reached the same conclusion.

Amongst the east Tyrone veterans were leading IRA figures like Jim Lynagh, Pádraig McKearney, Seamus McElwain and Paddy Kelly. Encouraged by the arrival of the Libyan arms, they were very much of the view that the battle was there to be won – if the will to win it was also there. Their tactic was to create flying columns designed to bring about 'liberated zones' – areas commanded by the IRA, and not the British Army or the RUC.

This policy of creating 'liberated zones' had been in play for some time. On 7 December 1985, the IRA's East Tyrone Brigade attacked the RUC station at Ballygawley, killing two RUC officers and destroying the base with a bomb. The same unit followed up with a mortar attack on Castlederg RUC station, which injured four people. Another attack was launched at the unmanned Birches RUC station on 11 August 1986, during which a 200lb bomb demolished the station.

If the year 1986 was pivotal for the takeover of Sinn Féin by Adams and McGuinness, it was equally pivotal for Freddie Scappaticci, who was to play a seminal part in the overall Adams–McGuinness strategy of defining IRA tactics. By that stage, he had already been two years in the job as OC ISU, having replaced John Joe Magee, who, although no longer in charge, was still an ISU member. During Scappaticci's reign as OC ISU, the killings continued unabated.

According to Ian Hurst and Greg Harkin, the nutting squad was responsible for killing at least thirty-seven people, with Scappaticci having an input into most of these deaths. Before he had become OC ISU, there had not been a nutting-squad killing since that of Patrick Scott, a twenty-seven-year-old from Belfast, who was shot dead on 3 April 1982 – almost two years before Scappaticci took over the reins of command. After he replaced Magee, Scappaticci oversaw the killings of fifteen people before he was stood down from his post in January 1989.[2]

An important development in Scappaticci's career as a British agent occurred in April 1986, when the Army Council gave permission to Northern Command to vet all IRA operations, since some had resulted in unnecessary civilian deaths: 'There had been some bad operations, politically bad operations, and this was done to correct that,' recalled one rural activist. 'McGuinness [the northern commander] got authority from the Army Council to vet operations. Before that, area commanders would run through their plans in very general terms, for example, "I have a policeman or a Brit patrol," with the chief of staff or director of operations. Now people had to go into the detail of the operation.'[3]

Of all the Army Council directives issued during their almost thirty-year war with the British, the April 1986 one was potentially the most damaging for the IRA because, *if* Martin McGuinness, or someone of a similar status on the Northern Command, was working for British Intelligence, then, effectively, the Army Council would have handed over the day-to-day running of the armed struggle to the British. Again, *if* Martin McGuinness had been the alpha tout, then the priority of British Intelligence would have been similar to that of their Second World War predecessors (whose Bletchley Park codebreakers had cracked the German Enigma Code), in that their objective would have been to inflict the maximum damage on their enemy without alerting them to the fact that they had been fatally compromised. And, just as in that war, this would have translated into allowing some IRA operations to proceed unhindered so that the leadership would not suspect that they had been completely infiltrated. Were this the case, the vista that would emerge is one of British Intelligence sanctioning the killing of members of their own security forces by the IRA. Some might think that a preposterous suggestion. Some might think that floating the possibility that Martin McGuinness was the alpha tout is equally preposterous. Others might like to consider that a consequence of that April 1986 order was that the ISU were ordered by Martin McGuinness to vet all operations being planned by the IRA's Belfast Brigade. The OC of the ISU, Scappaticci, and his pals in the TCGs, were now in full control of the IRA's war in Belfast.

Whitey Bradley was 'enraged' that all actions in Belfast had to be vetted by the ISU. From his point of view, he was entitled to be angry because he had first-hand experience of exactly how precarious the situation had become. On 30 June 1988, his ASU attempted a rocket propelled grenade (RPG) and rifle attack on North Queen Street RUC/ Army Barracks. The Belfast TCG had been forewarned about the operation, most probably by Stakeknife, and had accordingly instructed the SAS to lie in wait for the IRA volunteers. As soon as the ASU opened fire, the SAS returned fire with automatic weapons, including a belt-fed heavy machine gun. One volunteer was wounded and was spirited across the border for treatment. He made a full recovery. Unfortunately, bullets passed through the Volvo car that had been used to transport the volunteers to the barracks and hit Kenneth Stronge, a passing taxi driver. Shot three times, Stronge died of his injuries on 4 July 1988.

Commenting on Scappaticci being made privy to upcoming operations, Bradley said, 'It is now known, of course, that Scappaticci had been a British agent since at least 1979, and perhaps earlier. By requiring all Belfast operations to be vetted by Internal Security, the OC was unwittingly providing British intelligence with knowledge of all IRA plans in Belfast. Therefore, from about 1986 until Scappaticci fell out with the IRA in 1991, British intelligence was, to all intents and purposes, deciding which IRA operations to allow to run in Belfast and which to block. Little wonder there was almost no successful operations of significance by the Belfast Brigade in those years.'[4] That's not to say that there were no major operations during this time. The Belfast Brigade sometimes sanctioned operations without passing them on to the ISU, and a perfect example of this was the killing of two detective police officers in the Liverpool Bar in Belfast in August 1987.

Bradley's assertion that British Intelligence was running IRA operations in Belfast was backed up by a former Belfast IRA leader, 'Peter Murphy', who also decried the fact that the ISU vetted all operations: 'We spent most of our time trying to evade the attention of plain-clothes Brits. They were usually all over us. And nearly every op we put out resulted in the volunteers being caught. We now know why. Scap and the FRU were deciding which ops to stop and which to let through. What chance had we?'[5]

Meanwhile, outside of Belfast, Martin McGuinness vetted all operations. From the outbreak of the Troubles in 1969 until, but not including, the Loughgall ambush in 1987, eight IRA volunteers had died in the East Tyrone Brigade area, with six perishing as a result of botched mortar and bombing missions. Two others, Colm McGirr (23) and Brian Campbell (19), were shot dead by the SAS while approaching an arms dump outside the town of Dungannon on 4 December 1983. After the Army Council's April 1986 order, until the advent of the 1994 ceasefire, that number increased dramatically, with twenty east Tyrone IRA volunteers being shot dead in security-force ambushes. The last deaths occurred on 16 February 1992, following an attack on the RUC station at Coalisland, when four volunteers – Peter Clancy, Kevin Barry O'Donnell, Patrick Daniel Vincent and Seán O'Farrell – were killed.[6] It was reported that twelve SAS soldiers fired over 500 rounds at the IRA volunteers during the ambush.

On the front line, ASU commanders and volunteers were baffled and aggrieved at the 1986 order, feeling that security was being blatantly compromised. And, just as North Derry IRA volunteer John Scullion had baulked at revealing details of his operation to Frank Hegarty on McGuinness' orders, so Luke McCartney also cringed at the prospect of having to run the details of all brigade operations past McGuinness: 'I remember Martin telling me that he had to vet all ops … can't remember the exact date, but it was in the mid-eighties, yeah, about then. It was fucking crazy as far as I was concerned. There was one day, an ASU saw a sniping opportunity and "clipped" a Brit. The op wasn't run past Martin 'cause he wasn't in town. When he came back, he cracked up at me. I just said, "What's the big deal? It was a good op. Isn't that what this is all about?"'[7]

The East Tyrone ASU leader, Jim Lynagh, was no less upset than McCartney, and he had a blazing row with the chief of staff, Kevin McKenna, about having to divulge the specifics of a proposed attack on Loughgall police station. As events went on to show, Lynagh's concern was well founded.

12

LOUGHGALL

'It is better to be feared than loved, if you cannot be both.'

Niccolò Machiavelli, Italian author and philosopher

Of the ops that were let through, the most damaging in terms of IRA casualties was the 8 May 1987 Loughgall ambush, during which eight IRA volunteers and a civilian were mown down by the SAS. While there is little evidence that Scappaticci played a part in the actual IRA operation, he did have a leading part to play in the IRA court of inquiry that followed the ambush.

Clearance for 'Operation Judy', the codename for the Loughgall ambush, was obtained from Tom King, Secretary of State for Northern Ireland. From the outset, 'Judy' was defined as an 'Op/React', a euphemism for 'set-piece killings' or, put another way, the taking of no prisoners. The former Police Ombudsman for Northern Ireland, Dr Michael Maguire, described Op/React as being marked by 'the deployment of specialist police or military units, evidence of fore-planning on the confrontation (usually informer information), little apparent attempt to arrest rather than kill, and massive use of firepower against the deceased.'[1]

'Colm McGarrigle', a republican from Tyrone, had a distinctive view of 'Judy': 'The likes of Jim [Lynagh] and Pádraig [McKearney] were always conscious that they might walk into an ambush. They knew no quarter would be given by the Brits. They accepted that like soldiers. What they didn't accept was the Brits trying to say there was no war, that the SAS were carrying out some sort of civic duty by killing people, that they always acted to uphold law and order. That's balls. The digger and van that carried the volunteers to Loughgall had been under observation for over two miles and could have been stopped at any time; arrests could have been made at any time. Yet, they allowed the vehicles to drive into the kill zone. Call it for what it is and be done with it: legalised murder.'[2]

On 8 May 2017, the *Irish News* reporter Connla Young wrote about an interview he had conducted with one of three IRA members who had escaped the Loughgall slaughter. The interviewee, whom Young referred to as 'Scout One', revealed that members of the IRA unit had grave doubts about going ahead with the operation. Chief among the doubters was twenty-one-year-old Declan Arthurs, the driver of the digger that was to ram the gates of the police station with a bomb in the vehicle's bucket. Arthurs had a foreboding that things were not right. The area was too quiet. Scout One told the *Irish News* reporter that Arthurs had spotted a police car which was supposed to be inside the police station as he drove the bomb in the digger into the village, and had decided not to go ahead with the attack on the first run but to drive on to the outskirts.

While Arthurs and a second volunteer then drove into the hamlet to check things out, Paddy Kelly, OC of East Tyrone, took the fateful decision to proceed with the operation. After a final sweep past the police station, the IRA unit turned the digger bomb and the HiAce van they were using to transport the rest of the attackers at the far end of the village and made directly for the barracks. Arthurs lit a fuse leading to the 400lb bomb and rammed the heavy security gates at the station. However, as some of the other IRA volunteers leapt out of the HiAce van, they were cut down in a hail of bullets. Others did not even make it out of the van and were riddled where they sat. In all, the SAS fired over 1,200 rounds into the IRA volunteers. IRA volunteers Paddy Kelly, Jim Lynagh, Pádraig McKearney, Declan Arthurs, Séamus Donnelly, Tony Gormley, Eugene Kelly and Gerard O'Callaghan were killed.

Scout One and Scout Two, whose job it was to pick up the IRA men involved in the attack and spirit them away, quickly realised something had gone wrong. They drove into the village, only to come face to face with the SAS team. Scout One said that an SAS soldier stood two to three feet in front of his vehicle and pointed an MI6 Armalite at him. 'I know for a fact to this day, when you look into someone's eyes, they knew we were involved.' However, as British reinforcements arrived, the SAS pair 'disappeared' and a regular soldier told the IRA men to turn their cars and leave the village. They were lucky to get away.

For the regional head of Special Branch, Frank Murray, 'there was much to celebrate. On the evening of the ambush, as Murray's officers and Special Forces officers returned to their barracks, Murray opened a special bottle of brandy he had been reserving for just such an occasion with a friend.' Reports also suggest that the SAS unit '"celebrated with champagne" on their return to Mahon Road Barracks'.[3]

Loughgall represented the IRA's biggest loss of life during their campaign, and it led to an IRA court of inquiry. To drill to the core of events, the IRA sent in their best investigators, amongst whom was the OC of the ISU, Freddie Scappaticci. Accompanying Scappaticci on this court of inquiry's panel were Gerry Harte, a leading East Tyrone volunteer, and Patrick O'Callaghan, the Northern Command operations officer. Apportioning blame and getting to the bottom of what actually happened was always going to be a daunting task.

The attention of the court was concentrated for quite a while on a local republican, Colette O'Neill, who had made a phone call as the IRA unit set out on their mission, the implication being that she had phoned the security forces and warned them about the impending operation. The problem with this contention is that the SAS had clearly been in position for some time before the ambush took place. In local IRA circles, some believed that the actual informer had to be a high-ranking republican with a detailed knowledge of the operation. The renowned journalist Ed Moloney had a conversation with an IRA Army Council member in May 1990, during which the IRA man told him that Liam Ryan (an East Tyrone IRA volunteer) had carried out the intelligence work for Loughgall and that Ryan had insisted he had compartmentalised everything and, crucially, no single participant would have known all the details. According to the Army Council member, 'He [Ryan] felt that [the leak] had to be at a centralized level; he would have concluded that it had to be higher up than Tyrone.'[4]

Doubt is cast on this by a source on the British side. In his book *Charlie One*, Seán Hartnett, a County Cork man, wrote of how he had served in the British Army's Joint Communications Unit, Northern Ireland. Besides detailing his undercover communications activities – which included breaking into and bugging houses and telephones, and fixing miniature cameras to the tops of telephone masts so that any IRA activity in the streets below could be monitored from a central television bank – Hartnett also met resident members of the SAS in his barracks. He recalled a conversation he had with 'George', an SAS soldier, who was one of the shooters in the Loughgall ambush. According to Hartnett, George said, 'I was first deployed to Northern Ireland in 1976, straight from the deserts of Oman where the SAS had been fighting the insurgency.'[5] George elucidated further, 'Anything that could be bugged or tracked was targeted. Paddy Kelly and Jim Lynagh were put under the most intense surveillance I've ever seen and monitored 24/7. But it wasn't at that level that we found our "in".'[6]

Warming up to his story, George said, 'One of the [security-force] operatives followed a relatively low-ranking member of the IRA support group, more on a hunch than anything else, after a meeting he had with Paddy Kelly. He saw him drive past a number of locations and became suspicious when he noticed there happened to be a digger at each of them. We concluded that another attack was imminent. One of the locations was a farm near Loughgall, which was a small, mainly Protestant village. Given what an easy target the RUC station there would make, we decided that was it, and mounted an immediate surveillance operation and planned an ambush.'[7]

George seemed to relish telling Hartnett the story of the ambush, relaying how the SAS planned to let the digger break through the police station's fencing, then, as the IRA piled out of the van, shoot them dead: 'Once we could see the men had weapons, it was open season, and everyone took the opportunity. Things did get out of hand, no doubt about it. The official reports afterwards say there was 600 rounds fired, but in reality, I'd say there was at least twice that.'[8]

George went on to disclose that some of 'the lads' inside the police station were slightly injured when the bomb in the digger exploded, but 'Once we knew they were okay, we were all pissing ourselves laughing that the station had been blown up after all.'[9]

Hartnett asked George, 'So there was no mole involved at all?'

'It was just good surveillance and nothing else, whatever the rumours might say about it. Of course, that didn't stop the IRA's own internal security squad looking for a rat, ruthless bastards that they were.'[10]

This could be seen as being a little hypocritical on George's part. After all, he and his friends had wiped out eight IRA men without offering them the opportunity to surrender. Perhaps it never crossed his mind that the SAS could themselves be described as 'ruthless bastards'? And yet, it is hard to disagree with him: the ISU *were* ruthless bastards whenever they found a rat.

Shamelessly, and seemingly without remorse, George told Hartnett, 'There was talk of an inquiry on us too, which we were keen to avoid, of course. It would have looked very bad. We probably could have taken prisoners but, on the other hand, we felt a long overdue message had to be sent to the IRA.'[11]

The long-overdue message was not lost on IRA volunteer Colm McGarrigle, who explained that the British had drawn up a three-pronged strategy to defeat the East Tyrone IRA. This, he said, included bringing in a shoot-to-kill policy in relation to the IRA, the arming of loyalist murder squads, and the fostering of loyalist death squads to kill not just republican activists but also their family members. McGarrigle said that British Army undercover operatives controlled members of the UVF and UDR hit teams: 'We knew who the hitmen were, and we were more than capable of hitting them back, but our northern commander [Martin McGuinness] wouldn't let us go after them.'[12]

When asked why McGuinness had handcuffed the IRA, McGarrigle said that he wanted purely uniformed targets. He didn't want out-of-uniform killings, even if they were UVF or UDR, and yet the loyalist paramilitaries were shooting ordinary nationalists at will: 'Young people, old people. It didn't matter, as long as they were Catholics. They shot dozens of Catholics. It was sickening. Every time an innocent nationalist was murdered, it became more embarrassing and more sickening – especially when we knew we could take these guys out.'

When probed about who appointed Freddie Scappaticci to the IRA court of inquiry into Loughgall, McGarrigle replied that it would have been a GHQ-led inquiry, so presumably the chief of staff or the adjutant-general. After it was put to him that Scappaticci's appointment was a measure of the esteem and trust in which the ISU man was held, McGarrigle responded by saying that he was seen as a competent and experienced investigator – the best there was, in fact. However, given the outcome of the inquiry, he firmly believes that the British engineered it so Scappaticci would be part of the court of inquiry.

The inquiry itself, according to McGarrigle, took the form of 'question-and-answer' in various locations. 'This wasn't an open court situation. People were questioned in houses in Tyrone, south Armagh and Belfast by members of the inquiry panel. Over 100 people were questioned.' This went on for almost two weeks and 'all the important people' were spoken to, before Patrick O'Callaghan, the senior officer in charge of the whole process, called a halt when the court began to 'get bogged down in stuff that wasn't particularly relevant'.

However, by this point, Scappaticci and, through him, British Intelligence had been made 'aware of every pick of it [the Loughgall operation]. By the end of the CI [court of inquiry], Scap would've known every republican involved in the op, where members of the ASU had billeted on the night before the op, where the weapons were held and picked up, who hijacked the digger, where the run-back house was – everything.'

The court of inquiry came to the conclusion that Colette O'Neill had informed the British about the operation, and the new leadership who had replaced the men killed in Loughgall were told that she was to be shot dead. However, McGarrigle defends O'Neill, saying that 'she was told before the op, probably by Paddy Kelly, to inform the north Tyrone boys to stay out of east Tyrone on the day of the massacre and she did what she was told'. He concludes that there was no proof that she informed on the East Tyrone men, but 'The court didn't see it like that. They thought she had notified the Brits the operation was on for that Friday.'

McGarrigle wasn't the only one with doubts. According to him, 'I don't think Gerry Harte believed she should be killed, though I'm reliably informed that Scappaticci was pushing hard for her execution. Look, I wasn't privy to the deliberations of the court of inquiry. What I do know is that they recommended this woman be executed.' The execution never took place because 'the new IRA leadership, the people who had replaced the lads at Loughgall, were not convinced she was "wrong". In fact, they didn't believe for one second that she was a tout. She was a highly trusted and respected republican who had been on the East Tyrone Brigade staff for years, and the new leadership refused to kill her – and they were right.' McGarrigle believes that if she had been killed, 'it would have destroyed the IRA in the area. People would've been disgusted and walked away from the struggle. There's no doubt about that. The IRA would've been finished.'

When it was suggested to McGarrigle that the British may not only have had a plan to wipe out the volunteers at Loughgall but a secondary plan that was designed to sicken the remaining IRA volunteers in east Tyrone by engineering this woman's execution and, in that regard, cause mass resignations, his reply was unequivocal: 'Absolutely. And they had their man sitting right up there on the court of inquiry – Freddie Scappaticci, the man who was pushing hardest for her execution.'

As for Scappaticci, there was never any hint of him being a traitor. McGarrigle had met him a couple of times, but not enough 'to form an impression of him'. However, he did recall, 'I heard on the grapevine that strong reservations had been aired about him in south Armagh. Word was sent up to Belfast that south Armagh thought Scappaticci untrustworthy, but nothing was done. That said: he was never allowed to conduct IRA business in south Armagh again.'

It appears that even with potentially damning evidence against Scappaticci, the Belfast leadership still had full faith in their man – but he wasn't their man.

13

TORTURERS

'There were lots of others who didn't survive it [torture]; they're buried down the countryside somewhere by these people.'

Brendan 'The Dark' Hughes

Freddie Scappaticci could be loyal to those whom he regarded as friends. Diarmuid O'Toole, for example, said that Scappaticci 'knew a lot about me, but he never turned me in'. Yet, conversely, when it was put to O'Toole that nobody suspected Scappaticci was 'wrong', he hesitated: 'No, no, one man did. Big John had suspicions when no one else had. He asked me what I was doing, and I said I was working with Scap and he said, "Well, don't have anything to do with him. He's not clean."'[1] Despite Big John's warning, O'Toole continued to work alongside Scappaticci with no negative consequences. But there were plenty of volunteers Scappaticci did turn in, and there were times when his persuasiveness alone did not work on suspects and more robust methods were employed.

In his ground-breaking book, *Voices from the Grave*, Ed Moloney refers to testimony of nutting-squad torture given by Brendan Hughes following his release from prison. Hughes had taken on the role of director of GHQ operations, as well as director of intelligence, upon his release in December 1986. A straight-talking man, he outranked Scappaticci and those in the ISU; he was also critical of members of the ISU: 'These people tortured guys.'[2] Some individuals who had been tortured came to Hughes and told of their experiences with 'Burke and Hare', two notorious ISU men known for their brutality. In testimony he gave to the Boston College Historical Archive, Hughes related how he had prosecuted a case against these men at an IRA court martial, which concluded that both men be dismissed with ignominy.

'Fergal McArdle', a founding member of the Provisional IRA and a former GHQ staff officer, also vehemently opposed the practice of ISU members torturing suspects: 'I was on the court of inquiry panel with "The Dark" and Billy McKee into the ISU torturing of a lad called Paddy McDade. It was our verdict that the entire Internal Security Unit should be stood down and that two men should be court-martialled. They had burned McDade and others with cigarettes and cigars and, as far as I was concerned, they betrayed everything that Irish republicanism stood for. We made our recommendations, and I don't know what happened after that, but the ISU wasn't stood down. It should have been, I'm certain of that.'[3]

In 2022, an emotional McDade told this author his harrowing story: 'Everybody feared the security team, everybody feared them. Everybody knew, when you're going to see them, you're in trouble. You didn't know if you were coming back, or not; you didn't know what was in front of you.

'In 1986, a guy called Eamonn, who was later outed as a tout, picked

me up in the New Lodge Road area and drove me down south. We got
to a place called Charlestown, in County Roscommon, a small village.
I didn't know the name of the village at the time and only found out a
few months later, when I was in Castlereagh [interrogation centre] and
Special Branch told me that was where I'd been held. Not only that, they
told me exactly where I was, the cottage I was in, the shed I'd been in,
where I got beaten for three days – Tuesday, Wednesday and Thursday.
I was to be one of the disappeared.'

McDade believed that Eamonn told the British what was happening.
On the trip south, 'we were stopped at a Brit checkpoint, and they got us
out. Eamonn went away. Didn't come back for fifteen minutes. He said
the Brits took him away, queried his driving licence. He was obviously
telling them where he was going so that they could tail him.'

As soon as he arrived in Charlestown, McDade knew he was in
trouble. 'I just clicked because I saw "Burke and Hare" and John Joe
Magee. I don't know if Scap was there but there was a fat fucker there,
but he wasn't Scap – I didn't know who he was. Next thing they put a
gun to my head and were, like, come with us. So I got into another car,
where they put me down on the back seat and drove away … So, they
took me to a farm shed, took me out of the car, stripped me naked, got
a clothesline and started tying me up. Tied me up like a turkey, trailed
me into the cottage.'

Once they had him inside, 'they made me lie on a tiled floor the
whole time, blindfolded me, put a hood over my head, and started
stamping on me … on my head, face and all. They kept standing on me.
And they were shouting at me about stuff I knew absolutely nothing
about. I knew nothing. I kept telling them. I didn't know. At this stage,
I'm crying. I'm pleading with them. The next thing, bang, scars on my
ankles, fag [cigarette] butts.'

Despite having a hood over his head, McDade could see through the cloth that the men torturing him were Burke and Hare. 'See during the whole thing, it was like a day out to them. Nothing. It was a normal thing to do that. And the wire, the clothes wire they had tied me up with, I was still tied like that for three days, into my arms, into my ankles: excruciating it was.'

There was no break in the interrogation for McDade. 'Twenty-four-hour interrogation. All night. Bollock naked. I shit and pissed in the sleeping bag they made me lie in, upside-down. The sleeping bag covered the top half of me upside-down, and it was tied at the bottom.'

This was part of the torture technique in a process that was intended to break McDade. 'They wanted a result; they wanted somebody thrown out on the street [found shot dead]. They wanted to come back and say, "Hey, listen, we got our tout." And the sleeping bag was part of the torture 'cause they kept lifting me up in it and dropping me on the floor. That's why when the kids or grandkids throw their arms around my neck, I freak. It's the fear.'

It seemed that his interrogators thought that McDade was planning an interview of some kind with a television crew. 'They kept saying "You're going in front of a television crew. Just admit these things and you'll be okay, that's it. That's it. It'll be over and done with. Just admit these things." I said I wasn't involved. I knew nothing about them. I knew nothing about the things they were accusing me of. Like, why would I sit in front of a TV crew, and I kept saying this. That's where it got heaviest again. I kept denying it. The more I kept denying it, the more beatings I got. Beating the fuck out of me. Standing on me. Couldn't breathe.'

During his entire ordeal, his torturers failed to give McDade so much as a drink of water. At one point Burke 'got a hot cup of tea and he fucked that around me'. But despite the horror of what was happening to him, McDade refused to break. When asked if he had ever thought of admitting to what they wanted, he said, 'Admit to what? I didn't know what they were talking about.'

It is a testament to Paddy McDade's integrity and deep sense of right and wrong that he fought off what must have been an overwhelming temptation to end his torture by telling the inquisitors what they wanted to hear. Then, 'after two days, things started to slow down. Things stopped … Thursday, it started to die off. Somebody had told them they'd got the wrong man. Enough is enough.'

After he was released, 'Two men, total strangers, dropped me off at the bus station and told me to make my own way home. I had to go to Roscommon. From there, I got a bus to Sligo and then a bus to Bundoran. There I went into Joe O'Neill's pub 'cause he knew me, and he was very welcoming. I stayed overnight in Joe's pub and got the bus back that Saturday morning.'

The effects of these three days on McDade's life have been long-term. 'On two different occasions, I met a psychiatrist called Mangan, from Musgrave Park Hospital, and he said I had Post-Traumatic Stress Disorder. When I think of what I went through … I didn't know if I was ever going to come back, or not … It's getting me more so now, thinking about it. It wrecks me. They humiliated me. They took away my dignity as a human being. And the nightmares, the cold sweats in the middle of the night … I'd spring up in bed, choking, and I'd be upside-down in that stinking sleeping bag and usually I'd be crying.

'The doctors told me … I sat with people: barristers, solicitors and they all said the same thing; this is a war crime; what they [ISU] done to you was a war crime. They beat you for three days and they [British Intelligence] knew … When I went to Castlereagh a few months after the torture, a cop says to me, there's no point us beating you, Paddy, you were beaten hard enough down in Charlestown in the big farm shed. I didn't know I was in Charlestown. They [British Intelligence] knew where I was the whole time. They said, "You'll get a solicitor here, Paddy, but you didn't get one down in Charlestown."

'Then, to top it all, when I got out, Freddie Scap says to me, "What was it [Castlereagh and interrogation] like, Paddy?" I said they were all telling me I was in Charlestown, and Scap looked at me and said, "What?" Then he says, "Were you talking, like? Did you talk to them?"

'I said no. I'm convinced he was in Charlestown, I can't prove it, but I believe he was there.' After McDade denied telling the police anything, Scappaticci laughed off the incident.

About a week after his ordeal in Charlestown, 'a fella came to my door and said I'd to go down to Dicey Riley's bar on the New Lodge Road, that there were a couple of people who wanted to speak to me there. So I went down and there was Hare and a well-known IRA officer from west Belfast standing at the upstairs bar. And I asked them what they wanted. The well-known IRA officer said, "If you tell anybody what happened to you, we'll shoot you dead. Have you got that?" I nodded. Then he said, "Now, fuck off." I walked away.

'So I kept my mouth shut and weeks went by. Couldn't go to work, couldn't get it out of my head, so a couple of months went by and somebody came to my door and wanted to speak to me. It was Big Dan McCann [who was shot dead by the SAS while on an IRA operation in Gibraltar] and Big Dan said, "I need to know what happened to you."

'I said, "Dan, it doesn't matter."

'"I need to know what happened to you," he kept repeating. He brought me down the street, into a house down the street and other IRA volunteers weighed in and they said, "Paddy, sit down here. Talk and tell us what happened to you." So, I started telling them what happened to me and from there, things proceeded to the court martial.'

At the court martial, 'Ruby Davidson and Whitey [Bradley] appeared as witnesses for me 'cause they saw the bruises and the burn marks. The Dark was the prosecutor and there were all sorts of old-time republicans on the court martial, men who had given their lives to the republican cause, who had principles.'

Burke and Hare 'denied everything. Denied ever touching me. "It wasn't me." ... In the end they were found guilty and dismissed from the IRA with ignominy. But they were back within months.

'The one thing the court martial did do was to see John Joe Magee stood down to the rank of volunteer and Scap promoted to his job, as OC of IS. Then Scap became my best mate! He would've run miles from me before Charlestown, but afterwards he was all over me. We even played football together in the Andersonstown Leisure Centre.'

It is an interesting fact that McDade claims that on the occasions when members of the ISU were brought to Castlereagh for questioning nobody questioned them when they got out. 'None of them were ever asked what happened to them, or if they spoke to the cops in Castlereagh. Everyone else was dark-roomed, but not them. Whitey [Bradley] was raging about what happened to me and, when he found out, he walked in and confronted them as they were drinking in the Davitt's club, and he said, "Who the fuck questions youse? Do you question yourselves in the mirror?" In them days nobody investigated the security team.'

Unsurprisingly, McDade's opinion of the ISU, which ran investigations from the late 1970s to 1989, is not complimentary. 'They were a bunch of dipsos who sat in a bar and discussed what they were going to do with people. The people they murdered ... they can't come back and say, we weren't touts. These people sat in bars after torturing people and

had a drink. The bottom line is, they were hand-picked by the leadership of the IRA. Everything changed in the IRA, but the security team
never changed, and that's going back to internment.'

McDade finally got an apology from the IRA GHQ in 2002 for
what he went through, but for him it 'didn't mean anything. They were
shit scared of me sitting on the TV and telling the truth. You see, there
was a massive inquiry in 2002 about people being taken away by the
security team. I told them about young [Anthony] Braniff and they
were shocked. Shocked, they were. In them days nobody investigated
the security team.'

McDade underpinned his view that nobody investigated the
security team by agreeing with Whitey Bradley's assertion that Freddie
Scappaticci effectively vetoed all IRA operations in Belfast from 1986
to January 1989, in his role as OC of the ISU: 'Other people have said
the same thing to me. After 1986, nothing went down in Belfast that
the security team didn't have prior knowledge about. Every major op
had to go through Northern Command, and the security team were an
extension of Northern Command, and Scap was in charge of the security
team. So he/the security team knew everything about every op, from
who was on them, where the intelligence for them came from, and then
they briefed the returning volunteers after the ops had been carried out.
I was reliably told the only jobs that were successful were the off-the-cuff
ones, opportunist jobs, or ones that the Brits allowed to go ahead.'

Confirming what McDade and others were saying, an IRA volunteer
had this to say about what the security forces knew about operations
in Belfast: 'Jack Holland read through the notes of Ian Phoenix and
told me that a senior IRA figure close to all key figures in Belfast was
reporting regularly to him on operations. Holland said the information
was so serious that it was impossible for the IRA to conduct a war.'[4]

And, lest there be any doubt about it, British Intelligence's role in the McDade affair was also far from benign. Their penetration of the IRA and the ISU was so complete that they would have been fully aware of McDade's interrogation and they would have known that, had he been forced into making a false confession, he would have been shot dead. This possibility does not seem to have worried them because the gardaí were not informed McDade was being tortured in Charlestown. It seems that the TCG considered it better to let the IRA kill an alleged IRA volunteer rather than risk compromising an invaluable agent like Scappaticci.

What sticks out in the Paddy McDade fiasco, and many of the executions carried out by the nutting squad, is that there are no good guys and bad guys in the intelligence game: they are all bad. Like their counterparts in the ISU, British Intelligence were prepared to use every trick in the book to turn volunteers, to get them on *their* payroll. Moreover, despite attempts by former British intelligence officers to construct a different narrative, the nuts and bolts of spy-craft are still human weakness, blackmail and intimidation. The trick is to discover the dark secret that dare not show its face and then utilise that secret to blackmail/bully opponents into becoming informers and agents.

∗∗∗

Some turned informer because they simply did not want to go to prison. One such man was Joe Fenton, who agreed to work for Special Branch rather than risk imprisonment on charges of moving explosives for the IRA.

Thirty-five-year-old Fenton was a personable man, the sort who was good company if out for a drink with the lads. He is also one of those historical figures who reeks of pathos. Fair-haired and moustached, he was an estate agent who would go out of his way to help the clients who frequented his Ideal Homes offices, across from the Falls Park. He had a young family to look after and that was his main priority, although, in real terms, the guy was a lamb among a pack of wolves.

Like most state agents, Fenton did not want to work for either Special Branch or the FRU, although if you believed an unnamed Special Branch officer, you would be inclined to take a different view: 'Joe loved his work and got a great deal of pleasure after operations were compromised. He was a very willing agent and tried on at least two occasions to entrap senior republicans. But it was probably only a matter of time before he was caught out and by late 1988, he was under suspicion.'[5]

Joe 'loved' his work so much that he applied for a visa to start a new life in Australia with his wife and four children. When his visa application was rejected – allegedly because Special Branch told the Australian authorities he was an IRA terrorist – it was back to square one for Fenton, working for Special Branch.

Author Martin Dillon describes what happened next: 'When Fenton's plans [to emigrate] failed, he found himself once again in the shadowy world where he was being addressed by a Special Branch sergeant and an Englishman named "Don". I have been told by a source within the security services that "Don" is one of a number of MI5 liaison officers who oversee Special Branch operations or devise operations which are run by Special Branch operatives. Major operations are discussed within the Task Co-Ordinating Group, which comprises of Special Branch, MI5, E4A, Army Intelligence (plain clothes) and the SAS.'[6]

What Don and his Special Branch associates in the TCG realised was that the proprietor of Ideal Homes was ideally placed to inflict serious damage on the IRA. As an estate agent, he had access to empty houses that customers had asked to be put on the market and he placed these houses at the disposal of the IRA. For the Belfast IRA, this was like a gift from God. No longer did they have to ask their supporters to use a cluttered bedroom or a dingy back room. Instead, all they had to do was go to Fenton and he would give them the keys to an entire house. Brigade staff and ASU meetings were regularly held in the homes provided by Fenton, and such was his generosity that he offered keys to some married IRA leaders so that they could have sex with their girlfriends. Little did any of these men know that Special Branch had placed hidden cameras and listening devices in those houses. The film, when retrieved, must have made for interesting viewing, and good blackmailing material in some cases.

Not only did Fenton offer keys to empty houses but he was also, on occasion, able to provide transport for IRA ASUs. According to a senior republican, 'Fenton came under suspicion when the leadership first began shipping the Libyan weapons to the Northern ASUs. A number of consignments headed for Belfast were mysteriously intercepted by the RUC, and it was obvious an informer was at his or her work. The common link in all the losses was Fenton, who turned out to have been directly or indirectly involved in the purchase or acquisition of the vehicles used to transport the weapons from the southern dumps.'[7]

As a consequence of Fenton's bounty, over twenty IRA members were apprehended in possession of firearms and several bombing missions into Belfast city centre were thwarted, with the bombers being arrested. However, his tenure as an informer and agent was coming to an end, especially after Brendan Hughes took an interest in him: 'I was actually the person that found Fenton. I got out of prison, had nowhere to live and a friend of mine, Fra McCullagh, brought me to an estate agent called Joe Fenton. They then brought me to a house in Rockville Street. And I just immediately got suspicious that, here's me out of prison, brought to a house and told that it was mine, it was my house. And I didn't, I didn't take it, I didn't take the house … instinctively, I got suspicious.'[8]

To offset any notion that he might be an agent, Fenton had also endeared himself to the IRA by providing highly confidential intelligence on members of the security services. He supplied the names of police officers, their vehicle-registration numbers and their home addresses. In an interview for his book, Martin Dillon asked Hughes why no one thought to ask Fenton where he was acquiring such top-quality information? Hughes struggled to find an adequate answer: 'He [Fenton] was trusted by his IRA guardian [Belfast Brigade OC Harry Burns], who probably believed that Fenton was right to protect his sources.'[9]

In refusing to divulge his sources of information, Fenton must have known that he was playing a dangerous game, one that could cost him his life. He would have known that the IRA was not some sort of gentleman's club where etiquette was always observed: if you crossed these guys, they were more than capable of killing you. He must also have known that in refusing to reveal his sources, he ran the risk of finding himself sitting on a chair in the corner of a darkened room with Scappaticci whispering death threats in his ear and, if he was really lucky, there would be ashtrays in the room.

Hughes, when asked by Dillon how important Fenton was to British intelligence services, answered that he was too valuable to be handled simply by Special Branch and that MI5 were also involved with him: 'He [Fenton] told us [his IRA interrogators] that. He was so important that we now realise just how much they were willing to sacrifice to keep him in place. They were prepared to give us the lives of ordinary cops to keep suspicion away from Fenton.'[10] This is an extraordinary accusation from Hughes because it prompts the question: had Special Branch, through Fenton, passed to the IRA the personal details of police officers, knowing that the IRA would almost certainly use those details to assassinate those officers?

According to Brendan Hughes, Special Branch 'gave' the IRA Gerard and Catherine Mahon, a married couple who had occasionally secreted arms for the IRA. The Mahons were shot dead on 8 September 1985. Hughes said of the couple, 'We now know through the interrogation of Fenton that he was told to give us Gerard and Catherine Mahon to remove suspicion from himself.'[11] Hughes' statement in regard to the Mahons is backed up by Ian Hurst: 'Fenton admitted [to Internal Security] in his confession that he had directed Scappaticci and the IRA towards the Mahons to deflect attention away from himself after a number of safe houses were compromised. Acting on Fenton's information, Scappaticci and three other members of his unit took the Mahons to Norglen Crescent to be executed.'[12]

Continuously looking over his shoulder, waiting for an abductor's gun to be stuck in his ribs, Fenton saw his credibility, won by his fingering of the two Mahons, take a hammering when, in 1988, an ASU was caught when making mortars in one of his empty houses. From other IRA informers and from bugs in so-called safe IRA houses, Special Branch would have known that Fenton was running out of road. According to Ian Hurst, 'Freddie Scappaticci, in reports to his handlers, warned that Fenton was indeed suspected of helping the security forces when a tracking device was found inside a weapon stored in one of his vacant properties.'[13] Then, in 1989, his estate-agent business closed due to unpaid rent, making him less of an asset for Special Branch. Now there seemed to be no way out for him; too many operations had been compromised. Knowing that the game was up, Fenton went to England.

In real time, Hughes had had a full-on row about Fenton with Harry Burns, who had lost an arm, a leg and an eye in a premature explosion in Cushendall, County Antrim, in 1976. According to Hughes, 'I had a major run-in with Harry Burns in his own house ... Harry swore by Fenton. But then Harry warned Fenton that I was checking into him. Fenton done a runner, he went to England on the pretext of going to a boxing match and was away for about ten or eleven days. I was running internal security on the GHQ staff. Fenton returned. He was told to return by his handlers, that everything was all right, Harry would fix it up ... Fenton returned to Belfast and was immediately executed by the IRA before I could get to interrogate him.'[14]

On Friday, 24 February 1989, Joe Fenton was arrested by the IRA, brought to 124 Carrigart Avenue in the Lenadoon area of west Belfast and made to sit facing a wall in a darkened room. The owner of the house, merchant seaman Jimmy Martin, was not arrested for Fenton's abduction and murder, but he was eventually picked up after police raided his house on 7 January 1990 and freed another Special Branch informer called Sandy Lynch. During his police interviews, Martin admitted that he had 'lent' a room to the IRA for their interrogation of Fenton the previous year. Martin named John Joe Magee, Freddie Scappaticci and another person whom he called 'Eddie' as the people conducting Fenton's interrogation.

Martin recalled that, after a rowdy night in the interrogation room, two men, Scappaticci and Eddie, came downstairs at about 10 a.m. on Saturday 25 February and Scappaticci asked for something to drink. Toast was also made and brought upstairs, where Fenton was being held. According to Martin, 'There was still a bit of noise upstairs. It seemed to be constant. The ceiling was vibrating.'[15]

In a later police interview, Martin spoke of Scappaticci looking out of the downstairs kitchen window as a young lady approached the house. When she entered the kitchen, Martin left the room. The female and Scappaticci then left the house, but not before he popped his head into the living room to tell Martin, 'We're away.'

Martin then told police that he heard multiple footsteps coming down the stairs and going out the front door. When asked what happened next, he said that he heard three or four shots. 'I then heard kids shouting outside the door and I went to the door, and I heard the kid next door saying to her mummy there's a dead body. I had a fair idea who it was.'[16]

Martin spoke to police of how he later saw the television cameras on the scene and he realised the man in his house had been shot dead. When asked if he tidied up after Fenton and the IRA had left his house, Martin replied that he had taken unused bandages and gloves out of the room, and that Scappaticci had said somebody would come to take what was left away. According to Martin, nobody came.

In another interrogation, Martin identified the female who had come into the house and left with Scappaticci, saying that he had been at her wedding, as had Scappaticci. It is clear from the evidence surrounding the shooting dead of Joe Fenton that Freddie Scappaticci had been in Jimmy Martin's house, and, according to Martin's police interviews, was part of the ISU team who grilled the Special Branch agent. At the end of several days of intense interrogation, Jimmy Martin was charged with the murder of Joe Fenton.

It was little wonder that Brendan Hughes was so suspicious of the events surrounding Joe Fenton's death. What questions might he have asked him had he been given the opportunity? How on earth would you, Joe Fenton, from west Belfast, know the names, the vehicle-registration numbers and the home addresses of police officers? Is your intelligence source from the security services? If so, how, when and where did you meet them? What prompted them to give *you* this intelligence? Why did you not come to us earlier with these names and addresses? What are you holding back from us? Who is your handler? How is he/she contactable? Fenton's interrogation may have gone on for days, weeks even, but in the end, he would have been broken. As it turned out, Scappaticci and the ISU succeeded in getting him to admit to being an informer, so it is probable that he would have had a great deal more to tell them had he not been executed due to time constraints.

Ian Hurst claims that it was Special Branch who pulled Fenton out of Belfast and moved him to England. However, 'Fenton – like Scappaticci, some years later – believed he could bluff it out. He asked Andrew Hunter, the Conservative MP, for help. Hunter contacted police, who were absolutely clear about what would happen if Joe Fenton returned to Northern Ireland. Hunter, then a member of the DUP, said later, "Special Branch told me that if he came home, he would be killed very quickly."'[17]

Brendan Hughes agreed with Hurst that Special Branch knew Fenton would at least be arrested by the IRA, but most likely executed: 'After we shot him, we uncovered an extremely sophisticated bug in a house which Joe Fenton had provided as a safe house. In that house, members of the IRA discussed Fenton's fate and the evidence against him. Therefore, his handlers knew that IRA suspicion was so great that he was likely to be found guilty and executed.' Despite what Hurst claims, Hughes argues that 'They were still prepared to send him back. They sent him back to cover their tracks because they had someone of equal importance in place. Fenton was only a pawn to them.'[18]

Hughes' faith in those whom he had respected all his adult life was shaken. 'I just didn't know who to trust anymore. The people I had trusted with my life, I couldn't trust anymore. Gerry Adams, I couldn't trust, and other people around me in Belfast, I could not trust them either. I knew there was robberies taking place; I knew people were getting immunity from arrest; I knew there were touts there, I knew there was corruption there. And that's what led me to Dublin. I knew my life was in danger, nothing loyalist, nothing British, but from IRA personnel.'[19] Hughes later told journalist Ed Moloney of having confided his concerns to Gerry Adams in the latter's house, in front of 'XY'. Hughes talks of 'a major, major blow-up' and of XY storming out of the house. Afterwards, Adams told Hughes he was paranoid.

It could be alleged that, for the Belfast TCG, the two Mahons and Joe Fenton were expendable. As has been outlined earlier, lawyer Kevin Winters, BBC documentary-maker John Ware and others have said that Chief Constable Jon Boutcher of the Kenova Inquiry alluded to the fact that Scappaticci *always* passed on the details of his involvement in IRA interrogations and killings to his handlers in time for their victims to be saved. It is alleged that Scappaticci had told his Special Branch handlers about the upcoming executions of the Mahons and, indeed, had indicated on two occasions that Fenton would also be killed – yet the Belfast TCG allowed these murders to proceed, proving that they were just as ruthless as the IRA.[20]

For Joe Fenton, it was all over. The tides of war had caught up with him. One cannot help but wonder what sort of lives the Fenton family would have made for themselves if he had been successful in his application to emigrate to Australia, or if it ever crossed Fenton's mind that, just as he 'gave' the Mahons to the IRA on the instructions of Special Branch, the same state agency was more than capable of giving *him* to the IRA? It probably never did. Yet, he was, for them, the irksome flea that needed to be crushed, the burned-out salesman with no product left in his tattered suitcase. Best to allow the IRA to put him out of his misery, let them think they were on top of things.

At his graveside, parish priest Fr Tom Toner had some choice words for all concerned: 'The IRA is not the only secret, death-dealing agent in our midst. Secret agents of the state have a veneer of respectability on its dark deeds which disguises its work of corruption. They work secretly in dark places, unseen, seeking little victims like Joe whom they can crush and manipulate for their own purposes. Their actions too corrupt the cause they purport to serve.

'To you the IRA and all who support you or defend you, we have to say that we feel dirty today. Foul and dirty deeds by Irishmen are making Ireland a foul and dirty place, for it is things done by Irishmen that make us unclean. What the British could never do, what the Unionists could never do, you have done. You have made us bow our heads in shame and that is a dirty thing. The IRA is like a cancer in the body of Ireland, spreading death, killing, and corruption.'[21]

14

IT'S ONLY BUSINESS

'No one saves us but ourselves. No one can and no one may. We ourselves must walk the path.'

The Buddha

'Wee Freddie saved Wee Willie,' Luke McCartney said. The former IRA leader was referring to Scappaticci's intervention to save the life of his fellow agent Willie Carlin in March 1985. Technically speaking, McCartney was right, but, of more importance than Scappaticci's role in saving Carlin's life was the Derry TCG's decision that Carlin was to be pulled out. It would not be the last time a TCG would intercede to save one of their agents.

Born in 1948 and known to his MI5 handlers as 'Agent 3007', Carlin had left his native Derry for Catterick in England and joined the Queen's Royal Irish Hussars at the age of seventeen. In the 1950s to 1960s, work in the nationalist north of Ireland hovered between scarce and non-existent, and joining the British Army was not unusual. It guaranteed an income, much-needed money that could be sent home to family. And no one batted an eyelid at some little soldier walking up the street or going into the pub with his father for a beer. Everybody had to live.

A few years after joining up, Willie married a Derry girl, Mary McGonigle. Life was good for the young couple, with postings to the British Army on the Rhine and to Bovington Camp in Dorset, where Willie was promoted to sergeant. By 1 April 1974, their son Mark was four years old, and their new arrival, Michael, was just three days old. In his book, *Thatcher's Spy: My Life as an MI5 agent inside Sinn Féin*, Carlin writes that, weeks previously, he had been approached by a mysterious man called Alan Rees-Morgan, who introduced himself as a member of a clandestine intelligence organisation which reported to the minister of defence and the prime minister, Margaret Thatcher. Rees-Morgan told Carlin that he wanted him to go back to Derry to collect political intelligence on the intentions of Martin McGuinness and Sinn Féin.

Unschooled in the subtleties of espionage but undoubtedly courageous, Carlin agreed to Rees-Morgan's request. It was a frightening prospect for the young soldier, with Rees-Morgan telling him, 'You'll have to live the life. You'll have to try to become a republican – one of them. You won't be armed, and the army won't know about you, nor will the RUC. If we find out your life is in danger, we'll pull you out. However, if you're caught, the government will deny all knowledge of you because they don't know about this project. You will in fact be a secret.'[1]

With Mary yearning to go back to her native city, the Carlin family returned home to Derry, finding a house in the Gobnascale estate. Little did Willie Carlin know, when he stepped onto Irish soil once more, that his assignment would go some way to offsetting the likelihood of Martin McGuinness being an informer because, simply put, if McGuinness *was* working for British Intelligence, *he* would have been keeping them abreast of developments in Sinn Féin – as well as the IRA – so there would have been no need for Carlin's insertion.

There was considerable interest in how Carlin was getting on, not least from Margaret Thatcher, who frequently chortled when inquiring about the intrepid spy. However, in the first years after moving back and settling in Derry, Carlin had little to report to his handlers and failed to make the transition from seemingly innocent civilian to fully fledged member of Sinn Féin.

One of the locations where Carlin would have met his MI5 handlers was a safe house on the outskirts of Limavady, seventeen miles outside Derry. While sometimes he met his handler, 'Ben', in the safe house, more often than not he met him in a hotel or a pub because the MI5 contact liked long lunches, washed down with 'half-uns' of malt whiskey. On one occasion, Ben had arranged to meet Willie in the Londonderry Arms in the County Antrim seaside village of Carnlough. On his way, as Carlin drove past a house in Limavady that he knew to be an MI5 safe house, a red Peugeot drove out of the gates and headed straight towards him. When he looked at its occupants, he saw that Martin McGuinness was in the passenger seat, his head bent as if reading something. For Carlin, the shock was overwhelming, and he stopped the car at the first opportunity to catch his breath. Naturally, he asked himself what McGuinness was doing in an MI5 safe house. His friends in MI5 were reluctant to provide him with answers and, years later, Carlin offered, 'I knew McGuinness was opposed to the hunger strike and, by joining the dots, I thought whatever happened in the house that day might have been part of on-going meetings between him and representatives of the British government.'[2] Here, Carlin is making a good attempt to explain what was, for him, a puzzling situation. However, it does not stand up to scrutiny. Whatever McGuinness was doing in the MI5 house, it was nothing to do with the hunger strike because one of the problems with the 1981 hunger strike was that there was no direct contact between the republican leadership and the British government. Any contact McGuinness had with the British in relation to the hunger strike went through Derry businessmen Brendan Duddy and Noel Gallagher, who acted as intermediaries. Besides, the primary contacts during the hunger strike were conducted by phone.

Eventually, Carlin was trusted enough to be allowed to join Sinn Féin and, as a community activist, proved to be a useful addition to the Sinn Féin team. He was also a useful addition to the FRU, who had taken over his stewardship from MI5. In June 1984, Carlin, with McGuinness' approval, was made treasurer of Derry Sinn Féin. It was an important job and one which found him handling four non-disclosed party bank accounts with large amounts of money in each. Not only were there hidden bank accounts, but he also discovered at least six business owners who had approached the IRA to blow up their failing operations.[3]

Things were going as planned until, on 1 March 1985, Carlin got word from his handlers that the ISU were on to him. His primary handler, known only as 'The Boss', told him, 'Look, I'll deny this if it ever comes out, but you deserve to know. Your ex-contact from MI5, Michael Bettaney, "Ben" [he of the long, whiskey-guzzling lunches] as you knew him, passed your details on to an IRA prisoner in a prison in England and dropped you in it.'[4]

In an interesting exchange, Carlin asked his mentor how he knew about the intentions of the IRA's nutting squad. The Boss leaned forward and whispered in Carlin's ear, 'I know your Sinn Féin career was on the up and up. You really do need to trust me because one of my teams in Belfast handles the very man in charge of that squad and he's on his way right now to lift you, and that's how you know.'[5] The Boss then told Carlin to go home and persuade his wife to leave Northern Ireland with him.

On the way, Carlin was accompanied by an FRU operative called 'Ginger', who told him that the man who passed on the information was an FRU agent who did not know the Derryman, but who had made his handlers aware that Willie would be arrested that night by the IRA and that it would be he, the agent, who would be 'nutting' him. It is clear that Scappaticci had let it be known to members of the FRU that unless Carlin was removed from Derry, Scappaticci and his cohorts in the ISU would kill him and it would be Scappaticci who would be pulling the trigger. There is no ambiguity here: Scappaticci is stating a fact. But he *knows* that even if he murders Carlin, he is immune from prosecution. He *knows* he is above the law.

Carlin and his family were spirited out of Derry and Ireland on board Margaret Thatcher's private jet. And so, for Agent 3007, it was all over. Unlike so many of his fellow agents, he had been saved by the intervention of the TCGs. Or perhaps it had been Margaret Thatcher herself who had stepped in to save his life and had insisted the TCGs did not allow Scappaticci and the nutting squad to kill him. This is entirely feasible because Carlin wrote that Thatcher was aware of what was happening in real time and was livid that he had been exposed as a spy for the security forces.[6] Perhaps she had grown fond of little '007', having read his reports from Derry.

Carlin recounts having met Thatcher shortly after his extraction: 'The next thing I recall is a "wee" woman entering through the black door to our left. I say "wee" woman because she was no taller than I am and I'm only 5 ft 5 in. It was none other than Margaret Thatcher, and yes, she did carry a handbag over her left arm. "Now, who have we here?" she said as she swept into the room followed by another lady. "You must be William? Can I say that I am extremely proud of what you achieved in the service of your country and apologise sincerely for the way you have been treated."[7]

Life from that point on was one where the little Derryman would look over his shoulder to see if he was being followed, or if someone was going to walk up behind him to put a bullet in the back of his head. On 14 May 1985, he found out something about the man who had saved his life. It was Mary Carlin's birthday and, along with their protection team, the Carlins celebrated with a party. As the night wore on, Mary and the children went to bed, while Willie and his protection team sat chatting. The subject of who in the IRA had tipped the FRU off to Carlin's imminent arrest came up and one of the protection team, Desi, said that "'Peter" [Jones] handles him and says his number is 6126 or something. They say he's a right bastard on big bucks.' Another of the team said, 'he was an Italian who the boss called Stakeknife. They say if he turns up at your house in the early hours, he's likely to be the last person you'll ever see.'[8]

Carlin recalled an interesting encounter with the then Chief Constable of the RUC, Sir Ronnie Flanagan, about Freddie Scappaticci. When he was attending a charity boxing match in Belfast in 2001, he bumped into Flanagan who, on recognising Carlin, exclaimed, 'Jesus! Willie Carlin!', shook his hand and asked for a private chat. Carlin took the opportunity to ask about the events of his escape from Derry. He was curious about the man who had saved his life and tipped off the FRU that he was about to be lifted by the nutting squad. He asked about the 'soldier' called 'Stakeknife'. The Chief Constable's relaxed attitude suddenly changed. He leaned in and whispered to Carlin, 'Listen, son, you stay well clear of that. He was no soldier and that's all going to go bad. You have nothing to do with it, do you hear me?' His response left Carlin with nothing but more questions about why 'Stakeknife' was clearly a subject to be avoided.[9]

On Ash Wednesday 2019, Carlin met with two members of the Kenova team, charged with investigating the activities of Scappaticci/ Stakeknife. He had mixed feelings. On the one hand, he was concerned for the families of those victims who had been dispatched by Scappaticci and the ISU. Yet, Scappaticci had saved his life and he felt indebted to him. In the end, Carlin decided to tell the truth as he knew it.

**

IRA volunteers frequently looked death in the face when out on operations. Yet, in an era awash with contradictions, they feared and despised the IRA's ISU more than they did the British Army or the RUC's Special Branch. People like John Joe Magee, Freddie Scappaticci and a dozen others (most of whom are now dead or senile) personified 'The Terror', the self-mutilation of the Provisional IRA's revolution. No case illustrates this more than that of Anthony McKiernan.

An IRA man from 1971 until 1987, McKiernan had been an 'Engineering Officer', someone who used to make 'mix' – highly volatile homemade explosives. He was also someone who could put together a bomb or a booby trap. In the early 1970s, McKiernan was a well-known IRA volunteer in the north Louth/south Armagh area, someone who had taken part in IRA cross-border operations against the British Army. He returned to Belfast in 1972 and took a leadership role in the IRA there.

On 18 January 1988, the forty-four-year-old father of four was arrested by the IRA and shot dead the next day for allegedly being an informer. In a statement, the IRA claimed that he had supplied information to the security forces which resulted in the seizure of arms. Even by IRA standards, it was a strange killing.

The former IRA volunteer Frankie Garland, a lifelong friend of Scappaticci, had this to say about Anthony McKiernan's execution: 'The autopsy report said he had enough vodka in him to get a regiment of Cossacks blocked. Where did he get the booze from? Who gave him it, and why?' The coroner's report stated that, 'He had consumed so much [alcohol] he was likely to die from it alone.'[10] In a conversation with this author, the former IRA man opined that perhaps McKiernan was drunk when he was arrested by the IRA and that might have accounted for the booze in his system, but he soon rejected this because McKiernan had been in IRA custody for over twenty-four hours before he had been shot dead and the drink would have dissipated in his system during that time. Moreover, he said, the IRA could be sticklers for procedure, especially where court martials or courts of inquiry were concerned, and had McKiernan been that badly intoxicated, it would have invalidated any confession he might have made and no IRA court would have accepted the evidence of such a drunken man. Garland went on to suggest that, as he was being held by the ISU, the only explanation for him having so much alcohol in his system was that somebody in the nutting squad must have given it to him.

Given the evidence of the suspect's intoxication, the issue of Army Council approval for McKiernan's execution was problematic. Was it given against the backdrop of a suspect who, presumably, could not string two words together because he was so drunk? In other situations where informers had been broken by the ISU, such as that of Alexander

'Sandy' Lynch (two years later), it was made known to Lynch that a member of the Army Council would be coming to make sure he had made his taped and written confessions of his own accord and had not been subjected to torture. Was such a procedure initiated with McKiernan? To this day, no member of the McKiernan family has heard Anthony's confession. Why was it not made available to them?

One explanation for McKiernan being drunk is that he was given as much alcohol as he wanted as an act of compassion, a means whereby he could be anaesthetised against the fate that was before him. Garland did not reject this possibility. Another explanation is that the ISU water-boarded McKiernan with vodka. This suggestion might sound ludicrous, but not according to investigative journalist and author Martin Dillon. Dillon wrote that it had become apparent there was a 'mole' at the highest level in the Belfast IRA and that McKiernan suspected the informer was an ISU volunteer called Brendan 'Ruby' Davison. Detailing McKiernan's last hours, Dillon said, 'In "The Monkey's" [McKiernan's nickname] case, operatives attempted to disguise the manner of this death. They held him over a bathtub and "waterboarded" him with alcohol until he admitted he was a mole. Once he confessed, his interrogators poured a large quantity of alcohol down his throat, effectively ending his life.'[11] But Dillon does not provide a convincing reason for his theory, particularly considering the victim was clearly shot.

The former Markets resident Marian McMullan did not accept that McKiernan was an informer. She drew on her cigarette and exhaled, before saying, 'Touts get paid, don't they?' Without waiting for an answer, she continued, 'Anthony tapped [borrowed] 50p for a bet in the bookies the day before he was taken away to be murdered by Scap. Nobody was paying him. He wasn't a tout.' She nodded knowingly; it was obvious that McMullan was familiar with the circumstances surrounding the IRA killing. 'And it was Scap who took Anthony away. But rather than come for him himself and leave a trail of evidence behind, he sent his young son to Patricia McKiernan's house and the wee boy told Anthony, "My da wants you. He's outside in the car."

'Like, see Scap and Anthony? They knew each other dead well; they'd grown up in the Markets together and had joined the 'RA at the same time. And their kids slept over in each other's houses.' McMullan took another draw from her cigarette before repeatedly punching it into an ashtray. She glanced out of the window and said forlornly, 'Anthony put on his coat and went out to meet his lifelong friend, Freddie Scappaticci. That was the last time any of his family saw him alive.'

When asked what she thought had happened then, she said, 'He was taken to Smokey Deery's flat and then up to Beechmount. And that was where they murdered him – and it was all Scap's doing.'[12]

In February 2006, Anthony McIntyre, who knew both Scappaticci and McKiernan, had this to say: 'Those who knew Anthony are not convinced he was an informer. His comrades pointed to his long-standing commitment and dedication to the freedom struggle and were highly suspicious of the allegations made against him after his death. Now, eighteen years on, the circumstances surrounding his death seem even more dubious. Answers are urgently required.'[13]

In an article on The Blanket website, McIntyre also pointed out that Sharon Murtagh, McKiernan's daughter, had challenged the IRA to provide proof that her father was an informer, saying that, in 2002, the McKiernan family were visited by a prominent member of the IRA, who promised a review of their father's case. Despite the promise, the family heard nothing else from the IRA. So, in April 2006, the McKiernans asked renowned peacemaker Fr Gerry Reynolds to initiate contact with the IRA in order that more light may be shed on the death of their loved one. The IRA rejected Reynolds' approach, although a leading IRA member did visit the family after the priest's failed initiative and again promised an inquiry. That was the last time the family heard from the IRA.

Anthony McIntyre stated, 'The McKiernan family must be made aware of the exact case against Anthony. The Provisional movement cannot now say that they have full confidence in any of the information supplied by Scappaticci against any individual. Indeed, a shadow hangs over any court martial and execution that Scappaticci was involved in, while he was working as an MI5 agent and also as head of IRA intelligence and security.'[14]

What stands out about McKiernan's brutal killing is Scappaticci's ability to sever personal relationships from business. It is not known if McKiernan pleaded for clemency, but had he been inclined to throw himself at Scappaticci's feet and cry out for mercy he would have discovered that old times and old friendships meant nothing.

During our conversation, Frankie Garland felt inclined to psycho-analyse Scappaticci: 'Wee Freddie was a sociopath. He'd no regrets about any of the people he'd stiffed or arranged to be stiffed. Him and me and Tommy Gorman and the lads used to play indoor football in Andersonstown Leisure Centre, and we two would've had a bit of craic over a coffee afterwards and, do you know what? It always struck me, he liked working for IS; he liked the power it gave him, and I guess, when you boil it all down, he took pride in his work, he took pride in doing a good job.'

When asked to define what he meant by 'a good job', Garland answered, 'Simple. In the number of touts he caught and had "stiffed" [shot dead]. In his own mind, he was doing his duty as an IRA volunteer.'

When it was pointed out that Scappaticci was working for the British at the same time, he replied, 'You're missing the point … he was also working for the IRA, at least that's the way he saw it.'

It is possible that Scappaticci had convinced himself he was some-how behaving honourably. He might even have believed that he hailed from a higher caste of tout than those lesser touts whom he habitu-ally condemned to death. Perhaps he thought of himself as a forward-looking fellow – looking forward to his next victim? For Freddie Scap-paticci, it was all only business, the product of an orderly life, where everything was compartmentalised and detached. And if the someone happened to be a lifelong friend, too bad: they had to take their medi-cine – or their vodka.

Vodka was the last thing on IRA man Sandy Lynch's mind as he was marched into a darkened upstairs room in west Belfast's Lenadoon estate on 5 January 1990. He felt a hand on the back of his head and was pushed face-down onto a bed. A voice said, 'IRA Security.' The voice belonged to Freddie Scappaticci.

15

THE SANDY LYNCH AFFAIR

'Laws are silent in times of war.'

Cicero, Roman orator and statesman

Alexander 'Sandy' Lynch was a married man with no children, who lived in 33 Leckagh Drive in the County Derry village of Magherafelt. The unemployed labourer had been in the IRA for two years and had operated in an intelligence unit under prominent IRA man Kevin Mulgrew, from Belfast's Ardoyne area. It appears that he was not vetted by the ISU before being accepted as a volunteer because, unbeknownst to the IRA at that time, Lynch had been an INLA volunteer for seven years before joining the IRA but had been expelled from that organisation because he was suspected of being a police informer.

Sandy Lynch's story in relation to Stakeknife goes back to 9 November 1989, when he passed on information to Special Branch about an imminent IRA gun attack on the security forces in the New Lodge district of Belfast. As a result of Lynch's information, an undercover RUC team raided the house where the attack was supposed to be carried out and, in the confusion, Constable Ian Johnston was shot dead by his RUC colleagues. A Sinn Féin councillor for the area claimed that Constable Johnston had been mortally wounded because the RUC were pursuing a 'shoot-to-kill' policy. The thrust of the Sinn Féin accusation was that there were two undercover units on the ground, and one ended up firing on another, causing Johnston's death.

According to the former Sinn Féin director of publicity, Danny Morrison, who was later sentenced to eight years' imprisonment for Lynch's abduction, 'Lynch told the IRA [during his subsequent interrogation] that his Special Branch handlers were furious, had blamed him, and were pressing him to set up for assassination two north Belfast republicans, Seán Maguire and Kevin Mulgrew, in reprisal.'[1]

The fact that the police were aware of the impending IRA operation, and afterwards found arms in the house, led to an ISU investigation which increasingly focused on Sandy Lynch, who was arrested and interrogated by Freddie Scappaticci about the incident. He was released in December 1989. Lynch may not have realised the nutting squad was homing in on him, but his Special Branch handlers did, because Scappaticci would have told his FRU handlers, who would have passed on the intelligence to the Belfast TCG, which was primarily controlled by the Special Branch. This prompted someone in the security services to set a trap for the IRA by using the witless Lynch as bait.

The chain of events that led to the arrests of ten republicans, in-cluding Danny Morrison, may have started on 9 November 1989 with the friendly-fire killing of Constable Johnston, but it gathered speed on Wednesday, 3 January 1990 when Lynch was called to a meeting with his Special Branch handlers, who told him that they had intelligence indicating that he was once more about to be picked up and grilled by the ISU. The handlers proposed that Lynch go along with the IRA plan and promised him that they would rescue him before he was executed.

It is debatable whether Lynch grasped the peril of the situation that potentially awaited him if he agreed to become the Branch's worm on the hook. Did he really know the measure of Freddie Scappaticci and the ISU? Did it cross his mind that his handlers were playing games with his life?

Shortly after meeting with his handlers, Lynch arranged to meet IRA officers Kevin Mulgrew and Seán Maguire in a house in the Ardoyne. They met just before 7 p.m., whereupon Mulgrew told Maguire to bring Lynch to see a 'job', a euphemism for an operation. The two men drove to west Belfast, parked in the Lenadoon area and made their way to 124 Carrigart Avenue, the house that belonged to Jimmy Martin and his partner, Veronica Ryan – the same house in which the luckless Joe Fenton had been held before he had been taken out and shot dead.

Lynch entered the property first, with Maguire behind him. The house was in darkness. As Maguire preceded Lynch upstairs, someone followed in behind. Lynch believed that someone to be Scappaticci. In a statement to the police made before 29 October 1991, he recalled seeing Scappaticci in Fat Harry's pub in Belfast's Castle Street and also knowing him from his pre-Christmas interrogation.

Lynch followed Maguire into a dark room. People entered behind him. Having been pushed down onto a bed, he heard a voice saying, 'IRA security', then his coat, shoes and watch were removed and his hands tied behind his back. His head was pulled back from the bed and a bandage with two cotton balls to cover his eyes was wrapped around his face and tied at the back of his head. Following this, three or four people stood him up and he was searched from head to toe, the ISU people even going so far as to scrutinise his ears and nostrils and between his toes. He was then told to stand with his legs apart and a bug detector was run over his body. According to Lynch, Scappaticci said that the bug detector was going 'haywire'. This was followed by Scappaticci stating, 'The cunt's wired to fuck.'[2] IRA sources later speculated that the bug detector went 'haywire' because everyone in the room, bar one volunteer, was 'wired' – that is, they were all on the security forces' payroll, which would explain Special Branch's confidence in their ability to rescue Lynch before he was executed. Lynch's trousers were pulled down to his ankles and he was made to sit in a corner.

The interrogation began with someone telling Lynch that the IRA had been investigating him for eight weeks and they were certain he was the informer who had given away the operation in the New Lodge area on 9 November 1989. Lynch denied the allegations. The interrogator told Lynch what was in store for him: he would not be allowed to sleep; he would not be allowed to go to the toilet; they would be talking to him in teams, with one team talking while the other rested. The interrogation would be relentless and never-ending.

In a calculated display of command and control that must have left him trembling, Lynch felt someone standing behind him. That someone had his elbows on the informer's shoulders and his chin perched on the top of his head. A familiar voice asked, 'Do you know who I am, Sandy?'

'Yes.'

'You should, because we had talks before Christmas. You know me but I don't give two fucks, because where you're going, you'll not be telling anyone.'[3]

Lynch realised that Scappaticci was still in the room.

Scappaticci was one of those people who could not walk across a gym floor without throwing a haymaker at an inviting punchbag, and

he told Lynch that if he had his way the latter would 'get a jab in the arse
and waken up in God's country [south Armagh]'.[4] (Scappaticci may not
have known it, but there were IRA volunteers in God's country who
thought that *he* was worthy of the jab in the arse.) A doyen in the art of
deception, he went on to tell the gullible Lynch that if it were up to him
he would be hanging upside down in a cow shed and he would skin him
alive, and no one would hear him squealing. Despite being terrified,
Lynch held out and admitted nothing. Scappaticci left the room and
was replaced by a man whom Lynch believed to be from Northern
Command, but not Martin McGuinness.

When is a lifeline not a lifeline? That was the question facing Sandy
Lynch, who was now a mumbling, crying wretch whose mind had
been turned to jelly by Freddie Scappaticci's graphic description of him
hanging upside down in a barn and being skinned alive. Then along
came Mr Nice, who offered him a way out: confess your sins, and all
will be forgiven. The Northern Command man's offer of an amnesty to
Lynch was limited: he had one hour to throw himself at the feet of the
IRA and beg for mercy. Lynch says, 'He then asked me not to be sitting
there and feeling sorry for myself. He said the first words would be the
hardest but to admit it and he would do what he could for me. He said
the IRA aren't as hard-hearted as people painted them.'[5]

With five minutes of the amnesty left, Lynch broke and admitted he
was a police informer.

Everything changed. Scappaticci had returned and, in a sudden
change from sharpening his skinning knives, he now said he would
put a good word in for Lynch with the Army Council. The Northern
Command officer was no less conciliatory. Everyone suddenly wanted
to help the informer. It seemed to Sandy Lynch that Scappaticci was
supervising everything, although the chief interrogator's main concern

was overseeing a written statement of admission that Lynch was being urged to write. He told Lynch to keep the contents of his admission vague but to enumerate the IRA operations he had compromised. Lynch says that he made the written statement early on Saturday morning.

Eventually, Scappaticci came back and informed Lynch that the Army Council needed a recording of his confession as well. After several attempts, Lynch, with Scappaticci's help, completed the task. Scappaticci then told Lynch that someone from 'the leadership' would come to the room and ask him if he had written the statement and made the tape of his own free will and if he had been abused in any way.

With the interrogation over, Lynch sat on the chair for most of Saturday with his hands untied. By the afternoon, Scappaticci had left the scene. Then the Northern Command officer told Lynch that he too was pulling out, but that other IRA volunteers would be looking after him. Fresh jailers took over from those who had first interrogated Lynch. That Saturday evening, stew was sent up to the jailers, but there was no stew for Lynch.

For Jimmy Martin, all the scuffling and shouting that was coming from upstairs was none of his business. This was familiar territory for him because he had been in this situation before with Joe Fenton. This time around, he had been approached by an IRA man outside his home on Thursday and asked if he would 'lend' the organisation a room for Friday night and he agreed. Then, on Friday night, the usual triumvirate – 'John Joe, Eddie, and Scappaticci' – came to his house and sat in his living room.[6] Approximately ten minutes later, Lynch and his IRA escort arrived and went upstairs, whereupon the three ISU men fell in behind.

The plan to ensure that Lynch was not shot brought together some unlikely bedfellows. In an explosive article in the *Sunday Life*, seventeen years after Lynch's abduction, journalist Greg Harkin wrote that Scappaticci was central to the conspiracy to abduct Lynch and then to facilitate his rescue: 'Scappaticci, working for Army Intelligence, was in on the plot. Three separate, reliable sources – none known to the other – have now confirmed that his other interrogator was also working for Special Branch.

'When he was being searched, Lynch told CID officers later a bug detection device used by "Scap" went off. "I heard a voice which I believed to be Scappaticci. He was swearing and saying the anti-bugging device was going haywire." *Sunday Life* can reveal that it was the second man who was wearing the bugging device.

'It would be normal IRA policy to abort an interrogation if a detection device responded in the way that it did. Scappaticci and the other man chose to continue. Here we had two agents starting the interrogation of another agent.' The bug detector used by Scappaticci was later described by a forensic scientist as 'a radio frequency detector housed in a small plastic box'.[7] The forensic scientist said of the detector, 'On connecting this battery to the item, the item was found to be in working order.'

Again, according to Harkin, during the forty hours that Lynch was detained in Carrigart Avenue, 'Scappaticci's Army handler had several heated telephone conversations with Special Branch, believing that Lynch's life was in danger. Special Branch insisted that they had the situation under control.'[8]

The evidence at the subsequent trial of those charged with Lynch's abduction and detention tells us that, while all this furore was taking place, Special Branch had eyes on Jimmy Martin's house and a major security-force operation was in progress. Certainly, there were people in strategically placed cars watching Martin's house. Then, at around

5.15 p.m. on Sunday 7 January, the trigger that would prompt security-force intervention walked along Carrigart Avenue.

Danny Morrison, the Sinn Féin publicity director, who was allegedly a member of the IRA Army Council, approached the Martin house. Accompanying Morrison was fellow republican, Anto Murray. Ever alert to the possibility of walking into a trap, Morrison noticed a car parked at the entrance to a school. He felt uncomfortable when he saw a courting couple in the vehicle and remarked to Murray that the car was suspicious. He was right. No sooner had he and Murray entered the Martin household than police cars and jeeps appeared out of nowhere. Realising that he had stumbled into a set-up, Morrison ran straight through the house and out the back, before climbing into the next-door neighbour's yard, entering the living room and sitting down. Morrison told the family, the Dalys, that there was a raid and to say that he had been visiting.

Mary Daly sat looking at Morrison. She recognised him immediately from his press profile, and the stress of the situation quickly prompted an asthma attack. The police entered the house and Constable Geoffrey Power describes the scene: 'The living room door was open, I could see an old woman lying on a chair just facing the living room door, a young woman was on her knees at the old woman's head working with a mask to her face. There was a man holding her hand and sitting on the arm of the settee to the old woman's left side.'[9]

Meanwhile, Anto Murray had gone upstairs in the Martin house and kicked open the bedroom door. He brought Lynch out onto the landing, while at the same time trying to destroy evidence by pulling out the tape from a recorder. Murray told Lynch that 'they' were there to take him to a press conference, and that he should go downstairs and keep his mouth shut and that everything would be all right.

Lynch entered the living room, whereupon he saw three men seated showing intense interest in a football match on television. Veronica Ryan and Jimmy Martin were also in the living room. The police then kicked in the door and entered the room. Soon afterwards, Lynch was removed by police from the scene. Anto Murray, Gerard Hodgins, James O'Carroll, Danny Caldwell, Ann Gorman (who'd been visiting her neighbour Mrs Daly), Veronica Ryan and Jimmy Martin were arrested. Morrison was also arrested and removed from the Daly household.

Sandy Lynch's Special Branch handlers had kept their word to him: they had freed him and, in the process, arrested Morrison and several top republicans. They, and the TCGs, had shown that they could control a dangerous situation in which one of their agents' lives had been under severe threat from the IRA. However, less than a year earlier, Joe Fenton had been questioned by the same IRA unit in the same house, and had been killed. Over the previous fourteen years, the TCGs sacrificed dozens of suspected informers to cloud Scappaticci's role as an agent. But there are no answers to the questions of why Fenton was expendable and Lynch was not, and why a decision was taken to rescue Lynch when, in doing so, Scappaticci's cover would be jeopardised. By all accounts, plans were well developed to save Lynch no matter who came to 124 Carrigart Avenue.

Following his arrest, the situation was looking ominous for Jimmy Martin. He had become involved in this matter because he wanted to 'do his bit' for Irish freedom, but now he was finding out the hard way that Mother Ireland could be a merciless mistress. Unlike Morrison, Hodgins (a former IRA hunger striker), Murray and the other IRA suspects, who never answered questions under interrogation, Martin had no such hesitation and actively tried to minimise his role in the fiasco. From his point of view, he was a small-timer. After all, he had not been involved in Lynch's interrogation, had not been in the upstairs room with the agent and had not actually come face to face with him until after the police had pulled up in the vehicles outside his house. He started off his interrogation with 'No comment' in answer to the question, 'Did you think that what you done, allowing the PIRA to use your house at the weekend, was right?' but, under further questioning from detectives, he opined that he would not have allowed the IRA to use his house if he had thought what was going to happen was anything more serious than giving 'a young hood a couple of slaps or something'.[10]

However, matters got worse for Martin when, during another interrogation, he spoke about the killing of Joe Fenton. At first he denied that Fenton had been in his house prior to his execution on 26 February 1989. Then, inexplicably, he said, 'Just supposing I say this happened in my house, what will happen to my wife?'[11] With that one question, Martin confirmed to detectives that Fenton *had* been in his house before being shot dead. After some persuasion, Martin confessed that the same man who had approached him for the loan of a room to question Lynch had also asked him for a room to question Fenton, and that he had agreed on both occasions. He then said that at 7.30 p.m. on Friday 24 February 1989, Scappaticci and 'Eddie' came to his house with bandages and sat in his living room. Martin recalled, 'Believe it or not, it's nearly the same pattern. There was a knock at the door, and they must have been expecting them because they were up like a shot, and everybody went upstairs.'[12]

Martin told the police that Scappaticci came downstairs at about 11 p.m. and made tea. He recounted how, 'There was a lot of scuffling. It seemed to be hot and heavy and heavy verbal shouting. That seemed to carry on for longer than Lynch. He [Fenton] seemed to be getting punched or something. After about an hour, it quietened down.'[13]

During another interview, Martin gave the police more details about Fenton's killing. He recalled the girl arriving at his home, in what he reckoned was a prearranged meeting as Scappaticci was waiting for her in his kitchen. At that time, it was routine for females to carry handguns on their persons for the IRA because they were less likely to be stopped and searched by the British Army or police than males. Martin presumed that they must have been waiting for a car to come before Scappaticci said, 'We're away.' Not long after that, Martin heard feet coming down his stairs and took it that the upstairs had been vacated. Within a short space of time, he heard Fenton being shot dead.

When later asked if he thought Lynch would suffer the same fate as Fenton, Martin said, 'I knew he'd be shot.' There was no turning back from those words and, on 12 January 1990, Detective Inspector Tim McGregor charged Martin with the murder of Joe Fenton and with his unlawful imprisonment. In answer to the charges, Martin said, 'No, I wish to see my solicitor first.'[14]

Other members of the Martin family were initially charged with making their property available to the IRA, with the unlawful detention of Lynch and with conspiracy to murder the agent. Also charged with conspiring to murder Lynch were Hodgins, Morrison, O'Carroll, Murray and Caldwell. Freddie Scappaticci was not charged with anything.

Knowing that he had all but introduced himself to Lynch and that the latter would tell police he had been at the scene, and suspecting that there may well be material evidence that could connect him with Lynch's interrogation, Scappaticci fled Belfast. Over the next two years, Dundalk and Dublin in the Republic of Ireland would become his home. For a man of symmetry and order, whose very existence had been structured by the routine of family life, work and being a spy-catcher for the IRA, Scappaticci must have felt like he had been transported to an alien galaxy. He must also have been asking himself if the game was up – if the IRA would hold an inquiry into the Lynch affair and, if so, whether he would come out the other end of it alive.

Senior IRA figures *were* toying with the idea that an informer had been involved in the Sandy Lynch business. They must have been asking themselves who knew about Lynch's arrest and where his interrogation would have been taking place, and, more pointedly, who amongst those armed with the details was still at large. There were piranhas in the pool of suspects, none more so than Freddie Scappaticci.

16

WHO KNEW WHAT?

'When the waterholes were dry, people sought to drink at the mirage.'

Evelyn Waugh, Brideshead Revisited

By the late 1980s, the IRA were running out of ideas about how to fight the British. The so-called 'Tet Offensive' had foundered on the rocks of betrayal and political expediency. Still, in September 1990, a defiant IRA spokesperson said there would be no ceasefire until the British withdrew from Ireland. Such were the reversals that, in 1990, only ten British soldiers were killed, and this plummeted to five the next year. This inability to inflict telling damage on the enemy added to the sickening array of what IRA foot-soldiers called 'fuck-ups', operations where civilians died.

In May 1990, two Australian tourists, Nick Spanos and Stephen Melrose, were wrongly identified as British soldiers and killed by ASU volunteers in Holland. On 24 July 1990, three RUC officers – Joshua Willis, William Hanson and David Sterritt – were killed in an IRA car-bomb attack at Killylea Road in Armagh town, but the blast also killed a nun, Sister Catherine Dunne, who was driving in the opposite direction to that of the RUC men. Martin McGuinness apologised to Sister Dunne's family for her accidental death.

Records show that there was a litany of incidents involving civilians working for the security forces. One such attack was carried out on 24 October 1990, when the IRA in Derry held the family of Patsy Gillespie hostage and forced him to drive a bomb to the Coshquin British Army vehicle checkpoint, which was adjacent to County Donegal. When Mr Gillespie reached the barracks, the IRA detonated the 1,000lb bomb by remote control, killing him and five British soldiers.[1]

On the same night, the IRA forced a sixty-eight-year-old civilian, James McEvoy, to drive a car-bomb to the British Army checkpoint at Killeen, outside Newry. McEvoy raised the alarm, jumped out of the car and escaped injury, but one soldier, Ranger Cyril R. Smith, was killed when the bomb exploded, and thirteen other soldiers were injured.

Such was the political revulsion at these operations – even amongst the most ardent of republicans – that the need to find a peace accord on the island of Ireland became irresistible. But was everything as it seemed? Some questioned what appeared to be the self-destructive tactics being employed by the IRA, and the British/Irish Human Rights Watch was one such body. On 28 August 2006, the human rights organisation sent a dossier to the Police Service of Northern Ireland Historical Enquiries Team (HET) in which they alleged that British intelligence services may have been the masterminds behind the human-bomb operations. The report said, 'at least two security force agents were involved in these bombings and allegations have been made that the "human" bomb strategy was the brainchild of British Intelligence. Questions arise as to

whether the RUC, An Garda Síochána, and the Army's Force Research
Unit had prior knowledge and/or subsequent knowledge about the
bombings. These questions in turn lead to concerns about whether
these attacks could have been prevented and why no one has been
brought to justice.'[2]

Posing under his pseudonym 'Martin Ingram', Ian Hurst commented, 'This report, from a very credible source, brings up the question of
informers working at the top tier of the IRA who were allowed to commit crimes up to murder while working for the state. I stand by what I
said in the past about "J118" [Hurst alleged this was Martin McGuinness' intelligence services code number] and challenge anyone to debate
it with me in a public forum.'[3]

Meanwhile, in the border town of Dundalk, Freddie Scappaticci,
John Joe Magee and several of the other ISU volunteers who had been
involved in Lynch's arrest and detention, were trying to make the best
of their exile. Scappaticci was being visited regularly by his ever-loyal
wife, Sheila, and doting children. Friends from the Markets also visited
him and gave him money.

One discernible feature of Scappaticci's personality was his ability
to remain calm but, no matter how relaxed his façade, living out of a
suitcase would have been anathema to him. That said, life on the run
was better than going back home, where he would almost certainly be
remanded in custody for the abduction of Sandy Lynch. A watershed
moment for Scappaticci would have been the hearing of the depositions at which a judge would decide if there was enough evidence
against those already charged with Lynch's abduction to go to full trial.
Given the strength of the testimony against the defendants, this would
have been an elementary process and a summary of the evidence,
in written form, would have been delivered to the defendants and

forwarded to the outside leadership. In simple terms, this meant that anyone reading the depositions would know that Freddie Scappaticci's thumbprint had been found on the battery in the bug detector used on Sandy Lynch, and that Lynch had identified him as being one of his interrogators.

Like all those involved in the Sandy Lynch affair, Scappaticci had been suspended from active service while the IRA investigation into who informed on the interrogation was taking place. What made matters worse for Scappaticci was that Danny Morrison had written from prison to the outside IRA leadership advising them that there was an informer in the ISU. But Scappaticci never panicked or wavered: if there was a suspected informer in the ISU, the finger of culpability would not be waved in his face. Moreover, if any suspects needed questioning, the man who mined secrets like De Beers mined diamonds was ready and willing to carry out that task, even if he was across the border. His priority was to find a way to get back to Belfast without having to go through the rigours and tribulations of a High Court trial. Helpfully, he was frequently contacted by his Belfast solicitors, who also happened to represent some of those charged with Sandy Lynch's abduction, and, consequently, he had up-to-date information on the quality of evidence against him.

The trial of those charged with murdering Joe Fenton and falsely imprisoning Sandy Lynch started in January 1991. On 9 May, all of the defendants were found guilty by the Lord Chief Justice, Sir Brian Hutton. As expected, police forensic officers offered evidence that Freddie Scappaticci's fingerprint had been discovered on a Duracell PP3-type battery, which was found inside the bug detector used on Lynch. In his summing up, Judge Hutton referred to Scappaticci's leading role in Lynch's interrogation, noting that 'Scappaticci was giving the instructions at this time. Scappaticci told him to write the statement, keeping it very vague. They [the IRA] had all the details and he was not to go into detail. Scappaticci told him to start with his name and address and that he was making a statement of his own free will.'

Other people were also scrutinising the evidence against Scappaticci: his mentors in the FRU. Writing off Scappaticci was not an option that they were prepared to contemplate, but his return to Belfast would have been fraught with danger if the IRA had even a shadow of a doubt about his loyalty. For the FRU, the question was: how could the IRA be convinced that he was not 'wrong', and what would it take to have him reinstalled in his former role in the ISU? There were several hurdles to jump.

Given Judge Hutton's remarks about Scappaticci's involvement in Sandy Lynch's interrogation, it was inevitable that Scappaticci would be arrested by the RUC if he returned to Belfast. However, getting himself released from RUC custody would have been the least of Scappaticci's problems, since they were all on the same side. Getting past the IRA should have been infinitely more difficult, yet that was not to be the case.

From the IRA's perspective, if Scappaticci were released from police custody that should produce a siren call that things were not right. By their own rules, he should then have been dark-roomed and asked what explanation he had given the police regarding the thumbprint on the battery of the bug-detection device. Any explanation would have been taken apart and the question as to why the RUC did not charge him with Lynch's interrogation would have remained unexplained. This would have called into question his loyalty to the republican cause and the IRA. There would have been whispers outside the dark room, 'Is he a tout?' Scappaticci's interrogators might have decided he needed to be taken to south Armagh for a deeper debriefing.

What would have exacerbated the situation is the fact that the evidence against Scappaticci did not stop with the bug-detection device. Sandy Lynch had made it clear in his written statement to the police that he had recognised Scappaticci's voice during his abduction and questioning. Had there been no thumbprint and, were it the case that a court would have been relying exclusively on Lynch's vocal identification, Scappaticci might have been acquitted for lack of evidence. However, Lynch's claim that he recognised Scappaticci's voice bolstered the evidential value of the thumbprint, which would have made it challenging to assert that Scappaticci had not been involved in Lynch's interrogation. And, while the statement of a co-accused could not be used against a fellow defendant in court, the fact remained that Scappaticci was identified to the police not only by Lynch but also on multiple occasions during Jimmy Martin's interviews – both in connection with the Joe Fenton murder and the Lynch abduction. So, no matter which way the evidence was viewed, it could be contended that a *prima facie* case existed against Scappaticci. Yet he was not charged.

This extraordinary, if conflicting, chain of events is made even more remarkable by the fact that Scappaticci was not dark-roomed and was spared a heavy IRA grilling. Why was this? Did old-boy rules kick in here? Was there an unwritten law that the nutting squad do not interrogate their own members? It seems like it. What emerges from this imbroglio is that Freddie Scappaticci had chutzpah; his construction of a false alibi is testimony to that assertion.

After meeting his handlers in Dublin, Scappaticci decided on a strategy that he hoped would see him return to Belfast without being charged by the police or arousing the suspicion of the IRA. A senior RUC officer, Chief Superintendent George Caskey, advised the FRU that, for Scappaticci to return to Belfast successfully, he needed a viable explanation as to how his fingerprint got on the battery of the bugging detector. Needs must, and what can only be described as a hare-brained idea took root: why not ask Veronica Ryan to confirm that Scappaticci had been doing electrical work in the Martin household before the Lynch affair, thus inferring that that must have been why his fingerprint was on the battery? It was a long shot, but it was all there was at the time.

Accordingly, Scappaticci set the wheels in motion by having someone approach Veronica to ask her to give a statement to police. She duly obliged and made the aforesaid statement to the prominent local solicitor Oliver Kelly. It is worth pointing out that Veronica did *not* say she saw Scappaticci handling the battery before it had been used in the bug detector. Equally, she did not explain how the battery ended up in the device before Lynch's ordeal began.

By any measure, Scappaticci's concocted alibi was leaky, and should his guilt or innocence have been tested in front of a High Court judge, His Lordship, or Her Ladyship, would have been entitled to ask the question: why would I believe Veronica Ryan, someone who had been charged, if eventually exonerated, in connection with Alexander Lynch's detention? The same judge may well have asked: who really put the battery in the device – the man whose thumbprint is on it, or some unknown individual, whose fingerprint isn't on it, who may not exist, and who is most certainly not before the court? Another question: why would Scappaticci wait for more than two years before bringing this evidence to the attention of the police?

But the fix was on. When Scappaticci returned to Belfast in 1991, he was promptly arrested by police on a building site in the city centre and brought to Castlereagh holding centre, where he was questioned by, among others, Detective Inspector Tim McGregor. McGregor, a strait-laced cop, said to the BBC journalist John Ware that as soon as Lynch had been rescued, Scappaticci 'went on the wanted list, disappeared from public view'.[4] He also said that during Scappaticci's interrogation, 'To my surprise, he actually spoke. He denied being involved in the alleged kidnapping/interrogation and he accounted for this fingerprint being there and he said he was doing electrical work.'

This might seem extraordinary given that the IRA's *Green Book* could not be clearer when it comes to how volunteers should approach the police while in custody: 'SAY NOTHING, SIGN NOTHING, SEE NOTHING, HEAR NOTHING'. However, the reality was that, by 1991, the IRA's 'say nothing' order had been amended to evade the inference laws, which stipulated that silence under questioning could be construed as guilt.

With Veronica Ryan's statement in their possession, Scappaticci's then solicitors offered it to the police as potential evidence. Obviously Scappaticci supported Veronica's statement during his questioning. By any stretch of the imagination, this was a proliferation of nonsense, and DI McGregor may well have reached that conclusion, despite being informed, on submitting a file to the public prosecution service, that there would be no prosecution. In 2023, Kevin Winters commented on his then client's release, 'On reflection, years later, I have to say I seriously question that decision [not to prosecute Scappaticci]. On the face of it, there was probably sufficient evidence to charge him, to prosecute him and remand him into custody. We know now why that didn't happen. Because he was an agent.'[5]

This was in complete opposition to what had happened to Danny

Morrison. Here was a man who, unlike Scappaticci, had not even been in the same room as Sandy Lynch, had not so much as set eyes on him in Jimmy Martin's home, and yet was serving eight years in prison. It seems possible that, as Scappaticci was spinning his fairy tale in Castlereagh, someone from the British intelligence services whispered in the Public Prosecution Service's ear and implored them to 'let this one go', despite the police believing there was a strong case to be answered. Much to DI McGregor's frustration, it must have appeared that Scappaticci getting back into the organisation was more important than the rule of law.

Surprisingly, any doubts that might have been raised about Scappaticci's actions and reliability following the whole Lynch fiasco did not seem to be shared by the new ISU leadership. Peter Murphy, the former IRA leader, was asked if Scappaticci had been dark-roomed/debriefed by the ISU after being released from Castlereagh interrogation centre in 1991, and he replied that he did not believe that to be the case (this validates Paddy McDade's and Whitey Bradley's assertion that members of the ISU were not dark-roomed). This was inexplicable, given that Scappaticci was still nominally an IRA volunteer (he had not been formally dismissed) and that it was standard procedure for *all* volunteers to be debriefed after their release from British custody, irrespective of rank or circumstances.

Murphy was pensive. Choosing his words carefully, he declared that he did not know for sure what the IRA's approach to Scappaticci had been, but he speculated that 'deep down' the IRA leadership 'knew' Scappaticci was 'wrong' and had been working for the enemy, but they 'didn't want to upset the applecart'. If this is true, then it seems that the leadership's attitude was one of *laissez-faire*: do us no (more) harm, and we'll do you no harm. Moreover, Murphy said, things had moved on from the Scappaticci era; after his exile to the South, three new men were put in charge of the ISU and they were completely trustworthy.[6]

Murphy's suggestion that perhaps 'deep down' the IRA leadership knew Scappaticci was a British agent was not without foundation. Off the record, several leading IRA figures at Northern Command and GHQ level have made it known that they suspected Scappaticci was a British agent from 1991. What is staggering, then, is that they felt no inclination to interrogate him, to find out what damage he had caused them over the years. It is feasible, indeed probable, that the IRA knew interrogating Scappaticci would be a waste of time.

When quizzed if the reason why they did not want to arrest and interrogate Scappaticci was that he had blackmailed the IRA, threatening them with secret files or recordings if anything untoward should happen to him, Murphy replied that he had heard nothing to substantiate the existence of such files or recordings. Revealingly, he referred to another informer, fifty-six-year-old Denis Donaldson, who was shot dead while in hiding in his Donegal bungalow on 4 April 2006. According to Murphy, Donaldson had disclosed nothing about his activities as an informer to the IRA when he was debriefed in December 2005 after having been uncovered. The implication was that Scappaticci, an altogether tougher person than Donaldson, would admit to nothing either.

Perhaps, also, some in the leadership knew what damage he could do if he was revealed by them as an agent. According to Ronnie Anderson, the late senior FRU officer and one of Scappaticci's handlers, 'Scap gathered enough information on leading Provisionals and Sinn Féiners to ruin the Republican Movement forever.'[7] Tellingly, Anderson went on to say, 'Stakeknife provided intelligence which enabled his handlers to turn two very close relatives of another senior, and very well-known, republican – and recruit them as agents.'[8] Freddie Scappaticci was a ruthless man, that much is known, so, if he thought that the nutting squad had a 'jab in the behind' waiting for him, it seems plausible that he would have had a word in the ear of this senior republican and let him know that, if anything happened to him, a dossier would be released with the names and details of all the touts he knew about and had recruited, and that the senior republican's two brothers' names and details would be at the top of the dossier. Would the senior republican not be persuaded that risking his reputation and that of his family's name over someone like Freddie Scappaticci was a regressive move? Would it not be in everyone's interest to take a step back and leave things as they stood?

Moreover, even if the suspicion had been in the ether that Scappaticci was a super-tout, the sheer scale of his betrayal would have been extremely daunting for republicans to deal with. If Scappaticci was considered 'wrong' by this point, the IRA leadership may well have been asking themselves: how do we deal with a man who has been at the very heart of our organisation for fifteen years, one who presided over dozens of killings/murders and who has, most likely, conveyed our most intimate secrets to the enemy? Do we want to have this displayed before the world's press? Would we not look like complete amateurs, were all this to come out? Rather than kill him, would it not be better for us to freeze him out of any future IRA business?

This was a view held by Anthony McIntyre: 'He [Scappaticci] was too big to fail. They [the republican leadership] could not expose the fact that the guy who was tasked by the leadership to protect the volunteers and security in the IRA was doing anything but. There was also a self-interest in the IRA in not exposing him, in not shooting him, because it would have visited an awful lot of questions on the IRA and the leadership that had him in place for so long."[9]

Freddie Scappaticci's adult life had revolved around the IRA, so much so that in all his years of service there was nothing in his conduct or demeanour that led his IRA brothers to believe that he was other than a trusted comrade and confidant. His lifelong experience had been such that when he walked into a room full of IRA volunteers, people would come to attention; when volunteers congregated and bowed their heads in whispered conversations, space would have been made for Scappaticci to join them; when he walked into a pub, he could comfortably blend in with IRA personnel. He was part of the fabric of the Belfast IRA: he belonged to what was euphemistically known as 'The Republican Family'.

While the term 'The Republican Family' may sound rather patronising, it was far from it. Uniquely, the family offered a form of intellectual sanctuary when mayhem and madness ran riot; it was the one outlet that could rationalise both the sanity and insanity of the war. Besides, the bonds that tied The Republican Family together were not only fraternal but often hereditary. Thus, having enjoyed the warmth of the family embrace for so long, Scappaticci would have felt a deep sense of displacement when he returned to Belfast to find himself outside it.

This dislocation was publicly manifested in 2002. During an internal IRA inquiry into the ISU, as referred to in his interview with this author, Paddy McDade attended a meeting of republicans to discuss the campaign to get an apology to the family of former falsely accused IRA volunteer Anthony Braniff. When Spike Murray, the man heading up the IRA inquiry, walked into this meeting and saw Scappaticci, he ordered him, without warning, to leave the room. His humiliation complete, the few steps to the exit door would have been the longest of Scappaticci's life. For a man with such a high opinion of himself, this virtual branding would have been a public dagger in the heart, amounting to his formal expulsion from The Republican Family. But if Scappaticci was mortified at the rebuke, he did not show it. On the other hand, neither, it seems, did he challenge his dramatic fall from grace by insisting on an IRA court of inquiry, presumably in case something untoward popped up. However, his debasement led to some bizarre behaviour which, fortunately for Scappaticci, was concealed from the IRA by his pals in the intelligence services.

Everybody needs a hug sometimes; everybody needs to feel loved when life turns sour. But to whom could Scappaticci turn when he needed comfort? Not his workmates, not even his own family and most certainly not his replacement in the nutting squad. As things panned out, there was only one group who could offer him succour in his hour of need: the British Army.

In the early 1990s, Scappaticci was bumming about on the edges of the IRA, but he was providing little or no information to the FRU. For someone who was used to being the 'man in the big picture', this would have been quite a comedown, so much so that he began to question his worth. Enter General Sir John Wilsey, General Officer in Command, Northern Ireland.

In 1991, Wilsey's head of intelligence in Northern Ireland was Colonel Colin Parr, the man with primary responsibility for handling Scappaticci, and the same FRU officer who had gone to the police station to rescue Stakeknife when he had been caught drink-driving in the late 1970s. Parr was an interesting character. While on leave from chaperoning Scappaticci in April 1990, he had gone to the Masai Mara, a large game reserve in Kenya, where he conveyed his expertise in killing to members of the paramilitary Kenyan Wildlife Service. He also advised the Kenyan paramilitaries on the art of agent recruitment and management so that they could better set up ambushes to kill and 'disappear' animal poachers. He advised that 'Detection/arrest/kill ratios only have a prospect of major improvement if they can be based on pre-emptive intelligence.'[10]

Early in 1991, Parr came to Wilsey and asked him to meet with Scappaticci and calm his fears, because the latter was anxious that he would be in the eyeline of leading police officer Sir John Stevens. Stevens had been appointed by the British government to lead an inquiry into loyalist collusion with the same security-force personnel who ran republican agents. It also appears that Scappaticci wanted reassurance of his value. Wilsey agreed to meet Scappaticci, and the rendezvous took place in south Belfast. Unfortunately, for Wilsey, with the passing of time, news of the encounter reached the ears of the former FRU soldier Ian Hurst. Hurst didn't like the idea of the state acquiescing in the wholesale murder of its own citizens, and so he set about exposing what he saw as an obscenity.

Hurst was determined to do all in his power to shine a light on the FRU's and Scappaticci's nefarious roles in intelligence-gathering and murder. And so, on Saturday, 14 April 2012, Hurst, using the pseudonym 'Jeremy Giles', phoned General Wilsey at his home in Devonshire. What followed, given that Wilsey was speaking to an unknown person at the other end of a phone, demonstrates a naivety that almost calls into question the general's sanity. After introducing himself as 'Jeremy Giles', Hurst tells Wilsey that he is a reporter from Channel 4 and that he has some documents which feature the general. Hurst says, 'There are documents but there's also a recording of you admitting to being in a car with Fred Scappaticci.'

W: '*I* was in a car with him?'

IH: 'Yeah, in south Belfast. And it's recorded in some contact forms we have.'

W: 'That doesn't sound right to me. I don't know Fred Scappa … Who is he?'

IH: 'You don't know who Fred Scappaticci is?'

W: 'No. Not by that name. No.'

IH: 'Well, you know him as "Stakeknife".'

W: 'Oh, that chap. Yes, Sorry.'

After a bizarre conversation, Wilsey says, 'What happened is the head of Intelligence in Northern Ireland came to see me and said that Stevens [Lord Stevens] was burrowing around and that this Fred chap, whatever his name is, Stakeknife, was unsettled and would I go and see him and reassure him to the value of his work. And that's what I did.'

Hurst put it to Wilsey that he would not have contacted any other agent in the same way that he did Scappaticci. Wilsey agrees: 'Well, he was our best agent, as you know.' Later, after accepting extravagant platitudes from Hurst in relation to his book, Wilsey returns to the subject of Scappaticci: 'Well, you have to remember that the military background was such that we knew we had this source, Stakeknife, and it was the golden egg. It was the one thing that was terribly important to the army. So we never, ever, mention the words Stakeknife, or whatever he subsequently became.'

General Wilsey, no longer 'in theatre', was not averse to telling the mysterious caller how valuable Scappaticci had been to the British Army: 'So we were terribly cagey about Fred. And he was … probably the military's most valuable asset.' Wilsey went on to confirm that Scappaticci was 'much reassured' by their meeting.

When asked by Hurst as to Scappaticci's attitude to intelligence agencies other than the FRU, the general said, 'Fred did not want to go with the police. He thought they were sectarian, and he did not want to be handled by MI5 or MI6. He thought that they were a whole lot of university poofters and so on.'

Holding on to secrets did not seem to be General Wilsey's biggest strength. When pushed by Hurst, he initially refused to say who had been the head of Intelligence who had approached him about Scappaticci. 'Well, I don't think I better tell you.' But the reticence did not last long. 'Well, it was Colin Parr.' He said that Parr had also attended the thirty-minute meeting with Scappaticci.

The general seems to have been a helpful man, one who would go above and beyond the call of duty to assist someone in distress, and, when, in the early 2000s, Scappaticci was having trouble getting his legal bills paid after being outed as Stakeknife, he turned to Wilsey, who arranged for the Ministry of Defence to pick up his charges.

At the end of this revealing conversation, Hurst seemed bemused with Wilsey: 'If I've got any questions tomorrow, sir, if I think it over today, would it be possible that I could give you a ring?'

W: 'Yeah, of course. Give us a ring, yeah.'

IH: 'All right, sir. Well, I won't disturb your Saturday afternoon any further and hope –'

W: 'No, it's nice talking to you.'

IH: 'And you, sir.'

W: 'Say again your name?'

IH: 'Thank you. Bye.'

W: 'Bye.'[11]

And thus ended a most peculiar conversation between a British Army general and someone whose false identity he could not remember.

For his troubles, Hurst's house has been burgled and his computer and research material stolen. In his opinion, this was the work of the British intelligence services.

17

SCAPPATICCI BREAKS COVER

'It is easy – terribly easy – to shake a man's faith in himself. To take advantage of that, to break a man's spirit is the devil's work.'

George Bernard Shaw

The early 1990s was a testing time for the fledging Irish peace process. Secret talks had been taking place between the SDLP leader, John Hume, and Gerry Adams since 1987. On another front, Martin McGuinness and fellow Army Council member Gerry Kelly were engaged in clandestine talks with representatives of the British government. McGuinness was also in talks with the Irish government to find a way out of conflict. Their path to a complete cessation of the IRA campaign was paved with reckless operations.

On 20 March 1993, the IRA detonated two rubbish-bin bombs in Warrington, England, killing two boys: Johnathan Ball and Tim Parry. It was an attack that led to much condemnation of the IRA, but this did not succeed in forcing them to end their campaign. Barely a month later, the IRA detonated a one-ton bomb in Bishopsgate, London, killing one man and causing one billion pounds-worth of damage.

Having been rebuked and lost the confidence of his peers in the movement, and feeling disempowered and isolated, Scappaticci could provide little intelligence to his FRU handlers. The reality was that, despite having been reassured of his continued worth to the intelligence services by General Sir John Wilsey, General Officer Commanding (GOC) Northern Ireland, his worth *had* been diminished; he was not involved in killing suspected informers any more, nor was he vetting new IRA recruits or picking up any information about Army Council meetings or policy. In short, Wilsey had been padding Scappaticci's ego when he told him he was the British Army's 'golden egg'. This would not be the last time that Scappaticci would stick his head above the trenches when he should have kept it down.

A transformation was taking place in Scappaticci. The man who effectively ran the ISU for almost thirteen years would not have left himself as exposed as his post-Sandy Lynch incarnation. So what happened? What changed him?

Although, on the face of it, Scappaticci was of sound mind and body, he admitted in court almost thirty years later that, from the time he had gone on the run in the Republic of Ireland for Lynch's abduction, he had been receiving treatment for 'deep depression'.[1] In a court case in 2018, Scappaticci's lawyers said that there had been 'repeated diagnosis of him suffering from a depressive order'.[2] For Scappaticci, being rebranded a civilian was the equivalent of a dishonourable discharge from the IRA – and becoming an ordinary, decent citizen held no appeal for him. He wanted to intimidate people; to feel their fear when he walked into a room; to convince them he was still a powerhouse in the IRA; and, more than anyone else, it was the families of victims of the nutting squad whom he most wanted to feel his power.

This perverse trait manifested itself in the aftermath of the ISU slaying of twenty-three-year-old IRA volunteer John Joseph Mulhearn from the Falls Road, Belfast, on 23 June 1993. Dressed in a boiler suit, with hands tied, Mulhearn's body was found on the Tyrone side of the border. The IRA released a statement saying that he had been one of their members and had been informing since 1990.

Three weeks after the young man's murder, his father, Frankie, was handed a taped confession, wherein Joseph is heard saying, 'I'm a volunteer. My name is Joseph Mulhearn. I've been working for Special Branch this past three years.' The tape stopped and started several times and ended with Joseph saying, 'I bitterly regret this past three years. I would urge anyone in this same predicament to come forward as there is no other way out.'[3]

Weeks after Joseph's death, Scappaticci met the late Frankie Mulhearn, shook his hand, and asked, in a paternal way, if anyone was giving him hassle. Mulhearn takes up the story. 'I knew he was in the nutting squad. He told me he had been [in Donegal], where my son was held. When he got there, Joseph was only wearing a cross and chain – no clothes. He said my son looked really tired, and [Scappaticci] ordered he be given a wash, a shave and something to wear.' Mulhearn went on to say, 'He said that the first shot had hit him in the back of the neck and he shouted at the guy who had fired the shot to do him again. So apparently, the second shot hit him in the back of the head. That's something I never knew, and I never, ever, ever said that to anyone. But you can imagine how I felt. But he left anyway, and I went in and spewed up my guts.'[4]

At this point, the BBC *Spotlight* reporter, Darragh MacIntyre, told

Mulhearn, 'We've discovered that Scappaticci made a habit of speaking to relatives of alleged informants. We were told that four other families were allegedly approached by Scappaticci and then told exactly how their loved ones had died.'

Mulhearn was visibly taken aback, 'You're joking me. My God! That's unbelievable. This is unbelievable. I'd like to meet those people. That's unbelievable. Did he get some sort of kick out of it? I'd like to see Scappaticci going to court. All I want is justice for my son. I don't want anything else, but Scap's handlers need to be brought to court as well, because they're every bit as guilty as Scap would be.'[5]

Despite his running commentary on how Joseph Mulhearn was held and shot dead by the IRA, republican sources have said that Scappaticci was not at the scene of the young man's murder, that he was not allowed back into the IRA after Sandy Lynch's rescue. That said: he was clearly out to give the impression he was still active, still a threat to any who crossed his path – hence, his approach to Frank Mulhearn.

Previously, Scappaticci had curried favour and a pat on the back from the GOC, the man who had taken Ian Hurst's telephone call, General Sir John Wilsey. Now Stakeknife approached a grieving father, whose son had just been brutally slain, and told the poor man that he was the one good guy in the nutting squad, that while others had treated Joseph disgracefully, he had ordered that he be given a wash, a shave and some clothes – before ensuring he was dispatched quickly with a shot to the head.

Even as Scappaticci smarted at the way he had been cast aside by the republican movement, along came a reporter called Roger Cook, who had decided to do a television exposé on Martin McGuinness. *The Cook Report* often focused on confronting major criminals, sticking megaphones in their targets' faces and chasing them along streets and through car parks, demanding answers to incriminating questions. Cook had decided to use the same formula against McGuinness, providing Scappaticci with the perfect opportunity to air his views on his former friend.

Even though a year's research had already been done for the McGuinness programme, it is unlikely that the ever-confident Cook expected the republican to give him a running commentary on his life in the IRA. In the two programmes on 17 and 24 August 1993 respectively, Cook described McGuinness as 'Britain's Number One Terrorist' and introduced a variety of victims and disenchanted former IRA members as evidence of the Derryman's leading status in the organisation. Sir John Hermon, the former RUC chief constable said that McGuinness was 'very central to what was going on'.[6]

Eighty-two-year-old Rose Hegarty was Cook's most powerful contributor, claiming that McGuinness 'visited my home very frequently, practically every other day. He always urged me to get him [Frank] to come home, that things could be sorted out. He gave me an absolute guarantee that nothing would ever happen to Frankie. I just hate him, hate him, hate him like poison.'[7]

McGuinness refuted all the allegations made by the programme, saying it was 'the unsubstantiated claims of self-confessed liars, involving political opponents and the manipulation of grieving relatives'.[8] He went on to argue that he had acted honourably towards Frank Hegarty's family and had cautioned them that his life would be endangered if he returned to Derry.

Despite McGuinness' denial that he coaxed Hegarty back to Derry, 'British Intelligence sources always insisted otherwise. And they "knew", it has now emerged, because they were listening in on calls emanating from the Hegarty family in Derry to Hegarty's safe house in

Sittingbourne, Kent.'[9] Unbeknownst to the chairman of the IRA Army Council, members of the IRA's Derry Brigade also 'knew', because they had tapped the Hegarty phone and had been listening in on the McGuinness–Hegarty phone calls as well.[10] Derry republican sources have confirmed that when he found out the Derry Brigade had taped his conversations with Hegarty, McGuinness threw a fit and ordered the tapes destroyed.

For whatever reason, the British never released their tapes of the conversations between Hegarty and McGuinness. The reason that McGuinness was not arrested in connection with Hegarty's murder, despite the evidence against him, may have been because it would have endangered the peace process, given the central role he was playing in taking the gun out of Irish politics. If it was the case that the RUC did not question McGuinness about Hegarty because it would endanger the peace process, then that would mean he was above the law – a protected species.

Fuming at what he perceived was the timidity of the programme, Scappaticci phoned *The Cook Report* main office at Central Television in Birmingham and introduced himself as 'Jack', an IRA insider. He left a contact number, and Production Manager Pat Harris phoned back. Happy that 'Jack' was credible, arrangements were made for him to meet three reporters from *The Cook Report* – television director and producer Clive Entwistle, *Daily Mirror* reporter Frank Thorne and *The People* reporter Sylvia Jones – in the car park of the Culloden Hotel in Holywood, County Down, two nights after the second episode of the show had been televised. Recalling the meeting, Jones commented, 'We had no idea then who "Jack" was and made plans for Clive to be on hand as a security measure. For all we knew "Jack" could have turned out to be a McGuinness supporter wanting revenge.'[11]

While Entwistle and Thorne waited for Scappaticci in separate cars in the hotel car park, Jones was in the hotel lobby speaking to a senior police officer about the serious allegations made in *The Cook Report* and the meeting that was due to take place in the car park. Scappaticci arrived dead on time in his own car and got into Thorne's car. What he did not know was that the RUC chief constable, Sir Hugh Annesley, had a dinner appointment in the hotel that night and the car park was being swept by security police. The officer with Jones checked Scappaticci's car registration and, much to his horror, discovered that it was their ace of spies who was talking to the press.

After getting assurances that no photographs would be taken, Scappaticci agreed that Entwistle could join them and take notes, but more than notes were taken – Scappaticci's distinctive voice was recorded. The agent's first goal was to illustrate what happened to suspected informers when they were arrested by the IRA: 'The standard procedure is to strip them and they usually put a boilersuit on them, alright? Put them in a chair facing the wall, right? And then go from there. They have you sitting there, right; maybe the room's cold. They make you all sorts of promises and they [the suspects] think they're going home – but they don't.'[12]

After bringing the listeners into the horror chamber of the interrogation room, Scappaticci spent the next fifty minutes pulling Martin McGuinness' character asunder and outlining the peculiar nature of the IRA: 'McGuinness? I know him very well. I know him about twenty years, you know. He's in charge of the Northern Command. He's the Northern Command OC. There's a Southern Command, it has nothing to do with the Northern Command. The Northern Command basically takes in the nine counties of Ulster, right. He controls all of that. He's also on the IRA Army Council. There's a five-man Army

Council. He's one of them. Nothing happens in Northern Command that he doesn't okay, and I mean nothing.'[13] There were actually seven men on the Army Council, which Scappaticci would have known, but it's unclear if this was a simple slip of the tongue or if he changed the number on purpose.

Scappaticci went on to say that the alleged leading IRA men, Tom 'Slab' Murphy and Brian Keenan, controlled the campaign in England and on the European continent. Perhaps stung by his recent rebuff, Scappaticci then singled out his nemesis, Spike Murray, claiming he was McGuinness' adjutant and 'more militarily involved in Northern Command' than the Derry commander. 'Anything that would happen, Spike would have the say-so. Right?'

Turning to Frank Hegarty's murder, Scappaticci said, 'Hegarty was an affront. He [McGuinness] took it very personally. McGuinness was instrumental in getting him [Hegarty] back. He engineered getting him back and talking to him on the phone. Ivor Bell, ex-chief of staff, blocked Hegarty coming in. Bell didn't like his [Official IRA] background. He just didn't fancy him. When Bell went, Hegarty started working for a fella from Derry. He's now in Strabane ... Hegarty started helping out the QM side and got more deeply involved. He then came home, and McGuinness was the instrument of him being taken away and shot.'[14]

According to Scappaticci, when Hegarty returned to Derry he met IRA leaders in Donegal to 'clear things up'. But, for the IRA, the only thing to clear up was the manner of his death. He was an informer, someone who had given away a massive IRA arms dump, and the penalty was execution.

What prompted Scappaticci to put the boot into McGuinness can only be guessed at, but he did not disguise his hatred of the Derry republican. There follows a discussion on the role of McGuinness within the IRA, during which Scappaticci says, 'He is ruthless. He has the final say on informers, whether that person lives or dies.' Here, Scappaticci is handwashing, portraying himself almost as a mere observer in how the IRA dealt with informers, someone who had no part to play in whether a suspect was shot dead or was spared. Sometimes what is not said is as important as what is, and Scappaticci is careful to avoid any mention of the overseeing role the TCGs played in the executions of suspects.

Scappaticci was asked about 'getting his story on screen'. The informer replies, 'Well, you see, things that I would be giving you would be people's lives being taken, you see.'[15]

After the meeting ended and Scappaticci departed, the police officer who had been speaking to Sylvia Jones asked the reporters not to discuss what the IRA man had said until they had transcribed the taped conversation and shorthand notes, and presumably let him listen to the tape and see the notes. The next day the same officer met the reporters again and advised them that Scappaticci's identity had to be protected at all costs, that he was a 'very, very, important' informer and that 'one slip could cost him his life'. After this appeal, the reporters agreed not to run with the story, but to bank it for another day.

Meanwhile, back in the Rat Hole in HQNI, Lisburn, the FRU had got wind of Scappaticci's dealings with the reporters and they were not impressed. He received a furious roasting from his handlers and was ordered not to speak to the journalists again. Scappaticci defied the FRU and turned up the next morning for another meeting in east Belfast with the reporters. However, it soon became clear to the journalists that the informer was not going to give them any further information, and they surmised that his FRU handlers had got to him.[16]

A Belfast criminologist, commenting on Scappaticci's bizarre behaviour said, 'It is not unusual for people who have been stripped of their positions of power to act irrationally. With power comes control, and with control comes importance. So, take away his power and control and Scappaticci is no longer important, he loses his vaunted status as a top IRA man; he is now just an ordinary guy in the street, no more, no less; he is replaceable. Crucially, his *raison d'être* changes, in that his has been an ordered life, a large part of which was his involvement in the nutting squad. That's over. Now he has time on his hands and a vacuum in his life. He's no longer as valuable as he once was, not only to the IRA, but also to the intelligence services – and that grates on him. The intelligence services weren't ignoring him, he simply didn't have access to the same high-grade intelligence, so there would've been fewer contacts. Thence his bizarre behaviour, as exemplified by his insistence on meeting the GOC and his damning interview with the Cook team. He's loose and he's dangerous – especially to the intelligence services. His interview with the Cook reporters could have been a shot across the bow of the security services. It's possible he was making a statement: I can hurt you, so don't ignore me; I won't allow that.'[17]

***

The announcement of the IRA ceasefire on 31 August 1994 heralded the beginning of the end of the war in Ireland and it also signalled the standing-down of the IRA's ISU, but not before the unit killed Caroline Moreland, a thirty-four-year-old woman with three young children, who was found shot dead near Roslea in County Fermanagh. Nothing crystalises the wickedness of the IRA more than this appalling killing.

From the Beechmount area of west Belfast, Moreland, who was suffering from cancer of the spine, had habitually allowed her house to be used by the IRA – specifically, for weekly Northern Command meetings. Then, after a rifle was found by security forces in her home in July 1994, Moreland was turned by British Intelligence. She was subsequently arrested by the IRA and taken to a location on the border where, it is alleged, she was tortured and questioned for fifteen days. According to a tape that she recorded for the IRA, she was blackmailed by RUC Special Branch into becoming an informer: 'They [Special Branch] told me that I would go away for at least twenty-five years and that my children would be taken off me and put in care of social services. It was at this point I agreed to work for them.'[18] Moreland went on to say that she regretted agreeing to work for the British intelligence services, and urged other informants to give themselves up and throw themselves on the mercy of the IRA.

The IRA's cynicism in relation to Moreland's killing was boundless and was highlighted by journalist Ed Moloney, who explained how he viewed her death: 'Given the political delicacy of the moment, her fate was debated at a meeting in July of the IRA's Army Council [which had no women members], where the chairman at the time was Martin McGuinness. There was no disagreement about her fate. She would die for her moment of weakness because to let her go would send the wrong message to an IRA grassroots already uneasy about the talk of ceasefires and sell-outs.

'The real debate was about what to do with her body afterwards. McGuinness argued that she should be "disappeared", her remains hidden in a secret grave so no one – not least those in government and the media, sceptical about the IRA's bona fides, would know she had been killed.'[19] The bottom line here is that McGuinness' insistence that

Caroline Moreland should be 'disappeared' contradicts the idea that she was to be killed and left for all to see so that the IRA, on the brink of a ceasefire, would appear to be ruthless and uncompromising.

Moreland's killing, in such tragic circumstances, left many republican activists perplexed. With rumours of an IRA ceasefire in the air, there were republicans who looked intently at her death and wondered what was to be gained if, in a short time, the guns would go silent? Likewise, some republicans were sickened that a mother of three young children, who was terminally ill with cancer, should be so cruelly dispatched.

For the IRA leadership, calling a ceasefire without a British declaration of intent to leave Ireland was problematic. Men and women like Brendan Hughes, Ivor Bell, Tommy Gorman, Dolors and Marian Price, Anthony McIntyre and others in cities and townlands up and down the length and breadth of Ireland had dedicated their lives to the struggle and spent decades in prison. They remembered the disastrous 1975–76 ceasefire, which almost brought about the total defeat of the IRA. They also recalled that the new post-1975–76 IRA leadership had given them an undertaking that there would never be another ceasefire short of a British declaration of intent to withdraw from Ireland.

Despite some internal rumblings, on 31 August 1994 the IRA called 'a complete cessation of military operations' from midnight that night and said that they were willing to enter into inclusive talks about the political future of the province. The nationalist population welcomed a ceasefire that held out the promise of lasting peace. Cavalcades of cars and taxis traversed west and north Belfast, Irish tricolours flying out of windows, exuberant youths yelling out that the IRA had 'won'. The ridiculousness of that claim was not lost on those on both sides who had actually fought the war – the IRA's ISU and the ASUs; Colonel Colin Parr, Major David Moyles, Sergeant Peter Jones and their pals in the FRU; Stakeknife. All knew the IRA did not win the war and nothing illustrated this more than a British government announcement, in the immediate aftermath of the ceasefire declaration, that they had no intention of issuing a declaration to withdraw from Ireland, regardless of the IRA ceasefire.

18

OUTED!

'Scap is Stakeknife ... Stakeknife is Scap.'

Sergeant Ronnie Anderson, former FRU handler of
Freddie Scappaticci

The FRU demobilised Stakeknife in 1995. It must have been a poignant moment for him when he was informed that British Intelligence no longer needed his services. That's not to say he was not appreciated. Indeed, rumours have persisted that he attended a farewell shindig in FRU West, Enniskillen, where he was surrounded and lauded by his FRU buddies and where he gave a speech in which he said that informing on the IRA had never been about the money, but about Queen and country. The tittle-tattle had it that the FRU appreciated his endeavours and gave him a jolly good send-off.

Whether the stories are true or not, Freddie Scappaticci, for the first time since the formation of the Provisional IRA in 1970, was not tied to any army. First the IRA had banished him from the organisation,

and now the FRU had sent him to the scrapyard. A convoluted journey
had come to an end. In 1973, if we are to believe British Army Captain
E.P.G. Springfield, all the former republican leader had to do to be
released from internment was to sign an oath disavowing any future
involvement with the IRA, but he had refused to take that oath,
preferring instead to remain in prison rather than forego his principles.
Now he was an informer, a tout, the lowest of the low in the annals of
Irish republicanism.

He was also a troubled man, someone given to periods of depression, who paradoxically resented having been spurned by his former
comrades in both the IRA and the FRU. Still, there were other things to
keep him occupied. He had a loving wife and family; he had the big pot
of gold, said to be almost one million pounds in accumulated British
pay-outs; he had properties in Belfast and Portaferry.

He also had a penchant for Spain, according to a leading Belfast
journalist: 'We were in Torremolinos ... about ... 2004, and there was
this Irish bar and we [mother and daughter] went in. And this fella with
a Newry accent said to me, "Oh, you must be from Belfast. You must
know my friend." God's sake! How would I know his friend? Anyway,
we ordered a drink and later he told me he was the son of a Peeler
[police officer] and his friend's name was Freddie Scappaticci. He said
Freddie had often stayed with him in Newry, and in Torremolinos, and
they had been friends for years.'[1] It is doubtful if the IRA would have
approved of their top spy-hunter being on such friendly terms with an
ex-RUC man's son.

If Scappaticci felt a sense of accomplishment when he witnessed
Sinn Féin signing off on the Mitchell Principles on 9 September 1997,
he did not show it – but then, he was a man who knew how to hide
his feelings. These principles, named after the American interlocutor

and facilitator, Senator George Mitchell, were a framework which incorporated proposals that rejected violence as a means of resolving political disputes in Ireland. However, while Sinn Féin signed off on the principles, the IRA did not, attempting to keep the prospect of a permanent ceasefire at arm's length.

Among volunteers, there was confusion about the way forward. A split had occurred over a ceasefire in November 1997, with prominent IRA volunteers – including the chairman of the IRA Executive, Seamus McGrane, the GHQ QM, Micky McKevitt, and other leading activists – leaving the Provisionals to form the 'Real IRA'.

In December 1997, a Sinn Féin delegation, which included Gerry Adams and Martin McGuinness, walked through the doorway of 10 Downing Street to meet British Prime Minister Tony Blair. This was the first time an event of this magnitude had happened since the Anglo-Irish Treaty negotiations of 1921, when Michael Collins and Arthur Griffith had led a delegation of republican leaders into negotiations with David Lloyd George. Those talks had concluded with the signing of the Anglo-Irish Treaty and Collins being condemned to the status of traitor in hard-line republican circles. Wherever he was, perhaps Collins was smiling down on Adams as the latter shook hands with Blair and opened the portal to another negotiated settlement of the Irish conflict – one which, again, did not hold out any hope of the All-Ireland Republic.

Five months later, on 10 April 1998, the Sinn Féin leadership endorsed the Belfast/Good Friday Agreement that ushered in an end to the Provisional IRA's armed struggle in Ireland and beyond, and which held the prospect of a cross-community power-sharing executive in Northern Ireland. Once more, the word 'traitors' was being bandied about in relation to a republican leadership.

All in all, things could have been worse for Scappaticci. But then, things began to go wrong for him. On 8 August 1999, Liam Clarke, the Irish editor of *The Sunday Times* wrote about meeting the former FRU soldier Ian Hurst, whom he identified using the pseudonym 'Martin Ingram'. In the ensuing article entitled 'The British Spy at the Heart of the IRA', Clarke wrote that Hurst had revealed that he had been working the FRU desk in the Rat Hole in 1981 when he received a phone call from a police sergeant saying that a 'Mr Padraic Pearse' had been arrested for drink-driving and had given the sergeant their contact number. Clarke wrote, 'Steak Knife [*sic*] was and is the crown jewel of British intelligence in Ulster, a man at the heart of the IRA's war effort who had to be kept happy at all costs. His source reports are read by ministers. His output was, and remains, so prolific that two handlers and four collators work full-time on them.'[2] These claims of Hurst's were not an accurate reflection of Scappaticci's value to British Intelligence at this time, since he was no longer in the IRA.

Hurst went on to lay bare the animosity that existed between the various branches of the British intelligence services: '[Special Branch] told him [Scappaticci] that they would expose him unless he worked for them, they put out arrest-on-sight warrants, they accused him of holding information back. They even sweet-talked him, but they couldn't match the money we [FRU] were giving him and couldn't make him trust them.'[3]

Clarke's article exploded like a barrack-buster mortar bomb in the republican community throughout Ireland. Suddenly, people were looking at each other suspiciously, with the question 'Are you Stakeknife?' in the back of their minds. Very few evaded the speculation, with the leadership coming in for robust scrutiny. Yet, Freddie Scappaticci seemed to escape the attentions of the inquisition. He had not been involved with the IRA since 1990, and there was enough distance between then and Clarke's exposé to exclude him from the inner circle of suspicion.

Nonetheless, the fact that Hurst had gone public with his existence as an FRU agent must have been a deeply worrying development for Scappaticci even though, as reported by one of his handlers, he had taken out a kind of life-insurance policy by collating damning dossiers on the republican leadership. The enormity of Hurst's revelations ensured that the Stakeknife story was never going to be buried in an unmarked grave. Indeed, once Clarke's story was published in *The Sunday Times*, most republicans anticipated that it was only a matter of time before the source of that information expanded on the identity of the informer – and their anticipations were well founded.

On 11 May 2003, three Irish newspapers – the *Sunday Tribune*, the *Sunday World* and the *Sunday People* – along with the Glasgow-based *Sunday Herald*, identified Freddie Scappaticci as Stakeknife. The newspapers' editors said that they only printed his name after the Ministry of Defence had assured them that he had left Ireland and was beyond the reach of the IRA. Explaining why his newspaper had outed Scappaticci, the *Sunday Herald's* investigative editor, Neil Mackay, said that he had heard reports on 5 May that 'rogue British agents' planned to reveal Stakeknife's identity.[4] By 'rogue British agents' Mackay was referring to the British agent who went by the pseudonym 'Kevin Fulton', a former British soldier who had infiltrated the IRA before fleeing the wrath of the organisation. However, Mackay revealed that he had been speaking to at least two other British Army soldiers, both of whom were former members of the FRU.[5] In addition to Mackay's reason, the *Herald's* editor-in-chief, Andrew Jaspan, said that by 7 p.m. on Saturday night he had been made aware that the three Irish newspapers were going to publish Stakeknife's identity in their Sunday editions.[6]

Explaining the newspapers' rush to publication, Paddy Murray, the editor of the *Sunday Tribune*, said his newspaper had planned to run the story the following week, but events dictated that they bring it forward. 'When he was spirited out of Belfast, we decided to run with it,' Murray said. 'The MoD was quite clear that someone was going to name him. Our legal advice was simply "if it's right, run it". Our view ethically is what we were doing was exposing a wrongdoer, but ethically it made it easier he wasn't at risk.'

Freddie Scappaticci had been reading about himself in the newspapers and, far from having been spirited out of Northern Ireland by the FRU and adopting a new identity and life in England, he had been hiding out in the home of a former IRA prisoner from the Ardoyne area in the Glengormley area, just outside of Belfast. And rather than go into exile, he was intent on staying at home, on facing down the IRA and the media, and denying that he was Stakeknife.

Anyone who knew Scappaticci should have expected no less. He was a strong man, someone for whom self-preservation was king. If at all possible he was going to avoid putting up his hands and declaring himself a tout, and he knew that, had he fled Ireland in the wake of his outing in the press, he would have been admitting his guilt.

At stake was a way of life he had carefully cultivated over decades and the inevitable break-up of his family circle because, had he bolted to the British mainland to live, he could not have expected his grown-up family, who had their own lives, to simply up sticks and go with him. Then there was the shame of being exposed as a British agent. But rather than hold up his hands and publicly carry the ignominy himself, he allowed it to be borne by his blameless family – some of whom were ridiculed by members of the public, despite the fact that they were innocents. What was certain was that Scappaticci faced an uncertain future and the prospect of having to look over his shoulder for a vengeful IRA for the rest of his life. Nothing better illustrates how some republicans regarded Scappaticci than the view expressed by former IRA leader, Peter Murphy, who said, 'Looking back, Freddie Scappaticci was one of the most callous blackguards ever to pollute Irish history, on a par with the likes of Strongbow. There would have been few tears shed for him had he been nutted.'[7]

The world must have seemed to have fallen off its axis for Freddie Scappaticci. Certainly, it was never supposed to come to this. From the beginning of his association with the FRU in the late 1970s, right up to his meeting with General Wilsey in 1991, he had been assured that the British Army had his back, that his identity would never be revealed, that he would enjoy the financial fruits of his deceitfulness and that he would always be safe from the wrath of the IRA – and yet it was a former member of the FRU who had effectively exposed him.

The tremor that ran through the nationalist community when it was revealed that Scappaticci was Stakeknife was seismic, with people openly expressing their disbelief that such a high-profile republican could have been working for the British all along. Marian McMullan said, 'The over-whelming feeling of people was just … shock, y'know? Nobody had a clue. The first I heard of it was when wee "Geordie Mouse" knocked the door at about a quarter to seven [in the morning]. Geordie was a busybody; he broke into cars and stuff like that, and he said to my ma, "Stakeknife? It's Freddie Scap." And my ma said, "What?" And he said, "Aye." It was a total shock. There were people standing at corners talking. It was like … 1920, y'know; everyone was at their doors. At first, people were afraid to say it until the papers were all out and then everybody's going, "It has to be true." And the Provies were all standing in groups, in huddles, heads together, fingers pointing, talking very low, that type of thing. The Short Strand district was in uproar over it. There was always a kind of one-upmanship between the Markets and the Strand. It was an awful blow."[8]

A well-known Belfast journalist was in a bar in Belfast on the Saturday night before the story broke, and a reporter who worked for the *Sunday Mirror* told her of the imminent Scappaticci story, saying, 'The shit's going to hit the fan tomorrow.'[9] The journalist was working for the *Andersonstown News*, a local west Belfast paper, which would be sympathetic to the republican viewpoint. 'So I went in to work on Monday and obviously all mayhem had broken loose in the office and the Shinners [Sinn Féiners] were in and out of the office to Mairtín [Ó Muilleoir, the paper's owner]. They were obviously trying to co-ordinate what was gonna happen. But then they came back and said they were giving an interview, but Robin [Livingstone, the editor] was going to do it and the interview was carried out in [Belfast Sinn Féin councillor] Alex Maskey's home.' The journalist went on to say that the republican movement co-ordinated Scappaticci's media approach, which was to deny everything.

For Peter Murphy the shockwave was less profound: 'You've gotta remember, we knew there was a tout high up in the army. There were just too many ops getting caught, so it was no great surprise when it came out about Scap. When I thought about it, what did surprise me was that he got away with it for so long.'[10]

Another IRA source said, 'He was the bogeyman of the IRA: judge, jury and executioner. He didn't have to attend brigade meetings. He didn't get involved in the politics or the talking. But whenever something went wrong, Freddie Scappaticci was sent for.'[11]

If there was pandemonium in The Republican Family, there was trepidation in the IRA leadership because they had been plunged into an extremely difficult situation. Relatives of the dozens of victims killed on Scappaticci's recommendations would be entitled to demand an apology from the IRA, given that their loved ones had been condemned not just by the IRA but by a British agent, who had been one of their most prominent volunteers. And inevitably, the hundreds of IRA volunteers who had been interrogated by this enemy agent – and some were brutalised in the process – would be entitled to feel aggrieved and hard-done-by. But probably the biggest embarrassment of all for the republican leadership would have been the reaction of ordinary republicans and nationalists, who, given the sheer magnitude of Scappaticci's treachery, would have been forgiven if they were to ask themselves, 'What kind of people did we put our trust in for all those years?' And, more importantly, 'Why on earth should we continue to put our trust in them?' Against this challenging background, the IRA leadership, who perhaps knew that he was an informer, decided that the road of least resistance was to support Scappaticci and bolster his assertion that he was not Stakeknife.

This was the approach Scappaticci took even before the story broke. At 8.10 p.m. on 10 May 2003, the Saturday night before the newspapers printed their claims, journalist Greg Harkin, who, along with 'Martin Ingram', was writing a book on Stakeknife, walked up to Scappaticci's door and was invited in by the British agent. Looking fraught, Scappaticci tried to convince Harkin that there must be another Alfredo Scappaticci (he was Frederico) who had been involved in the IRA, because he was not an informer. 'Who's saying this, because they've got it wrong,' he said. 'I know a few other Freddie Scappaticcis, and there's probably more that I don't know, so there must be a mix-up somewhere. I'm Fred, but I'm not Alfredo or Freddie. It says that I'm getting this money. Would I be living here with this sort of money, if I had it?'[12] This was Freddie being Freddie: indignant, defiant, full of chutzpah, thinking that all he had to do was deny everything and the furore would eventually die down. Harkin was having none of it. As he walked away from the Scappaticci household, the journalist's instinct told him 'I had just met Stakeknife.'[13]

The next day, Scappaticci spent some eighteen hours being debriefed by his handlers in the Portaferry area (where he had a holiday home). Despite the FRU repeatedly warning him that his identity was going to be revealed, he remained adamant that he was not going to flee his native city. On his return to Belfast from Portaferry, Scappaticci immediately sought a meeting with the IRA leadership, assessing, correctly, that the repercussions of killing him for being an informer would have been catastrophic for the republican movement and, therefore, that it was in their interest to believe him and support him. Given the acute damage in the ranks that would be caused were the IRA to acknowledge Scappaticci's role as a British agent, they let Scappaticci live on the understanding that he would issue a strong denial that he was Stakeknife; the IRA would not contest this statement. Ironically, of the two IRA leaders who met him, one had expressed the opinion fourteen years earlier, in the aftermath of the Sandy Lynch abduction, that he was an informer – but this did not matter by this time.

But the IRA's complicity in a cover-up, and gritty determination on Scappaticci's part, was not going to be enough to dictate events. The hard reality was that Stakeknife's dirty war could no longer be contained in the Rat Hole, and, tellingly, it was one of his handlers, FRU sergeant Ronnie Anderson, who opened up the murderous operation to scrutiny.

Unlike Ian Hurst, his fellow FRU officer, Anderson had been one of

Scappaticci's primary handlers, someone who 'had numerous face-to-face meetings with Scappaticci and talked to him "hundreds of times" on the phone'.[14] In a breathtaking interview on 18 May 2003, Anderson told journalist Neil Mackay, 'He [Scappaticci] never wanted to be resettled with a new identity. What is happening now has always been his plan. The events are being steered by him. There is not much we can do if he doesn't want to be resettled. We could arrest him but that would only blow the gaff.'[15] Anderson went on to say that Scappaticci 'had been turned by us for about six years in the early 1980s when [he] was in the IRA's security team. I met him when we were planning an operation in south Armagh to save a tout who'd been compromised. Scap was brought in to speak to us before the rescue operation.'[16]

When Anderson's assertion was put to Peter Murphy, the latter could not hide his astonishment: 'He was brought in to speak to the FRU? In their barracks? Was he wearing a British Army uniform? Did he have a drink in the officers' mess?'[17]

If Anderson had misgivings about the TCG's strategy of allowing informers to be killed by the IRA, he was not airing it in public: 'I believe the dirty war was worth it.'[18] This is a statement from someone who knows exactly what he is saying. 'Bad things happened, and people died, but Scap saved lives as well. Decisions which led to loss of life to protect Stakeknife were taken by the Joint Irish Section – MI5 in Belfast and the Tasking and Co-Ordinating Group, which consisted of the heads of Special Branch, MI5, British army command and the ministry of defence and other government officials.'[19] This incredible revelation, when broken down, has Anderson fingering Scappaticci, but more damningly, he also accuses the TCGs and the wider intelligence services, whom, he says, took decisions which resulted in people being shot dead or 'nutted' in order to protect Scappaticci's identity. In essence, the former FRU officer is saying that British Intelligence aided and abetted the execution of British citizens by the IRA. Despite the enormity of his claims, the RUC did not think it necessary to question Anderson about any of this.

Another security source backed up what Anderson had to say about Scappaticci: 'The Brits were playing God, deciding who Scap could get rid of and who could be killed to save him. If there was an IRA man they needed to get rid of, or an agent past his sell-by date, Scap did the dirty work.'[20]

Driven to distraction by the unforeseen turn of events, Scappaticci tried desperately to gain control of the narrative by giving an interview to the *Andersonstown News'* editor, Robin Livingstone, on 12 May 2003. Scappaticci had a natural flair for bending the truth, and during this interview denied ever having been a spy for British Intelligence: 'Things have been dragged out in the press with not one iota of truth,' he said. 'Never once did anyone come to me and ask if there was any truth in it.'[21] He spoke passionately about the effect his exposure would have on his family, and finished the interview on a defiant note: 'According to the press, I am guilty of 40 murders. But I am telling you this now: after this is settled, I want to meet the families of the people that they say I murdered. And when I do, I will stand in front of them and say, I didn't do it. I had no part in it. And I will look them in the eye when I do it.'[22] The sincerity that Scappaticci tried so desperately to evince in this interview is matched only by his selfishness and heartlessness; nothing or no one was more important to him than himself.

On 14 May 2003, Scappaticci met journalists Brian Rowan and Anne Cadwallader in his solicitor's office on the Falls Road, where he faced the television cameras and once again denied he was a British agent. The IRA leadership – including the director of intelligence,

Bobby Storey – were waiting for reports on the press conference in An Cultúrlann McAdam Ó Fiaich, an Irish-language centre across the road from the solicitor's office. With the IRA having decided that, guilty or innocent, they had to prop up Scappaticci, republican leader Gerry Adams released a statement of support, saying that the media had been conned by British Intelligence and that no evidence existed to cement the claim that Scappaticci was an informer. Danny Morrison, having served his eight-year sentence for the Sandy Lynch affair, would later publicly indicate his scepticism of this position, but at this point he backed the IRA line, saying that the allegations against Scappaticci were 'bizarre and without proof. Until proven otherwise I'm very sceptical about stories which emanate from sources of British military intelligence.'[23]

All the conjecture about whether Freddie Scappaticci was an FRU agent was dissipated by former *Cook* reporter Sylvia Jones. To her credit, she decided to bring this odious charade to a close, and so, on 20 July 2003, she wrote an article in *The People* in which she recounted meeting Scappaticci on 26 August 1993. She wrote, 'A senior officer in the then RUC warned us in the strongest terms that everything possible should be done to protect Scappaticci because even the slightest slip could put his life in danger and threaten their most important source of intelligence.'[24] To reinforce her position, a recording of the *Cook Report* interview with Scappaticci was put on the Internet.

Following this, Scappaticci's only recourse was to leave the country of his birth without so much as a *mea culpa* on his lips. And as for those republicans who supported him in the face of overwhelming evidence, he didn't even tip his hat. It was over, and all the self-manufactured fury evaporated like steam from the spout of a kettle as he set off to a new life in England.

During his interview with Greg Harkin on 10 May 2003, Scappaticci had tried to deflect attention away from himself by claiming that there must be a mix-up and that he was not the Freddie Scappaticci they were looking for, that he was Fred. But everyone in the IRA and nationalist Belfast knew him as 'Freddie'; the only people who called him 'Fred' were his buddies in the FRU. Moreover, anyone who was familiar with Scappaticci knew immediately that the voice of the person on the *Cook Report* recording was his, regardless of whether he called himself Fred, Freddie, Alfredo or anything else. The irony is, had Scappaticci not lost his cool and sought out the *Cook* reporters in 1993 there is every possibility he might just have been able to bluff his way through this controversy with the help of the IRA.

It would be hard to come up with a more fantastic story than that of Freddie Scappaticci. He had convinced the IRA that he was their most faithful volunteer when, in fact, he was working for the enemy. He was not just a spy who came in from the cold but one who warmed his hands at the turf fire with the IRA's generals. But his race was run.

19

LIFE ON THE RUN

'I want everybody to come and have some chips ... fish and chips with King Gypo.'

Gypo Nolan, The Informer[1]

As a master in the art of deception and deceit, Freddie Scappaticci successfully stayed out of harm's way once he fled Ireland in 2003. Perhaps this is because the IRA gritted its teeth and decided not to pursue him. Conceivably, they had no choice but to let him live. Scappaticci's story is somehow reminiscent of that of Sir Anthony Blunt, the 'Fourth Man' in the five-man Cambridge spy ring that had infiltrated British Intelligence in the 1930s and 1940s. An expert on seventeenth-century art and a brilliant art critic, Blunt had been promoted to Surveyor of the King's Pictures in 1945 – while all the time spying for the Russians. Because his exposure as a spy would have rocked the British establishment, MI5, having discovered Blunt's treachery in 1964, offered him a way out: confess to being a Soviet spy and we'll give you a secret immunity deal. Blunt accepted and consequently stayed in his post for another eight years.

Fast-forward to 2003. While Scappaticci was no Blunt, had the IRA 'nutted' him the impact would have sent shockwaves through the republican movement. Had Blunt been exposed, the question would have been asked: how could this spy have got so close to the Queen? Similarly, in the nationalist community in Ireland, had Scappaticci been executed, the question would have been asked: how did this spy get to be so powerful and so close to the leadership? Given the permutations, Scappaticci may have presented the IRA leadership with a *fait accompli*: do a deal with me or face being exposed as a bunch of amateurs in comparison with the British intelligence services, which had been in existence, in one form or another, for hundreds of years. Another alternative, as mentioned previously, is that Scappaticci had warned the IRA leadership that he had audio and visual testimony in the safe-keeping of a confidant, and it would be released to the press should he be killed. Either way, the IRA was facing a predicament.

So where did he go? There were reports that he moved initially to Manchester to live with relatives, one of whom allegedly owned a coffee shop in the city centre. The late *Guardian* journalist Henry McDonald told this author that he had been in a car with a former British soldier who had made a point of driving past and indicating Scappaticci's Manchester home (the journalist refused to reveal the address).[2] A close Scappaticci-family acquaintance also said he had initially taken up residence in Manchester before moving to a gated area in London. Newspaper reports alleged that he stayed in Scotland for a while. A British journalist recently told this author that Scappaticci had been living in a city in the north of England and had an involvement in a builders' supplier's firm.

But even if the press did know where Freddie Scappaticci lived, they could not publicly disclose it because, on 5 December 2006, he got a High Court order banning the media from revealing his whereabouts or printing a photograph of him after 11 May 2003 (the day his photograph appeared in *The People*, having been taken during his interview with Greg Harkin).

In 2004, Scappaticci was arrested and then released by police officers from the Stevens Inquiry, which had been tasked by the British government with inquiring into sixteen cases of collusion between Stakeknife and the security forces. A spokesperson for the inquiry said, 'The activities and allegations surrounding Stakeknife are of great public interest, especially in Northern Ireland. This is due to allegations of collusion between paramilitaries and security forces.'[3]

Despite his narcissistic tendencies and the possibility that he may have suffered from dissociative identity disorder, Freddie Scappaticci was clearly a free thinker, and nothing demonstrated this more than the lifestyle he chose after he retired from active service as a British agent. What were his options? There were many, because it seems he was not strapped for cash. A former FRU officer stated, 'As well as annual and bonus payments, most of which would have been kept in a secret bank account, he [Stakeknife] would have received some sort of severance package when his cover was blown. From my experience he would have made around £2 million.'[4] Amazingly, even though he could comfortably have retired to a luxurious existence in sunnier climes, Scappaticci returned to the only life he knew – he went to work every morning, laying bricks and blocks on building sites in Britain.

Kathy McDermott, a close acquaintance of the remaining Scappaticci family, had a bird's-eye view of the effects of the patriarch's exile within the Scappaticci family. 'Eamonn [his son] took things very badly. He got tortured by some people in the Markets about his father. He didn't deserve it. He's a great fella, you know? He would put you in mind of his mother's side. All the Scappaticci boys are good people; they're quite fair in their dealings.

'To Freddie's and Sheila's credit, all their kids have done very well. Paul got a philosophy degree and he's now restoring books, stuff like that. A very intellectual fella. And Maria is a teacher. And Danny is building over in London. Eamonn is a carpenter here [in Belfast], and one of the girls is a care-assistant. The other girl works in Marks and Spencer's. They were a close-knit family.'[5]

When asked if the Scappaticci children had broken with their father after he had been forced out of Ireland, Kathy said, 'I think they broke over time, though not Danny, he would have bothered with his daddy to the end. Liz definitely broke quicker than the other girls, but Maria, she was the youngest, she probably had a closer relationship with her daddy than any of them because he was in the house more in the 1990s. He'd have done the school runs to pick her up and he never did that with the other children. There was thirteen years between Maria and the next youngest, Danny, and the other kids idolised her. They're such a lovely family.'[6]

On 24 October 2008, the Court of Appeal in Belfast quashed charges against the seven individuals convicted of falsely imprisoning and conspiring to murder Sandy Lynch. The rationale behind this decision was never really explained, other than that the three judges had two secret meetings with the Public Prosecution Service at which evidence that had been withheld from the defendants' counsel at the original trial was revealed, which made the convictions unsafe.

Lurking in the background, of course, was the spectre of Scappaticci, who had been the *agent provocateur* at Lynch's interrogation, giving the

FRU and British Intelligence a running commentary on developments in the Martin household in Lenadoon. Turning to the judgement, Danny Morrison said, 'My lawyer argued that we needed to know why the convictions were unsafe. I was convicted in an open court in a fanfare of anti-republican publicity, so equally the reasons for my conviction being overturned should be spelled out.'[7] Unfortunately for Morrison and his fellow appellants, there was no chance of the British intelligence services or their confederates in the Director of Public Prosecutions' office aiding in the outing of informers.

Morrison was understandably livid at the abuse of law. '[F]or years we had suspicions about one or two other IRA people who had interrogated Lynch. They had fled south after our arrests. There was forensic evidence linking some of them to the bedroom in which Lynch was being interrogated. One man had been named by Lynch as the chief IRA interrogator, Freddie Scappaticci. Yet, Scappaticci returned north after a few years, was briefly arrested and released, and Lynch was never brought back to be used as a prosecution witness against him.'[8] The fingerprint, coupled with Sandy Lynch's identification of Scappaticci as his primary interrogator, had clearly been making Morrison's blood boil. When he was on remand in Crumlin Road Gaol, or lying in his H-Block cell, Morrison would have been entitled to ask himself: why isn't Scappaticci in a cell beside me? Why is he is not charged when the evidence against him is so strong? Had he asked himself those questions, he may well have been inclined to put them to the outside leadership.

Understandably, Morrison's ire was later directed at the heart of British policy in Ireland, when he argued that the British government would protect Scappaticci at all costs 'because those in 10 Downing Street knew about Freddie Scappaticci and every other informer. He was discussed over dinner, with cigars and Chablis. Scappaticci was the prime minister's man, murdering weak and troubled and insecure and compromised IRA Volunteers, and civilian supporters, in order to perversely elevate his reputation as an IRA spy catcher. And it was all for nothing. For nothing. Immoral. It never deflected the course of Irish history, but deflected the course of ordinary lives, gave rise to ordinary suffering and long-lasting grief.'[9]

For the families of the dead, it was time to act, and, in April 2015, some families decided to initiate a Police Ombudsman of Northern Ireland (PONI) investigation into whether the security forces could have saved the lives of their loved ones but instead allowed them to die so that Freddie Scappaticci's role as an informer within the IRA could be protected. Kevin Winters, of KRW Law in Belfast, who represented the families in their police-ombudsman inquiry, commented on the British government-sponsored Sir Desmond de Silva investigation into the murder of the human rights lawyer Pat Finucane, and the degree of security-force collusion by loyalist paramilitaries: 'De Silva confirmed that collusion as a state practice did exist. It showed there was no oversight, no protocols, and the cynical view was that agents were allowed to thrive. By killing people at a low level in the organisation, they were ingratiating themselves into the paramilitary structure.'[10]

More meat was put on the collusion bone in a BBC *Panorama* documentary broadcast on 28 May 2015, when ex-Metropolitan Police Commissioner Sir John Stevens commented on the three government-sponsored investigations he had led, saying that there were 'thousands' of agents and informers in the various paramilitary organisations and that some had been involved in 'dozens and dozens of murders'.[11] In the same programme, the former and first police ombudsman of Northern Ireland, Baroness Nuala O'Loan, said, 'They were running informants and their argument was they were saving lives, but hundreds and hundreds of people died because those people were not brought to justice. Many of them were killers, some of them were serial killers.'[12]

The fact that there were no rules governing the running of agents and informers was no schoolboy error on the British government's part. In 1986, the head of Special Branch in Northern Ireland, Raymond White, was one of a delegation who met British Prime Minister Margaret Thatcher when she visited south Armagh. Commenting afterwards, White said, 'I just took the opportunity of saying that what we were engaged in was in the grey area that hadn't been legislated for in the management of any agent. You were asking that individual to act as a model terrorist and, as I say, do whatever the terrorist leadership were basically asking him to do. We [White and Thatcher] had a ten-minute conversation about that and the message at the end of the day was, well, carry on what you're doing, but don't get caught.'[13]

John Ware, the journalist behind the Panorama programme, went to the crux of the matter, asking White if he was aware that the intelligence services had been forewarned by Stakeknife about potential murders? Like all savvy cops, White had the tradecraft to know when he was being offered hemlock, so he sipped from the cup of water instead before replying, 'If I answered that question, I would be identifying the individuals that were there and as there's an on-going investigation to these things, that's an aspect I would leave on the table.'[14]

White's guile under questioning was not replicated by former FRU soldier 'Brian Redburn', who said, 'There were more people than Scap doing dirty work.'[15] In a 2000 Sunday Herald interview, Redburn said that FRU Brigadier Gordon Kerr had authorised his officers to hand over files and information to the loyalist UDA to facilitate the assassination of republicans. Redburn went on to admit, 'I can say with dead certainty that the FRU did conspire to murder certain individuals with loyalist terrorists through our work with UDA informers. There's no doubt about this. My unit was guilty of conspiring in the murder of civilians in Northern Ireland on about 14 occasions. We were able to take out leading Provos with the help of the UDA. It was a great military coup.'[16] This boastful and damning admission leaves British Intelligence, in the form of the TCGs, open to the charge that they aided and abetted in British citizens being executed by both the IRA and the UDA.

Immunity from prosecution was a measure of the power that those in the FRU and the TCGs had been gifted by the British government, and nothing exemplifies this more than the failure of the police to question Redburn about his incendiary claims, given that he implicated his unit in at least fourteen killings.

Obviously, the murder of suspected informers also had the imprimatur of the leadership of the republican movement and, given Martin McGuinness' propensity for straight talking, it was hardly surprising that he took a different view: 'Informers are very, very unpopular people and Irish republican people believe it is quite acceptable to take the life of anyone who is in the pay of the British crown. I don't see it as murder.'[17]

20

ALL THESE THINGS MUST COME TO PASS

'And once the storm is over, you won't remember how you made it through, how you managed to survive. You won't even be sure whether the storm is really over. But one thing is certain: when you come out of the storm you won't be the same person who walked in. That's what the storm is all about.'

Haruki Murakami, Kafka on the Shore, *2005*

In October 2015, the Director of Public Prosecutions, Barra McGrory QC SC, after receiving files from the PONI investigation, called on the Police Service of Northern Ireland (PSNI) to examine the roles Stakeknife, the Special Branch, FRU and MI5 had played in the wholesale slaying of alleged agents and informers. Chief Constable George Hamilton responded to the request by saying that he would be bringing in an outside police force to investigate the claims being made against Scappaticci and the intelligence services and, accordingly, in June 2016, 'Operation Kenova' was launched.

Chief Constable Jon Boutcher's first port of call was to pick his staff, and he assembled fifty detectives from around the world. The message that Boutcher wanted to display was clear for all to see: I'm not the British government's white-washer; there will be no cover-up.

During the course of his inquiry, Boutcher arrested former members of the security forces as well as IRA veterans. He also demanded, and got, access to security-force intelligence files that were never supposed to see the light of day. Additionally, he asked MI5 to 'give his Kenova team a statement detailing what it knew about crimes carried out by Stakeknife, including as many as seventeen murders.'[1]

An MI5 source revealed the organisation's antipathy towards Boutcher and the fact that he had uncovered papers 'which are very telling about the role that our man [Scappaticci] played in certain things. They are documents that the service kept that they probably should have got rid of. Boutcher has upset quite a few people in the service. He is not in a cosy relationship with them. The victims' families are his priority. People were doing things that may have been deemed operationally necessary at the time, but which may no longer be acceptable.'[2] Clearly, Boutcher valued truth over the 'service', a mortal sin in the eyes of those who treasured the service and who, it seems, regarded Boutcher as a traitor.

It was gruelling work, as demonstrated by Boutcher when he released a statement on 17 December 2018 in which he said that he intended to submit files to the Public Prosecution Service for consideration in 2019. The statement said that the Kenova detectives had trawled through 12,000 documents and carried out 129 interviews with witnesses, families and victims, as well as taking 1,000 statements. Suspects had been brought in and questioned about offences which included murder, torture and kidnapping going back to the 1970s. Tellingly, Boutcher also said that his detectives had spoken to individuals with links to the government and the various British Intelligence agencies that had operated in Northern Ireland. He also stated that his team was utilising 'ground-breaking techniques to review and uncover forensic evidence which was not previously available and that this has allowed us to drive the investigation further than has been previously possible. We have managed to obtain a number of new DNA profiles and unidentified finger marks which are highly likely to belong to offenders.'[3] Even if the DNA profiles and 'finger marks' could be identified, Boutcher's ability to press charges would be diminished simply because several of the ISU volunteers have died, John Joe Magee amongst them. One man who was still alive for most of the Kenova Inquiry was Freddie Scappaticci, although, by 2017, the march of time had dealt him a double blow, with the deaths of two pivotal figures in his life: his father, Donato, and his wife, Sheila.

Ninety-eight-year-old Danny Scappaticci was buried on 13 April 2017, his coffin draped in the Italian flag. According to IRA man Peter Murphy, Freddie attended his father's funeral: 'I used to power-walk around Milltown graveyard occasionally and this particular morning, I saw people congregated in the vicinity of the republican plot, so I decided to go over that way to find out what was happening. Who was there? Scap! But there was jeeps and Peelers everywhere. He was all suited-up, and wearing an overcoat, like a Burton's dummy, he was. I'm not too sure if he saw me or not, but I saw him.'[4] Abandoned to a life of loneliness and severe depression by his former friends in the FRU, and suffering from heart attacks, Freddie Scappaticci looked like a 'lost soul', according to Murphy.

On 31 October 2017, Sheila Scappaticci passed away. A highly respected and noble lady, her death was sorely felt by her grieving family and friends. Freddie had wanted to attend her funeral, but her children vetoed his attendance. Press reporters, presumably on the lookout for Freddie, had to be asked by relatives to leave the vicinity of the church where the funeral service was taking place.

The press was again following Scappaticci after 30 January 2018, when detectives from the Kenova Inquiry, looking for evidence of his involvement in numerous killings, raided his home in England and found 329 pornographic images on his computer, mostly of bestiality. The images had been accessed between late 2015 and January 2018. A case summary, signed off by the Special Crime and Counter Terrorism Division on 4 December 2018, stated that Scappaticci, when interviewed by police on 1 February 2018, confessed to viewing images of 'bestiality', saying, 'Oh, yeah, I admit it.'[5] He went on to say, 'Yeah ... it just seems to lift me ... see when you go down into the depths, because ... see, I tried to commit suicide.'[6] The former nutting-squad chief failed to mention that he had been renowned in the Markets area since the 1970s for his huge collection of pornography, but he did try to convince detectives that his main interests when on the computer were cars, the British Army, maps, combat, football, politics and girls 'with big breasts'. The police officers countered that by saying that there were no searches found for 'women with big breasts' or 'little breasts' or 'any breasts', and that the evidence pointed to him having more than a passing interest in animals and bestiality.[7]

On 5 December 2018, Scappaticci pleaded guilty at Westminster Magistrate's Court to a charge of possessing extreme pornography. In mitigation, his lawyers referred to 'repeated diagnoses of him suffering from a depressive order', adding that Scappaticci had suffered from 'deep depression' for thirty years[8] – which roughly corresponds with the time of his having gone on the run for his involvement in the Sandy Lynch abduction in 1989 and his banishment from the IRA. It was also put before the court that he had tried to commit suicide. Scappaticci's lawyers also said that he had a history of myocardial infarction and had suffered a stroke in 2014. Furthermore, it was claimed that Sheila and he had been separated for the last fifteen years – which should be interpreted as meaning from the time he first went into exile in 2003. This is true, in that they were physically separated due to his flight to England, but Sheila regularly visited him and comforted him, even though she suffered from motor neurone disease.

Chief Magistrate Emma Arbuthnot was feeling lenient, so she sentenced Scappaticci to three months' imprisonment, suspended for a year. She commented that he had not been before a judge in fifty years 'and that's good character in my book'. Others would disagree with her character assessment.

Commenting on the Scappaticci case, Jon Boutcher said, 'This result is an indication that whatever criminal behaviour is identifiable during my investigation, evidence will be presented for the purposes of prosecution.' True to his word, Boutcher prepared and eventually passed thirty-three files on former members of the IRA, the British Army and security services to the Public Prosecution Service in October 2019. A statement from the inquiry team was issued: 'Jon Boutcher, the head of Operation Kenova, and his team has [sic] prepared files containing evidence regarding a number of offences outlined in the investigation's terms of reference – including murder, kidnap, torture, malfeasance in a public office and perverting the course of justice.' To this day, the Service has yet to publicly state if charges will be preferred against anyone.

Meanwhile, on Armistice Day, 11 November 2019, the British prime minister, Boris Johnson, promised to end prosecutions against British soldiers accused of 'unlawful killings' during the Troubles if his party won re-election at the polls on 12 December 2019. This was electioneering on a grand scale but, upon re-election, Johnson remained true to his word and, on 24 May 2022, his Northern Ireland minister, Brandon Lewis MP, introduced a bill to parliament which would see British soldiers escape the rigours of the law for offences up to and including murder. However, if Prime Minister Johnson thought it would be a cakewalk to get his legislation across the line, he was sadly mistaken – the opposition to an amnesty has been ferocious, coming from the House of Lords, victims in both the unionist and nationalist communities, the Irish government, every political party on the island of Ireland and from dozens of legislators in the US.

The British government has suggested that would-be perpetrators would have to face their victims' families and confess their infractions before being granted an amnesty. But unless suddenly blessed with a bout of altruistic fervour, why would republicans or loyalists own up to offences, including murder, for which they are not charged and are unlikely ever to be charged? The same cannot be said for named and identifiable British soldiers who killed citizens while on tours of Ireland, Iraq or Afghanistan. These perpetrators could quite easily benefit from Boris Johnson's escape route by going to a government-appointed body, where they would face the families of those they killed and ask for an amnesty, which would invariably be given. On the same basis, those in the British Intelligence community who oversaw the activities of agents like Scappaticci would also be able to avail themselves of the keep-out-of-jail card. More to the point, the new legislation undermines the Kenova Inquiry because how can Chief Constable Jon Boutcher hope to bring about the convictions of those in the TCGs when an amnesty is theirs for the taking?

Irrespective of Boutcher's endeavours to bring the perpetrators to justice, Freddie Scappaticci continued on regardless with his life in England until his death in April 2023 – living proof that, as Niccolò Machiavelli reputedly said, 'The end justifies the means.'

EPILOGUE

In 'The North' or 'Northern Ireland' – take your pick – language is important. During the 'war' or 'Troubles', one side was peopled by the forces of law and order, the other with lawbreakers and terrorists. Alternatively, one side was peopled by Irish freedom fighters, the other with sectarian bigots and British mercenaries. When one group of soldiers took lives, it was 'unlawful killing'; when the other group of soldiers took lives, it was 'murder'. But what was the difference between the Loughgall ambush, where eight IRA volunteers were killed by the SAS, and the Narrow Water ambush, where eighteen British soldiers were killed by the IRA? Neither party gave the other side an opportunity to surrender and neither lamented those they had so callously slain.

The success enjoyed by the FRU would surely make for a grand knees-up at the annual regimental reunion. Yet, amid the backslapping, the guffawing and the toasting, it is highly unlikely that glasses would be raised for the likes of Frank Hegarty, Paddy Murray or Joe Fenton. These men were just some of the many informers whose lives could have been saved by intervention from the TCGs, but, in many cases, the spooks decided to allow such men to be executed by the IRA so that other moles, such as 'Stakeknife', could remain in place within the IRA's command structure.

Some might point to the fact that the TCGs did not actually kill anyone, and argue that this puts them on a higher moral plane than the killers in the IRA's ISU. Others might retort that just because they did not pull the trigger, this does not exonerate the TCGs from their culpability in mass murder, and that looking away, when intervention could have saved lives, is akin to liability. The evidence tells us that Scappaticci always told his handlers about an upcoming murder and, invariably, they decided not to intervene when the ISU shot their victims to death. And where was the governmental censure in all of this? There was none, because, secretly, the British government backed up the activities of the TCGs, as evidenced by Margaret Thatcher telling Special Branch officer Raymond White in 1986, 'carry on with what you're doing, but don't get caught'.[1] Unsurprisingly, they weren't caught, and it is a tribute to British ingenuity that, until lately, most people had never heard of the TCGs.

However, time has a way of catching up with everything, and the prospect exists that when the Kenova Report is finally released it will throw up some disturbing possibilities:

1. That the TCGs and British Intelligence could have prevented dozens of deaths (including some of their own agents) at the hands of the ISU but chose not to do so, instead allowing the IRA to execute the victims.

2. That a charge of aiding and abetting in multiple murders might be levelled at those in the TCGs and the British intelligence services, due to their failure to act to save lives.

3. That those in the TCGs and the British intelligence services who

allegedly allowed the IRA to carry out these murders displayed an appalling disregard for human life, while promoting themselves as a holier-than-thou bulwark against the excesses of the IRA.

4. That those police officers in the TCGs betrayed the first principle of policing, which is to protect life.

5. That charges of war crimes could be levelled at those in the TCGs and the British intelligence services for their refusal to intervene and, by not doing so, allowing people to be tortured and murdered by the IRA.

The clock is ticking down on the Jon Boutcher-led Kenova Inquiry, with an interim report expected to be released in late 2023. In a statement, Boutcher said, 'At the very outset of Kenova I made a promise to all the affected families that I would produce a public-facing report outlining our findings to give them the truth of what happened to their loved ones, including who was involved and in what capacity. I am committed to finding and reporting the truth openly and transparently and without fear or favour to any party.'[2]

However, at the time of writing, Boutcher is apparently being put under considerable pressure by British Intelligence to amend his report. According to one newspaper article, 'Intelligence agencies are seeking powers to block parts of the report from Operation Kenova, set up to investigate the role of Stakeknife, Britain's most significant undercover agent in the IRA, before it is published. Following consultations with the security services, the Cabinet Office has written to Boutcher asking for 'an extensive redaction process in which sections would be removed rather than redacted "word for word".'[3] In response, Boutcher said of his inquiry, 'police investigations are independent of government and not subject to any absolute governmental right of veto or censorship. The government cannot determine the validity of its own actions – only the independent judiciary can do that.'[4]

It remains to be seen if Jon Boutcher and his Kenova team will be able to resist the resolve of the British government given that, plainly, the latter is determined to conceal the role of the TCGs in the wholesale murder of British citizens.

There have been suggestions that Scappaticci was not actually Stakeknife and that, instead, this moniker is a collective British Intelligence project rather than an individual. This view is strongly contested by members of the FRU who handled Scappaticci.

When I accepted the commission to write a book about Freddie Scappaticci, the IRA's ISU and the actions of the TCGs, I had an inkling that it would take me to the bodies that were discarded like so much litter on isolated border laneways and dark Belfast streets. However, the more I delved into the research, the more I found myself shaking my head in wonderment. For example, while I obviously knew that Scappaticci had been outed as a British agent in 2003, I had no idea of the extent to which questions were being asked in republican circles, albeit *sotto voce*, about Martin McGuinness' trustworthiness. However, despite the doubts raised about him, especially over the Frank Hegarty affair, with the exception of one IRA leader, the IRA contributors to this book fell just short of accusing McGuinness of being an informer.

And what of the rest of the IRA's ISU? Its one-time commander John Joe Magee died in Dundalk, County Louth, in 1994. Brendan 'The Dark' Hughes, amongst others, has speculated that Magee was also an FRU informer, but no hard evidence has been produced to confirm this assertion. Accusations of working with the FRU have also been made against the man known as 'Burke' (in Hughes' 'Burke and Hare' analogy), who died in 2003. Despite having been dismissed from the organisation, 'Burke' was given an IRA funeral and, ironically, Hughes, who had successfully prosecuted him for the torture of Paddy McDade at an IRA court martial, gave the graveside oration. Again, in the absence of hard evidence that he was an informer, 'Burke' must be deemed innocent.

The actual date on which the IRA's ISU was stood down is thought to be in 1994. In all, the unit is believed to have killed at least thirty-seven people. While the victims' families mourned the loss of their loved ones, no one lamented the passing of the ISU.

There are media reports that the FRU was disbanded in 1995. However, while the initials may have changed, the core ethos and structure of the unit endured and, in 1997, it morphed into the Joint Support Group (JSG). Using tactics harnessed from the back streets of Belfast and Derry, the JSG ran numerous Iraqi agents during the British Army's occupation in Iraq from 2003 to 2011 and continued to work closely with the SAS.

As the IRA campaign was wound up, and after the PSNI had replaced the RUC on 4 November 2001, the regional TCG spymasters were stood down in 2002.

**

Nobody likes spies, but most regimes like the deterrent effect that comes from executing them when they are captured. It is no surprise then that, in an era when the rule of law was stretched to breaking point, it was accepted by republicans that informers and state agents would be executed by the IRA, if caught.

We now know that some of those shot dead were not informers

or agents, but rather individuals who were brutalised by the IRA into confessing to working for British Intelligence. We also know that, after initiating inquiries, the IRA has apologised to some families for the slaying of their loved ones. But what of those victims who were informers? Did they really deserve to pay the ultimate price?

Take Joe Fenton, for example. He faced a prison term after being caught moving explosives for the IRA and was blackmailed by Special Branch into working for them. When he tried to extricate himself from his acute situation by applying for visas for him and his family to begin a new life in Australia, Special Branch ensured that his application would be turned down and that he would still have to do their dirty work. And then there was Caroline Moreland, who was caught by the security forces hiding a rifle for the IRA and was blackmailed into working for Special Branch by threatening her with a twenty-five-year prison sentence and the idea that her children would be put into care. These people were not willing informers but rather expendables, coded numbers in a state-sponsored policy of coercion and intimidation. The intelligence services allowed Fenton and Moreland, and the other victims, to be murdered, and the IRA were only too willing to carry out those foul deeds.

What is missing from the equation is a recognition that those found lying on the side of a country road or in a back alleyway were much more than out-of-date utilities: they were human beings who were used, abused and tortured, and each of the warring parties had dirty hands when it came to their deaths. Furthermore, the fact that some, indeed most, of the victims experienced some form of physical or psychological abuse at the hands of the nutting squad invalidates any confession they may have made; torture is torture, no matter who practises it.

This leads us to the issue of apologies. Apologies do not bring back the dead, but perhaps they might be a small comfort to those families who have had to endure the stigma that their loved ones were informers: if they were working for Special Branch and British Intelligence, it was rarely by choice.

Freddie Scappaticci had little choice when he went to live in England in 2003, after his exposure by the Irish and Scottish press, and specifically by the *Cook* reporter Sylvia Jones. Credit must be given to her for cutting through all Scappaticci's ambiguities in her 20 July 2003 article in *The People*. Had that article not gone to print, Scappaticci would have 'brass-necked' it; he would have had no problem looking the families in the eye, proclaiming his innocence and declaring himself the victim of a British conspiracy to denigrate his name and integrity.

The paradox in all of this is that Scappaticci could have put forward a credible case that the only reason he became, and stayed, involved with British Intelligence was to save lives, and that each time he realised someone was about to be 'nutted' by the IRA, he informed his spymaster friends and gifted them an opportunity to intervene and save the condemned person's life. Scappaticci could justifiably have said that the fact the TCGs sat on their hands and allowed the IRA to execute dozens of people had not been his fault.

For all of that to play out, Scappaticci would have had to apologise for his involvement in the multiple murders of so-called touts. But did he care about the families' pain? To answer that question, we must revert to 12 May 2003 and to what he told the *Andersonstown News* when his name was first being aired in association with 'Stakeknife': 'According to the press, I am guilty of 40 murders. But I am telling you this now: after this is settled, I want to meet the families of the people that they say I murdered. And when I do, I will stand in front of them and say, I didn't do it. I had no part in it. And I will look them in the eye when I do it.'

Were those the words of a blameless man or of a narcissist who held the relatives in abject contempt? Some might say these were the words of someone who did not care tuppence about any of those who died at the hands of the IRA's ISU and the TCGs, the utterances of one whose only cause was his own self-preservation.

Freddie Scappaticci died in April 2023 in England. It was no accident that news of this death was released to the press late on the afternoon of 11 April, at approximately the same time as media attention was focused on US President Joe Biden's imminent arrival in Belfast. So, to the last, Scappaticci remained enigmatic. The news of his death was released to the world by Jon Boutcher, but only after being withheld by his intelligence-service mentors. No one knows where or when he was buried, or if he was cremated. No cause of death has been given to the media. Commenting on Stakeknife's death, the Kenova Inquiry chief said, 'We were made aware late last week of the passing of Frederick Scappaticci. We are working through the implications of his death with regard to our ongoing casework, which will be progressed in consultation with victims, bereaved families, advocacy support groups and a wide range of statutory and non-statutory bodies. We remain committed to providing families with the truth of what happened to their loved ones and continue to actively pursue criminal charges against certain individuals.'[5]

Prominent human rights lawyer Kevin Winters, who represents many of the families of those whose loved ones were killed, had this to say about Scappaticci's death: 'Some initial feedback from clients suggests annoyance about the timing of the death, coming as it does on the cusp of the [Kenova] report's publication later in the summer.' In a not too subtle swipe at the Public Prosecution Service, Winters continued, 'Not only that, but the PPS has been deliberating on prosecution decisions in 33 cases referred by Kenova three years ago. Families of victims will rightly ask questions. Their cynicism is heightened upon learning that news of Scappaticci's burial seems to have been kept quiet by the authorities over the Easter weekend. People just aren't happy.'[6]

It is fitting that the last word on Stakeknife should come from a man whom Scappaticci visited in the immediate aftermath of being outed. Diarmuid O'Toole passed away during the course of this book being written, but before he left us he had this to say in the wake of his former friend and comrade's death: 'He sat in my house and swore that all this stuff about him being Stakeknife was balls. And I believed him because I wanted to believe him. You've got to remember: I'd known him as a mate and a comrade for over thirty years. Everybody wanted to believe him. But now there's no doubt: Scap was Stakeknife.'[7]

ENDNOTES

PROLOGUE

1   Interview with 'John Scullion', a former IRA leader, July 2021, County Derry.

PREFACE

1   Interview with Dr Anthony McIntyre, Drogheda, 26 April 2021.

1   A MERCURIAL VOLUNTEER

1   Interview with Dr Anthony Rosato, Belfast, 3 August 2021.
2   Ibid.
3   Jonathan Bardon, *A History of Ulster* (Blackstaff Press, 1992), pp. 306–7.
4   Ibid., p. 306.
5   Liz Curtis, *The Cause of Ireland: From the United Irishmen to Partition* (Beyond the Pale Publications, 1994), p. 133.
6   Ed Moloney, 'Scappaticci: The Wilsey Tape', Broken Elbow website, 7 April 2017, https://thebrokenelbow.com/2017/04/07/scappaticci-the-wilsey-tape/.
7   Interview with Seán Flynn, Belfast, 4 August 2021.
8   Ibid.
9   Ibid.
10   Ibid.
11   Ibid.
12   *The Irish News*, 25 February 1964.

13   Ibid.

14   Interview with 'Frankie Garland', a former Markets resident and IRA volunteer, 28 April 2021.

15   Ibid.

16   Ibid.

17   Interview with 'Marian McMullan', former Markets resident, Belfast, 30 December 2020.

18   Ibid.

19   Interview with Seán Flynn, Belfast, 4 August 2021.

20   Interview with 'Jean Lennon', former Markets resident, Belfast, 25 May 2021.

21   Ibid.

22   Interview with 'Kathy McDermott', former Markets resident, 16 February 2021.

23   Interview with 'Frankie Garland', 28 April 2001.

2   BELFAST BURNING

1   Bardon, *A History of Ulster*, p. 630.

2   Max Hastings, *Ulster 1969: The Fight for Civil Rights in Ulster* (Gollancz Books, 1970), p. 150.

3   Interview with Seán Flynn, Belfast, 4 August 2021.

4   *Belfast Telegraph*, 7 June 1966, p. 6.

5   Robert W. White, *Out of the Ashes: An Oral History of the Provisional Irish Republican Movement* (Merrion Press, 2017), p. 44.

6   Interview with Tony Rosato, Belfast, 23 August 2021.

7   Interview with Fra McCann in White, *Out of the Ashes*, p. 58.

8   Interview with Seán Flynn, Belfast, 4 August 2021.

9   Interview with Dr Anthony McIntyre, Drogheda, 26 April 2021.

10   Interview with 'Marian McMullan', 25 May 2021.

3   NO JUSTICE, NO PEACE

1   David McKittrick, Chris Thornton, Seamus Kelters and Brian Feeney, *Lost Lives: The Stories of the Men, Women and Children Who Died as a Result of the Northern Ireland Troubles* (Mainstream Publishing, 2004), p. 48.

2   Ibid., pp. 49–51.

3   Ibid., p. 62.

4   Frs Raymond Murray and Denis Faul, 'The Mailed Fist: Record of Army and Police Brutality from Aug. 9–Nov. 9, 1971' (pamphlet), p. 14.

5   Ibid.

6   BBC Northern Ireland journalist Vincent Kearney interview with Micky Donnelly, in Martin Ingram [Ian Hurst] and Greg Harkin, *Stakeknife: Britain's Secret Agents in Ireland* (O'Brien Press, 2004), p. 61.

7   Interview with Derry City IRA volunteer, 20 July 2021.

8   White, *Out of the Ashes*, p. 87.

9   Ibid.

10   James Kitchen-White, National Archives (Kew) catalogue, DEFE 24/969/1. The date given for each internee is the date that they were interned.

11   Ibid.

4   MAKING MONEY

1   Gerry Bradley with Brian Feeney, *Insider: Gerry Bradley's Life in the IRA* (O'Brien Press, 2009), p. 214.

2   Interview with Dr Anthony McIntyre, Drogheda, 26 April 2021.

3   Ibid.

4   Interview with 'Diarmuid O'Toole', ex-IRA leader, 3 November 2021.

5   Ibid.

6   *Belfast Telegraph*, 15 August 1974.

7   Interview with 'Frankie Garland', 28 April 2021.

8   Interview with 'Barney McHugh', former employee of Scappaticci, 10 August 2021.

9   Ibid.

10   Interview with 'Diarmuid O'Toole', ex-IRA leader, 3 November 2021.

11   David Rose, 'Review', *The Observer*, 14 January 1996.

12   Ibid.

13   Ed Moloney, *A Secret History of the IRA* (Penguin, 2002), p. 172.

5   NUTTING-SQUAD RULES

1   Freddie Scappaticci, 'Stakeknife Secret Recordings', *The Cook Report*, 26 April 1993.
2   Interview with 'Daithi Harkin', Derry City IRA volunteer, 20 July 2021.
3   Ibid.
4   Ibid.
5   Bradley, *Insider*, p. 212.
6   Ibid., p. 214.
7   Ibid., p. 215.
8   Ibid., p. 214.
9   Ibid., p. 217.
10 Ibid.
11 John Wilsey, *The Ulster Tales: A Tribute To Those Who Served 1969–2000* (Pen and Sword Military, 2011), p. 58.
12 Stephen Grey, *The New Spymasters: Inside Espionage from the Cold War to Global Terror* (Penguin Random House, 2015), pp. 62–3.
13 Wilsey, *The Ulster Tales*, p. 57.
14 Interview with former IRA Belfast Brigade adjutant, 1 August 2021.
15 Wilsey, *The Ulster Tales*, p. 57.
16 Ibid., p. 56.
17 Ibid., p. 57.
18 Ibid., p. 54.
19 Ibid., p. 58.
20 Interview with former IRA leader, Tommy Gorman, 21 August 2021.
21 John Ware, 'How, and why, did Scappaticci survive the IRA's wrath?', *The Irish Times*, 2017.
22 Interview with former IRA volunteer, 12 August 2021.
23 Interview with Gerry Brannigan, 15 September 2021.
24 Interview with Freddie Scappaticci, Culloden Hotel, *The Cook Report*, 26 August 1993.

6   THE RISE OF THE TASKING AND CO-ORDINATING GROUP

1   Liam O'Flaherty, *The Informer* (Wolfhound Press, 2006), p. 97.

2   Dermot McEvoy, 'The Most Amazing Thing Michael Collins Ever Said', *The Irish Central*, 31 August 2021.
3   Ibid.
4   Kevin Fulton [Peter Keeley], *Double Agent: My Secret Life Undercover in the IRA* (John Blake Publications, 2006), p. 184.
5   Ibid., pp. 188–9.
6   Eamon Collins, *Killing Rage* (Granta Books, 1997), pp. 188–9.
7   Ibid., p. 238.
8   'Scandal of Ulster's Secret War', *The Guardian*, 17 April 2003.
9   Thomas Leahy, *The Intelligence War Against the IRA* (Cardiff University House, 2020), p. 146.

7   STIFF ALL TOUTS

1   Seamus Kearney interview with James English, *Anything Goes*, 15 May 2022.
2   James [Seamus] Kearney, 'Brothers in Arms', The Pensive Quill website, 12 July 2021, www.thepensivequill.com/2021/07/brothers-in-arms.html.
3   Ibid.
4   IRA statement, 14 February 1984.
5   Seamus Kearney, ' Stakeknife – The Case of Jimmy Young', The Pensive Quill website, 24 April 2023, www.thepensivequill.com/2023/04/stakeknife-case-of-jimmy-young.html.
6   Ibid.
7   Ingram and Harkin, *Stakeknife*, p. 81.
8   Martin Dillon, *The Dirty War* (Hutchinson, Random Century Ltd, 1988), p. 390.
9   Bradley, *Insider*, p. 208.
10   Geraldine Keenan, Saoirse32, 12 June 2005.
11   *IRA Green Book*, Court Martial, No. 17.
12   'The Spy Who Got Away With Murder', *Spotlight*, BBC, 30 May 2023.
13   John Ware, 'The Spy in the IRA', *Panorama*, BBC, 4 November 2017.
14   Interviews with 'William' and 'Feargus', 2022.
15   Ingram and Harkin, *Stakeknife*, p. 25.
16   The Saville Inquiry, Derry.
17   Interview with Ian Hurst, 8 April 2021.

18   Testimony of 'Witness 82', aka Major David Moyles, The Smithwick Inquiry, 2011–2013.

19   Ingram and Harkin, *Stakeknife*, pp. 63–4.

8   HIDING IN PLAIN SIGHT

1   Owen Bowcott, 'Families demand justice over IRA victims "executed" as informers', *The Guardian*, 1 June 2015.

2   'Stakeknife torture victim was sacrificial lamb', *The Irish News*, 14 November 2015.

3   Owen Bowcott, *The Guardian*, 1 June 2015.

4   John Ware, 'How, and why, did Scappaticci survive the IRA's wrath?', *The Irish Times*, 15 April 2017.

5   Fr Denis Faul, *Belfast Telegraph*, 2 July 1981.

6   Leahy, *The Intelligence War*, p. 151.

7   Aaron Edwards, *Agents of Influence: Britain's Secret Intelligence War Against the IRA* (Merrion Press, 2021), p. 227.

9   THE IRA'S *GREEN BOOK*: LIFE OR DEATH?

1   Interview with republican, 19 June 2021.

2   Ibid.

3   McKittrick et al., *Lost Lives*, p. 894.

4   Ibid.

5   Ibid.

6   Ibid., p. 991.

7   Collins, *Killing Rage*, p. 200.

8   The Reid/Adams dialogue went on intermittently for four years and eventually led to the beginning of the secret Hume/Adams talks in 1988.

9   Moloney, *A Secret History of the IRA*, p. 239.

10   Ingram and Harkin, *Stakeknife*, p. 175.

11   Interview with 'Matthew O'Cleary', a former Northern Command officer, 22 June 2021.

12   Interview with 'Mark Gallagher', a former Northern Command officer, 22 June 2021.

10 FRANK HEGARTY'S IRA SPONSOR

1   Interview with 'Diarmuid O'Toole', ex-IRA leader, 3 November 2021.
2   Ibid.
3   Interview with Freddie Scappaticci, Culloden Hotel, *The Cook Report*, 26 August 1993.
4   Interview with Matthew O'Cleary and Mark Gallagher, Northern Command IRA officers, 22 June 2021.
5   Ibid.
6   Interview with Ian Hurst, 8 April 2021.
7   Interview with Luke McCartney, Derry Brigade officer, 10 May 2021.
8   Ibid.
9   Ibid.
10 Ibid.
11 Ibid.
12 Interview with 'John Scullion', a former IRA leader, July 2021, County Derry.
13 Ibid.
14 Ibid.
15 Ibid.
16 Ibid.
17 Ibid.
18 Ingram and Harkin, *Stakeknife*, p. 118.
19 Ibid., p. 81.
20 Interview with Ian Hurst, 8 April 2021.
21 Ibid.
22 Interview with Freddie Scappaticci, Culloden Hotel, *The Cook Report*, 26 August 1993.
23 Ibid.

11 STAKEKNIFE TAKES CONTROL

1   Ed Moloney, *Voices from the Grave* (Faber and Faber Ltd, 2010), pp. 264–5.
2   Ingram and Harkin, *Stakeknife*, pp. 86–90.

3 Moloney, *A Secret History of the IRA*, p. 317.

4 Bradley, *Insider*, p. 220.

5 Interview with 'Peter Murphy', former Belfast IRA leader, 25 February 2022.

6 McKittrick et al., *Lost Lives*, pp. 1280–1.

7 Interview with Luke McCartney, Derry IRA Brigade Officer, 10 May 2021.

12 LOUGHGALL

1 Dr Michael Maguire, 'The Murders at the Heights Bar in Loughinisland', Police Ombudsman's Report, 2016.

2 Interview with veteran republican, 'Colm McGarrigle', IRA volunteer, 13 July 2021.

3 Edwards, *Agents of Influence*, p. 155.

4 Moloney, *A Secret History of the IRA*, p. 316.

5 Seán Hartnett, *Charlie One: The True Story of an Irishman in the British Army and His Role in Covert Counter-Terrorism Operations in Northern Ireland* (Merrion Press, 2016), p. 112.

6 Ibid., p. 116.

7 Ibid., p. 117.

8 Ibid., pp. 117–18.

9 Ibid., p. 118.

10 Ibid.

11 Ibid.

12 Interview with veteran republican, 'Colm McGarrigle', 13 July 2021. All following information from this man comes from this interview.

13 TORTURERS

1 Author interview with 'Diarmuid O'Toole', 3 November 2021.

2 Moloney, *Voices from the Grave*, p. 280.

3 Interview with 'Fergal McArdle', former IRA GHQ staff officer, 31 August 2021.

4 Interview with IRA volunteer, Belfast, 14 January 2023.

5 Ingram and Harkin, *Stakeknife*, p. 233.

6   Dillon, *The Dirty War*, p. 318.

7   Moloney, *A Secret History of the IRA*, p. 29.

8   Ed Moloney, 'Joe Fenton, The RUC Special Branch and the Destruction of the Belfast IRA', The Broken Elbow website, 15 May 2016, https://thebrokenelbow.com/2016/05/15/joe-fenton-the-ruc-special-branch-and-the-destruction-of-the-belfast-ira/.

9   Dillon interview with Brendan Hughes, *The Dirty War*, p. 323.

10   Ibid.

11   Ibid., p. 324.

12   Ingram and Harkin, *Stakeknife*, p. 233.

13   Ibid., pp. 233–4.

14   Moloney, 'Joe Fenton, The RUC Special Branch and the Destruction of the Belfast IRA', 15 May 2016.

15   James Martin's interview with police at the trial of Sandy Lynch.

16   Ibid.

17   Ingram and Harkin, *Stakeknife*, p. 238.

18   Dillon, *The Dirty War*, p. 325.

19   Moloney, *Voices from the Grave*, p. 286.

20   Ingram and Harkin, *Stakeknife*, p. 239.

21   Fr Tom Toner, Funeral of Joe Fenton, 28 February 1989.

14   IT'S ONLY BUSINESS

1   Willie Carlin, *Thatcher's Spy: My Life as an MI5 Agent Inside Sinn Féin* (Merrion Press, 2019), p. 31.

2   'A Dead Man Walking', *Belfast Telegraph*, 6 October 2019.

3   Carlin, *Thatcher's Spy*, p. 118.

4   Ibid., pp. 179–80.

5   Ibid., p. 193.

6   Ibid.

7   Ibid., p. 224.

8   Ibid., p. 235.

9   Ibid., pp. 251–3.

10   McKittrick et al., *Lost Lives*, p. 1108.

11   Martin Dillon, 'Sordid sex secrets of IRA chief who became major informer for MI5', The Independent.ie, 17 September 2017.
12   Interview with 'Marian McMullan', a former Markets resident, Belfast, 7 June 2021.
13   Dr Anthony McIntyre, 'Another Unjust Execution', *The Blanket: A Journal of Protest and Dissent*, 28 February 2006.
14   Ibid.

15   THE SANDY LYNCH AFFAIR

1   Danny Morrison, *The Guardian*, 13 January 2009.
2   Sandy Lynch statement to police, 29 October 1990.
3   Ibid.
4   Ibid.
5   Ibid.
6   James Martin's interview with RUC Constable George Fletcher, 10 January 1990.
7   Statement from forensic scientist Norman Stanley Newell, 11 April 1990.
8   Greg Harkin, *Sunday Life*, 12 July 2008.
9   Statement from RUC Constable Geoffrey Power, 19 September 1990.
10   Statement from RUC Constable Angela Coleman, 11 January 1990.
11   Ibid.
12   Ibid.
13   Ibid.
14   Ibid.

16   WHO KNEW WHAT?

1   Moloney, *A Secret History of the IRA*, pp. 343–8.
2   Henry McDonald, 'UK agents "did have role in IRA bomb atrocities"', *The Guardian*, 10 September 2006.
3   Ibid.
4   John Ware, 'The Spy in the IRA', *Panorama*, BBC, 4 November 2017.
5   'The Spy Who Got Away With Murder', *Spotlight*, BBC, 30 May 2023.
6   Interview with 'Peter Murphy', former Belfast IRA leader, 25 February 2022.

7   Greg Harkin, 'The Unmasking of Freddie Scappaticci, aka Stakeknife: the lies, intrigue, and smokescreens to keep the sordid truth hidden', *The People*, 18 May 2003.

8   Ibid.

9   Interview with Dr Anthony McIntyre, Drogheda, 26 April 2021.

10 Phil Millar, Declassified UK, 13 January 2022, https://consortiumnews.com/2022/01/13/the-spy-who-went-on-safari/d.

11 'Scappaticci: The Wilsey Tape', The Broken Elbow, 7 April 2017, https://thebrokenelbow.com/2017/04/07/scappaticci-the-wilsey-tape/.

17   SCAPPATICCI BREAKS COVER

1   Case summary, Westminster Magistrates Court, 5 December 2018.

2   Ibid.

3   Darragh MacIntyre, *Spotlight*, BBC, 9 June 2015.

4   Ibid.

5   Ibid.

6   Roger Cook, *The Cook Report*, Central Television, 17 and 24 August 1993.

7   Ibid.

8   Liam Clarke and Kathryn Johnston, *Martin McGuinness: From Guns to Government* (Mainstream Publishing Company Ltd, 2001), p. 222.

9   Roger Cook, *The Cook Report*, Central Television, 17 and 24 August 1993.

10 Interview with former IRA officers, Derry, 22 June 2021.

11 Sylvia Jones, 'Scappaticci told me IRA secrets before cop told me he was agent called Stakeknife', *The People*, 20 July 2003.

12 Ibid.

13 Ingram and Harkin, *Stakeknife*, p. 69.

14 Interview with Freddie Scappaticci, Culloden Hotel, *The Cook Report*, 26 August 1993.

15 Ibid.

16 Sylvia Jones, 'Scappaticci told me IRA secrets before cop told me he was agent called Stakeknife', *The People*, 20 July 2003.

17 Interview with a Belfast criminologist, Belfast, 10 March 2021.

18 'Caroline Moreland: IRA "and state" blamed over murder', BBC News online,

10 June 2015, www.bbc.co.uk/news/uk-northern-ireland-33069102.amp.

19 Ed Moloney, 'He was savagely cruel, but only McGuinness could end the terror', *News Letter*, 25 March 2017, www.newsletter.co.uk/news/ed-moloney-he-was-savagely-cruel-but-only-mcguinness-could-end-the-terror-1140311.

18   OUTED!

1   Interview with Belfast journalist, 9 June 2021.

2   Liam Clarke, 'The British Spy at the Heart of the IRA', *The Sunday Times*, 8 August 1990.

3   Ibid.

4   Interview with Neil Mackay, *Sunday Herald*, 20 September 2022.

5   Ibid.

6   Ibid.

7   Interview with 'Peter Murphy', former IRA leader, 25 February 2021.

8   Interview with 'Marian McMullan', 25 May 2021.

9   Interview with journalist, 11 June 2022.

10   Interview with 'Peter Murphy', former IRA leader, 25 February 2021.

11   Interview with former IRA volunteer, 9 June 2021.

12   Ingram and Harkin, *Stakeknife*, p. 244.

13   Ibid.

14   Neil Mackay, 'Scappaticci is lying: He is Stakeknife', *Sunday Herald*, 18 May 2003.

15   Ibid.

16   Ibid.

17   Interview with 'Peter Murphy', former IRA leader, 25 February 2021.

18   Neil Mackay, 'Scappaticci is lying: He is Stakeknife', *Sunday Herald*, 18 May 2003.

19   Ibid.

20   Ibid.

21   Freddie Scappaticci, *Andersonstown News*, 4 May 2003.

22   Ibid.

23   'Name first emerged at kidnap trial', *The Guardian*, 12 May 2003.

24   Sylvia Jones, 'Scappaticci told me IRA secrets before cop told me he was agent called Stakeknife', *The People*, 20 July 2003.

19   LIFE ON THE RUN

1   John Ford (dir.), *The Informer* (1935).
2   Interview with Belfast journalist, 21 September 2021.
3   Martin Breen, 'Stakeknife quizzed on shootings, *News of the World*, 8 March 2006.
4   Ibid.
5   Interview with 'Kathy McDermott', former Markets resident, 16 February 2001.
6   Ibid.
7   Danny Morrison, 'Dirty Fighting', *The Guardian*, 13 January 2009.
8   Danny Morrison, 9 No 10's murderer – Scap', *The Times*, 30 January 2016.
9   Ibid.
10   Owen Bowcott, 'Families demand justice over IRA victims "executed" as informers', *The Guardian*, 1 June 2015.
11   'Britain's Secret Terror Deals', *Panorama*, BBC, 28 May 2015.
12   Ibid.
13   Neil MacKay, *Sunday Herald*, 19 November 2000.
14   'Britain's Secret Terror Deals', *Panorama*, BBC, 28 May 2015.
15   Ibid.
16   Neil MacKay, *Sunday Herald*, 19 November 2000.
17   'Britain's Secret Terror Deals', *Panorama*, BBC, 28 May 2015.

20   ALL THESE THINGS MUST COME TO PASS

1   Ivan Little, 'Dogged Stakeknife probe chief won't take no for an answer', *Belfast Telegraph*, 19 December 2018.
2   Ibid.
3   Ibid.
4   Interview with 'Peter Murphy', former IRA leader, 24 February 2022.
5   Case summary for first appearance on 5 December 2018, in the Westminster Magistrates Court.

6   Ibid.
7   Ibid.
8   Ibid.

EPILOGUE

1   John Ware, 'The Spy in the IRA', *Panorama*, BBC, 4 November 2017.
2   www.kenova.co.uk/consultation-opens-into-kenova-plans-to-release-interim-report-of-findings
3   Sean O'Neill, 'Northern Ireland Troubles: Threat to censor report into IRA spy Stakeknife', *The Times*, 12 December 2022.
4   Jon Boutcher, 'Stakeknife investigator: "If I wanted to be popular I would have got a Labrador"', *The Irish Times*, 18 December 2018.
5   Statement from the Kenova Inquiry, 11 April 2023.
6   Statement from Kevin Winters, KRW Law, 11 April 2023.
7   Interview with 'Diarmuid O'Toole', 3 November 2021.

ACKNOWLEDGEMENTS

While I would like to name and acknowledge everyone who contributed to this book, the reality is that many of the interviewees only gave their accounts based on a guarantee that their anonymity would be respected. Accordingly, I have not named those individuals, especially those former IRA volunteers who gave their stories. There were others who also insisted on anonymity, men and women who grew up with Freddie Scappaticci and who, for whatever reason, still feared him. To both sets of interviewees, I would like to express my sincere appreciation and say that your contribution is greatly appreciated.

I would ask all the academics and journalists who contributed to this book to please accept my sincere thanks for their help. I can't thank you enough.

I would like to acknowledge my publisher and friend, Conor Graham of Merrion Press. I would also like to thank his staff, especially his editor, Wendy Logue.

I must also express my appreciation to my literary agent, Lisa Moylett of Coombs Moylett Maclean. Thanks for all your help and guidance, Lisa.

Finally, I want to acknowledge my family, who, as ever, stand solidly beside me. Love you.

Ricky O'Rawe